THE COMPLETE GUIDE TO
BUILDING AND OUTFITTING AN OFFICE IN YOUR HOME

CINCINNATI, OHIO

Disclaimer

Every precaution has been taken in preparing *The Complete Guide to Building and Outfitting an Office in Your Home* to make your home construction project as safe and successful as possible. However, neither the publisher nor the author assumes any responsibility for any damages incurred in conjunction with the use of this manual.

The Complete Guide to Building and Outfitting an Office in Your Home. Copyright © 1994 by Jerry Germer. Printed and bound in the United States of America. All rights reserved. No part of this book may be reproduced in any form or by any electronic or mechanical means including information storage and retrieval systems without permission in writing from the publisher, except by a reviewer, who may quote brief passages in a review. Published by Betterway Books, an imprint of F&W Publications, Inc., 1507 Dana Avenue, Cincinnati, Ohio, 45207. 1-800-289-0963. First edition. Pages 165 and 166 are reprinted (with some annotation added) from *Means Repair & Remodeling Cost Data, 14th annual Edition, 1993* by Howard M. Chandler, et al. Pages 83 (entire page) and 274 (entire page) of the original. Reprinted with permission.

98 97 96 95 94   5 4 3 2 1

Library of Congress Cataloging-in-Publication Data

Germer, Jerry.
    The complete guide to building and outfitting an office in your home / Jerry Germer.
        p.   cm.
    Includes bibliographical references and index.
    ISBN 1-55870-335-7
    1. Dwellings—Remodeling. 2. Home-based businesses—Planning. I. Title. II. Title: Building and outfitting an office in your home.
TH4816.G47   1994
643'.58—dc20   94-20676
                                              CIP

Edited by R. Adam Blake
Interior design by Brian Roeth
Cover design by Clare Finney and Angela Lennert
Cover photo courtesy of Hal Apple Design & Communications, and Mark Lohman Photography, Los Angeles

Betterway Books are available at special discounts for sales promotions, premiums and fund-raising use. Special editions or book excerpts can also be created to specification. For details contact: Special Sales Director, Betterway Books, 1507 Dana Avenue, Cincinnati, Ohio 45207.

METRIC CONVERSION CHART		
TO CONVERT	TO	MULTIPLY BY
Inches	Centimeters	2.54
Centimeters	Inches	0.4
Feet	Centimeters	30.5
Centimeters	Feet	0.03
Yards	Meters	0.9
Meters	Yards	1.1
Sq. Inches	Sq. Centimeters	6.45
Sq. Centimeters	Sq. Inches	0.16
Sq. Feet	Sq. Meters	0.09
Sq. Meters	Sq. Feet	10.8
Sq. Yards	Sq. Meters	0.8
Sq. Meters	Sq. Yards	1.2
Pounds	Kilograms	0.45
Kilograms	Pounds	2.2
Ounces	Grams	28.4
Grams	Ounces	0.04

ABOUT THE AUTHOR

Jerry Germer is a practicing architect and writer. He has written, edited, and illustrated numerous articles on solar design as Architecture Editor for *Solar Age*, 1983-1986. His recent freelance articles on building topics have appeared in *Home, Women's Day Specials, Fine Homebuilding*, and *The Journal of Light Construction*. His book, *Country Careers: Successful Ways to Work and Live in the Country* (John Wiley & Sons, 1993), explores the gamut of issues faced by self-employed persons working out of offices in their homes.

A native of Salt Lake City, Germer now works out of a converted attic office in his home in Marlborough, New Hampshire.

ACKNOWLEDGMENTS

To Drew Gillett and Mark Vincello, for help with environmental equipment; Terry Brennan (radon and air quality); Dick Wardell (financing); Tom Hamon (insurance); Frederick Edwards (window treatments); Lucie Germer, Betsy Budelman, Bruce Hesselbach, and Biff Mahoney (reviewing text and general encouragement).

DEDICATION

To Lucie, Max, and Cinda—for making the kind of home worth working from.

Table of Contents

Introduction

What does a former New Hampshire senator have in common with the creator of the character Roger Rabbit? Gordon Humphrey and Gary Wolf both work out of offices in their homes—along with 12 million others who work full time and 39 million who work part time from home offices.

You too may be drawn to a home office by the appeal of a half-minute commute free of gridlock and traffic smells, the chance to save on the cost of office space and working wardrobes, and the freedom to tailor your workspace to your own needs.

But are you sure you'll be able to work in your home, disconnected from the hustle and bustle of the commercial office? Do you know the best site in your home for an office, how it will affect the household, and what will be required to convert it into an efficient workspace? Can you work at home without slighting your family? Do you know what kind of electronic technology will be best for your home office?

In this book, I'll tackle the questions that bear directly on the physical space and steer you to reliable sources for areas beyond my main focus. For example, questions that relate primarily to how you manage your business are covered by the small business and working-at-home books listed in the appendix. No book could adequately keep up with the dynamic world of electronic office technology. Periodicals such as *Home Office Computing* provide your most current sources for this kind of information.

But, as *Roger Rabbit* co-writer Bonnie Wolf says, "Productivity is very closely related to having a functional workspace." Whereas the electronic revolution of the last decade enables you to carry out some office functions over a car phone or working with a laptop computer on a plane, these mobile office sites don't offer you a place to spread out materials, meet clients, or even think free of the noise and distractions of other people's activity. A well-conceived home office accommodates all of these needs, and this book will tell you how to plan, design, and construct one. In the following chapters you'll learn how to:

- Find the best place in your home for an office.
- Create an area designed to suit your own personality and style of working.
- Plan your office to give you an opportunity to work free of the distractions of the household.
- Present a professional image to visitors and clients.
- Plan and organize your space to make every square foot work for you.
- Outfit your space with furniture you purchase or build yourself.
- Select windows and window coverings to make the most of natural light while avoiding unwanted heat and glare.
- Choose energy-efficient heating and cooling equipment.

Because self-employed people tend to be generalists who manage a wide range of their own affairs, the book reads as if you will do everything yourself. But even when you choose to hire a contractor, you'll be able to make more intelligent decisions if you understand all of your options.

And options are what a home office is all about—something you have now that you didn't in a commercial office. Whether you intend your home office as a place to work part or full time, or a temporary base until you move on to other quarters, I hope this book will help you find your best route on the exciting road to creating your own special working environment. So now that you are in the driver's seat, let's go!

PART ONE

INITIAL DECISIONS

CHAPTER 1

IS A HOME OFFICE RIGHT FOR YOU?

Creating an office in your home that works for you, your business, and your household requires careful planning and a monetary investment small enough to outfit a spare room or large enough to construct a new addition. Whatever the scale, before you invest the money, time, and effort to do it right, you should know if it is right to do it.

After exploring some of the larger issues of feasibility—you, your business needs, your location—we'll get into the economic implications of home offices in the following chapter. So stand back from your dreams for a moment and consider some basic questions. The answers will prove important long after you are moved into your beautiful new office.

CAN YOU WORK ALONE?

If you are like most home office professionals, you will probably be working alone for some or most of the time. Won't it be great to free yourself from distractions and work at your own pace? Sure, but how about the sudden isolation? You are the only person and the only sound is the tap tap tap of your keyboard. You may adjust to the new mode without a hitch, or the adjustment might take a toll on your business, family relationships, and mental state. Or you may not ad-

just at all. Home offices do not suit everyone. Picture a typical workday.

It's about the third week. The computer cables and peripherals have finally been worked out. The excitement of being your own boss in your own space is starting to wear thin. Your spouse has left for work and the kids are off to school. It's so quiet. After a few hours of work, you stop for coffee. There's no one to share it with—and it's still quiet. You return to your work, eventually stopping for a lunch that you quietly make and eat alone. By midafternoon, you welcome the distraction of the kids returning from school. Eventually your spouse comes home and you are again surrounded by people.

After many more days like this you realize you miss the workday crunch you were so happy to leave behind. At its worst, loneliness can depress you and affect your work.

You may get an indication of how able you are to work by yourself in a home office from Worksheet 1-1 (shown on page 4). If you don't think working in isolation suits your personality, you might do well to rethink your plans or find ways to counter the effects of isolation. Many home-based professionals link up with others in interactive networks via modems. Others get out of their home offices to occasionally lunch with friends. Outside involvement with service organizations maintains the social connection for others.

I have worked out my own way to deal with isolation. Because I work best in the mornings, I plan to do most of my "productive" work between around 7:30 A.M. and noon. I often leave the office during the postnoon slump period and drive to town to do business errands and work out for an hour at the YMCA. Refreshed and reconnected to people, I return midafternoon, eager for another hour or two of work.

Loneliness may not be your only obstacle to working alone. If self-employment is new to you, you may find it hard to work productively outside a structured work environment. I have no problem when a pile of work sits waiting, but a difficult time when it comes to promoting new business. On a warm, spring day, I may give in to the urge to go outside and putter in the yard. Someone does have to pull those weeds, don't they?

One of the perks of working for yourself is the very opportunity to work when, how, and if you like. But without discipline it's easy to accomplish nothing, then feel guilty about it. If you come up short on the personal discipline part of Worksheet 1-1, you might be helped by the following suggestions of other home-based professionals:

- Set up and follow a regular work schedule. You don't have to be a slave to long hours, but do commit a minimum number of hours each day to work.
- Plan your work over a long period and try to adhere to the plan.
- Dress for work. This reinforces your self-image as a professional at work.
- Get an answering machine for your phone and let it defer calls during your most productive periods.
- Don't give in to distractions in or outside of the house.
- Make sure the office says "office" rather than "part of the home."

None of these rules are cast in stone. Writers are notorious for writing just as well in jeans and sweatshirts as in business suits. But to recent refugees from a structured office environment, jeans and sweats signal play, not work. And making the office look like an office, rather than a part of your home, will impart a professional image.

A PROFESSIONAL IMAGE

One last question to ask yourself before committing to a major investment in a home office is how it will affect the image your clients have of you and the way you see yourself in your new role. Will you be able to regard yourself as the same serious professional in your new setting, or will your new image be that of "housewife" or "househusband" who happens to work out of the home? One of the many changes that came about during the 1980s was the growing acceptance of home offices as serious bases of business.

Still, by being the only adult at home during the day, you do inherit certain baggage by default. Your spouse's income from working outside the home full-time provides, likely as not, the lion's share of the household budget while you establish your own business. The tradeoff lands you with the major responsibility for the household, which may include cleaning and maintenance, preparing meals, shopping, and possibly looking out for children. Is there a way out?

Yes. First decide jointly just how serious your enterprise is to be. If you and your partner agree that it is to be more than a hobby, then sit down together to schedule household chores.

Second, if keeping the home together still falls mainly into your lap, at least try to organize your day to allow a minimum number of uninterrupted hours "in the office." Value this time every bit as much as the doctor who can't possibly be disturbed while in surgery.

Children are the thorniest part of the problem. One of the motivations that attracts many

Worksheet 1-1

CAN YOU WORK OUT OF A HOME OFFICE?

You won't know for sure if you can work effectively on your own in a home office until you have actually tried it. The questions below may at least give you a rough idea of whether your personality and work attitudes support working in isolation. Circle the letter of the answer following each statement that most closely fits your personality.

1. If you volunteered 4 hours each month to help produce a newsletter:

   A. You would prefer to spend the time writing content.
   B. You would rather spend the time on the phone brainstorming content with an editorial committee.
   C. You would best like to spend the time meeting with the editorial committee in person.

2. If you had your pick of locations in an open office that contained other workers, you would prefer to locate your workstation:

   A. In a far corner, remote from the entrance and other workstations.
   B. In a corner near the main entrance door.
   C. In the center, within easy contact of other workers.

3. You do your best work when you:

   A. Are left alone with minimal interruptions from other people.
   B. Get occasional feedback from colleagues.
   C. Get constant feedback from colleagues.

4. On a snowy Thursday evening just before 5:00 P.M., the boss announces that due to expected heavy snows, the office will probably be closed the next day. Workers are encouraged to take work home to complete it over the long weekend. You would most likely:

   A. Get up as usual Friday morning and dive into the work with the intent of completing it by 5:00 P.M.
   B. Begin working on Friday morning, but with no specific schedule in mind.
   C. Take advantage of the new snow on Friday to go skiing, and plan to complete the work sometime before Monday morning.

5. When in the midst of a task requiring intense concentration, the phone rings. You most likely:

   A. Ignore it and let your answering device take the message.
   B. Answer the call, but ask if you can call the person back later.
   C. Take the call.

If your answers were mostly "A", you seem to be the kind of person who can work independently, are capable of structuring your own work activities, and don't allow needless interruptions to obstruct your progress—all traits of an effective home office worker. Answers predominantly in the "C" category suggest that you need contact and support of others to work effectively. You should try working for a few weeks on your own before committing yourself permanently. Answers in the "B" category are inconclusive. Can you structure an arrangement that allows you to work part time in a home office and part time in an office with other people?

entrepreneurs to work from the home is the opportunity to be closer to their families. Unfortunately, choosing this route results in a trap when you discover you can't spread yourself thin enough to cover all the bases. The result is an unfortunate compromise all around. The kids don't get quality attention, you can't get your work done, and clients regard you as unprofessional. One solution is to find in-home care for preschool children. Another is to drop them off at a day-care center. Both cost, but so does the time you need to run your business.

The second part of the image question is how your clients will regard you in your new workplace. Home-based occupations are not new. Until the 1950s it was common for medical doctors and dentists to have their office in their home (of course, they still made house calls then, too). In time, they moved into clinics, group practices, and hospitals, presumably for better access to increasingly sophisticated equipment. For the most part, the businesses that stayed in the home were those run by women, usually on a part-time basis, such as piecework sewing and beauty shops. The home as a business site with status became tainted. Professionals who chose to base at home faced the prospect of not being taken seriously by their peers or the public.

The perception lingers, but a counter trend is under way. Thousands of male and female white-collar professionals have left the corporate workplace voluntarily or as casualties of downsizing in a changing economy. Aided by communications technology previously available only to corporate offices, these professionals are now working wherever they want.

The struggle for legitimacy begins with self-image. If you think of yourself as a serious professional, the feeling broadcasts itself to others. Start with a workspace designed and furnished to signal "business" rather than "home." Next, do what you must to become professionally legitimate. If you are a real estate broker, get certified as a Realtor. Join a professional association for your field, such as the American Society of Landscape Architects (ASLA) if you are a landscape architect, or the American Society of Interior Designers (ASID) if you are an interior designer. Besides the advertised benefits, using the association's letters behind your name will give you professional status in the eyes of the public. Jerome, Arizona, business consultant Barbara Blackburn advises her clients to get visibility by joining organizations such as the Elks, Kiwanis, Rotary, and the Chamber of Commerce.

KEEP IT LEGAL

The legality of establishing a home office is a test of feasibility you'll want to check out early. Most municipalities restrict what you can use your property for in the form of zoning ordinances. Many permit "home occupations" — a carryover from the days when certain types of professions were common in residential areas. But even if a home office is legally allowed, you still may have to formally apply to your local planning or zoning board for a "permitted use" or similar provision.

Permission, if granted, will likely restrict your operation, limiting the kind of sign you place outside, how many employees you can have, outdoor lighting, and required parking spaces.

If the ordinance makes no provision for home offices, you may be able to get permission through a variance. In general, you will have to apply in writing, demonstrating that you have adequate off-street parking and your office won't dilute the residential character of the neighborhood.

Your application may consist of completing a form and submitting a site scale plan showing your property and how the buildings are situated. Off-street parking areas should be well identified. Show the location of a new office entry, if there is to be one, and the revised footprint (outline) of the house if your office is to be in an addition.

You may already have a plot plan that came

Figure 1-1: Attic Office for an Architect/Author. *Below the bank of windows at right center, a shed dormer creates headroom for a drawing table flanked by side tables. At rear, right, is a second workstation for the computer. The long table at left provides a sit-down work surface and file storage with bookshelves above. In the foreground is a glass conference table.*

with your deed. If so, adding the new information to it should be easy. If not, you'll have to start with the legal description of your property, as stated on the deed, and draw a plan from scratch. If you can't do this yourself, call on a surveyor, home designer, landscape architect, or architect.

The written application may ask for a list of names and addresses of each abutting neighbor within a certain distance of your property. The municipality will then notify these folks of your request by mail and inform them of the date of the meeting when your case comes up for review. On that date, you can present your case in person before the appropriate committee and hope any neighbors with a grudge won't use the occasion to scuttle your application.

As if zoning ordinances weren't enough, you may live in an area subject to a "protective covenant." Condominium associations and certain housing developments sometimes impose restrictions to ensure the consistency of the appearance of the units over time. If this is the case, you will have to find your way around the covenant even before tackling the local zoning ordinance.

Any addition you plan will have to conform to the setback rules of your zone (more about this in chapter 15).

ACCESS TO CLIENTS

Two more questions affecting feasibility bear early consideration: How will you reach clients and how will you get the resources you need to operate?

Your clients may be as close as your phone, fax, or modem for much of the time, and as near as a mailbox or shipping service for the remainder. If you have a car phone, you can probably stay within reach, wherever you are. But if your business requires face-to-face contact with clients, whether on their turf or yours, distance and location become important.

If you intend to meet your clients on their turf, the cost of travel and lost time will eat into your profits. When these costs exceed the amount your home office saves on rent over one more centrally located, you are losing money. Are there enough other advantages to basing at home to offset this expense?

If clients come to you, how far will they be willing to travel, and—more importantly—will they be able to find you at all? An address that requires a map to guide visitors probably expects too much, because a client who arrives frustrated from getting lost will likely take that hostility out on you.

You may have some leeway with client access. When I began working out of my own home office in 1990, I realized the rural location was a bit out of the way for some of my architectural clients, but no problem for the markets I served through my writing. I decided I would nonetheless build the office to accommodate visitors. I would receive residential clients and sales reps in my office. I planned on visiting commercial clients at their place of business.

So far, the strategy has worked. My office represents part of a larger home renovation. When someone thinking about adding to or remodeling their home comes for the initial consultation, I get sales mileage out of my remodeling efforts by showing prospective clients through the rest of the house. As we go from room to room, I show pictures of how the 1800s New England farmhouse looked before I remodeled it. The tour convinces them that I know my way around home design and helps me turn prospects into clients.

PROXIMITY TO RESOURCES AND SERVICES

Before you lock yourself into a home office base, make a list of all the regular supplies and services you will need, then consider how you will get them and how much of your time it will take. As the information age marches on, it gets easier to run an office without having to leave it. You can get office supplies and equipment through the mail. But getting it is one thing and servicing it is another. Most high-tech office equipment goes awry at some time. If it's small and portable, you can take it into a nearby service center. Servicing larger items and tracking down glitches in systems hooked together requires on-site attention. Can you get a technician to come to your home office when you need to?

If you can satisfactorily answer the questions raised in this chapter, then you meet the basic tests for home office feasibility. Another important concern is economics, the topic of the next chapter.

CHAPTER 2
HOME OFFICE ECONOMICS

You can decidedly work out of your home at less cost than renting an office by saving on commuting time, interruptions, rent, a wardrobe, and possibly taxes. But your savings hinge on how much you invest to create a home workspace. We'll look at some of the economic issues of creating and outfitting a home office space in this chapter and explore the actual costs of remodeling and outfitting the space further on.

THE COSTS OF AN OFFICE IN YOUR HOME

Establishing an office in your home entails three kinds of expenses:

- Office furniture and equipment
- Supplies (consumables)
- Construction costs for remodeled or new space

The first two categories are the same whether you locate the office in your home or a rented commercial space. You can get an idea of what they'll be from mail-order catalogs and local retailers.

Construction costs can vary widely, depending on your location and the amount of work required. In general, a spare room will be the least expensive home office, and an addition will be the most expensive. A rough idea of the construction costs for various office sites is included

in chapter 5. Chapter 18 tells you how to peg your costs more precisely, after you have picked a site and have a better idea of what will be involved to convert it into a finished office. For now, let's turn to some of the other questions surrounding home office economics.

HOW WILL A HOME OFFICE AFFECT MY HOME'S RESALE VALUE?

This question may not loom large in your mind if you don't foresee extensive remodeling or you expect to hang onto your home indefinitely. Still, if you are like most Americans, you'll change residences at least seven times in your life, so recovering the cost of any remodeling deserves consideration. Also, remember that the glory days of the 1980s, when homes appreciated 20% each year, are over. Today's rate of appreciation hovers somewhere around 5% — barely even with inflation.

The trouble is, it's impossible for me to predict how a remodeling job will affect your home's resale value. The comparative returns on investment for various home remodeling projects have not yet specifically addressed home office conversions. When sixteen members of the Better Homes and Gardens Real Estate Service were asked to calculate the payback of various remodeling expenditures, they reported the following:[1]

Room Project	Recovery Cost Potential (%)
New Bath	75 to 100%
New Room	70 to 90%
Remodeled Bath	60 to 80%
Remodeled Master Bedroom Suite	60 to 80%
Minor Kitchen Remodeling	45 to 70%
New Garage	30 to 50%
Finished Basement	30 to 45%
Sunspace	5 to 20%

A similar rating in 1993 by *Home Mechanix* magazine[2] divided the payback into work done by a contractor and work done by the homeowner:

Project	Recovery Cost Potential (%)	
	Contractor	DIY
Finished Basement	57%	161%
New Family Room	56%	148%
Finished Attic	50%	124%

Though these payback figures don't specifically address home offices, they point the way. Adding a room, for example, has a relatively high payback of from 70% to 90% in the first rating, and from 56% to 148% in the second. Most of the cost of creating a master bedroom suite is also likely to be recovered. Could we not therefore conclude that we would be on safe economic grounds with an office addition that could easily be reconverted to a bedroom? In the second list, if you do the work, both new family room additions and finished attics pay back more than their original investment. So building a new room yourself or finishing your own attic for an office that might easily convert to another use seems to be a wise investment.

These examples point to an important part of getting the greatest recovery bang out of your remodeling buck: Go for mass over personal appeal. The more you tune your home to your specific needs, the less it is likely to appeal to the general needs of prospective buyers. Here are a few other tips real estate experts have suggested for making home improvements with an eye toward resale:

• **Don't overimprove.** Find out what the other homes in your neighborhood are selling for and ensure that yours won't exceed this level by 15% to 20% after improvements.

• **Consider adding an addition.** A home office addition can be reconverted to a third or fourth bedroom if you live in a suburban or rural area where single-family homes are in demand.

• **Don't spend too much.** More than 20% of the value of the house spent on improvements is too much, advises interior designer Carole Eichen.[3]

• **Make it fit.** If your home office is an addition to the home, let it look like part of the home and part of the neighborhood rather than a business office. You can make the inside as business-like as you want.

• **Make it nice.** Improvements should enhance, not detract, from the original house (to do it yourself or not is the subject of chapter 6). Quality always outsells mediocrity.

Do these rules have exceptions? Of course they do. With home offices on the rise, in the future there may be an increased demand for homes including offices, whether or not the office portions can easily serve other uses. The demographic patterns of your area and neighborhood offer the best clue as to how much to remodel and how likely a dedicated office would appeal to prospective buyers.

FINANCING: WHERE TO GET IT

Once you set a remodeling and furnishing budget you must find financing. Because all interest is an expense, whether or not it is tax deductible,

Figure 2-1: One Half of a Two-Car Garage. *One half of a two-car garage can be converted to an office with many attractions: cathedral ceiling with skylight, a separate outside entry, and the opportunity for windows on up to three sides.*

it probably makes the best sense to finance improvements out of savings, if possible. The $5,000 I drew out of a checking account in 1990 paid for all material costs required to turn an unfinished attic above my garage into a finished 425 sq. ft. office. I kept the costs low by building my own furniture and doing all of the work myself (except for installing the gas heating unit).

But I don't expect everyone's shoestring to be as tight as mine. For outside financing, look first for ways to use the equity you already have in your home. Here are four possibilities.

Second Mortgage

If you need more than, say, $10,000, a second mortgage may be your best source of financing. A second-mortgage loan piggybacks onto your first mortgage and is released in one lump sum for a maximum term of 15 years. The maximum amount loaned will be based on a percentage of the market value of your home minus the balance you owe on the first mortgage. Interest rates set up on a fixed- or variable-rate basis are deductible from your income tax bill, much the same as interest on your first mortgage. Even so, you still have to pay interest on the full amount of the loan, regardless of the rate at which you pay it out for expenditures.

Getting an appraisal and title search can make applying for a second mortgage as messy, upfront, as it is for a first mortgage. Some banks allow you to use your property tax assessed value in lieu of a reappraisal. In any case, you get stuck with any closing costs.

Refinance Your First Mortgage

Refinancing may make sense when interest rates are at their lowest (releasing you from an existing high fixed- or variable-rate loan) or when the amount you seek exceeds the amount you may obtain through a second mortgage. Another difference: you can draw out the term to 30 years rather than the usual 15-year maximum of a second mortgage.

Refinancing means repackaging the remaining balance of the first mortgage into a new loan that includes enough for improvements. As far as interest rates, term, and closing costs are concerned, the game is played much the same as with a first mortgage. You won't escape paying for "points" and all of the other trimmings that pad out closing costs. When considering refinancing, be sure to compare the total interest cost over the full term of the loan with that of your present montage. If you have a high interest rate fixed loan now, refinancing into a new low rate fixed mortgage can save a staggering amount and more than pay for the costs of your planned improvements.

Home Equity Line of Credit

More and more lenders are offering home equity lines of credit, a sort of revolving credit in which your home serves as collateral. The biggest advantage is the availability of funds when you need them and in the amounts you need. You pay interest on only the balance of principal — an appealing prospect if you don't know how much you'll need at the outset and when you will need to make payments. Your payments on principal and interest start after you begin to draw on your line of credit.

Because the loan is secured against the equity you hold in your home, the amount of credit available to you depends on the amount of that equity, likely up to 80% of the appraised value less the amount owed on the first mortgage.

The term of a line of credit is often set for a fixed time, say 10 years, beyond which the plan may allow you to renew the credit line. If it doesn't, you can't borrow more money until the first loan is repaid.

The variable-rate interest rates on home equity lines of credit can only be a few percentage points above the prime rate.

As with mortgage loans, obtaining an equity line of credit requires setup costs, as well as a transaction fee, in some cases. For this reason, this option may not work to your advantage if you draw only small amounts against your credit line. You might find that the several hundred dollars paid for loan-origination fees spread over the small amounts you actually use make the cost of this money dear.

Fixed-Term Installment Loan

An installment loan for home improvement bears the highest interest rate and the interest is not tax deductible, as with the other options. Another drawback is the amount you can expect to borrow, probably $5,000, to be repaid within 5 years. The advantages of this loan, if any, are that it is reasonably quick and easy to obtain. You may pay a loan fee of $40 or so, but no other front-end charges. You might do just as well to borrow off of the credit line on your credit card.

Relatives

If none of these sources appeal, ask Aunt Hattie or Uncle Wilber. Certificates of deposit are bringing in paltry returns these days. If well-off relatives have much of their savings in these instruments, they may welcome a proposal from you to borrow and repay them at a higher rate of interest than they could get from a savings account, but a lower rate than you would otherwise pay. It's a win-win situation, if you can work out the kinks. Even if they refuse, you haven't lost anything and you won't have drowned in paperwork trying.

TAXING MATTERS

Claiming an Income Tax Deduction

Until the late 1970s, home offices got a free ride from the feds with respect to claiming tax deductions for home office space. When Congress woke up to the fact that the easy-handed approach was costing the Treasury a bundle, it tightened the screws with the Tax Reform Act of 1976, which set rules for home office deduction that still apply. The home office has to be used *exclusively* and *regularly* for *activities related to a trade or business*, and satisfy one of the following requirements:

- It is your principal place of business, OR
- It is used as a place to meet your clients and customers, OR
- It is a separate structure not attached to the home.

The Internal Revenue Service tightened the screws in 1991 by requiring home office workers to detail their expenses on Form 8829. The latest squeeze, at least for part-time home office workers, came on January 12, 1993, when the Supreme Court struck down a $2,500 deduction claimed by an anesthesiologist who used a spare bedroom 10 to 15 hours a week for record keeping and telephoning colleagues and patients. The court ruled that to be deductible, the home office ordinarily must be a taxpayer's most important place of business or one used regularly to meet with clients—a test that the doctor didn't meet, in the eyes of the Court. The ruling will undoubtedly affect a wide range of professionals who use their home office part time, including self-employed persons and employees who need—but aren't provided—an office by their employer.

The battle will be tougher for part-timers, who will have to demonstrate that their home office truly is their principal place of business. If you are a full-time home office worker, you should be able to take a deduction for the portion of your home costs that support your office, if you play by the rules.

Lawyers and accountants warn that anyone who submits Form 8829 should expect an audit. To cover yourself, figure the exact percentage of your total home's floor space used by your home office and keep meticulous records of all expenses. As far as space planning is concerned, the more you physically separate your office space from the rest of the home, the easier it will be to convince the tax folks it's a serious office, and not just an amenity to your home.

Local Taxes

However you choose to deal with the IRS, don't forget that any improvements you make to your home office also increase its real value and will likely boost your property tax bill. Lani Luciano warns in *Money* magazine that the tax hikes from improvements can be very high, because your local real estate assessor may add the total value of the job onto your house appraisal.[4] To protect yourself, Luciano advises that you get two or three real estate agents to give you a written estimate of how much, if any, the project increased the home's value. Use these estimates to persuade the assessor, but don't expect him or her to happily concur. Moving an interior wall to create an office space from two smaller rooms adds no space to the house, but enclosing a porch, finishing a garage, or adding on to the house does. Much room for argument lurks somewhere between these extremes.

INSURANCE

Chances are that you have already faced the grim reality of health insurance costs for self-employed professionals. Though it may cause your head to ache, health insurance isn't the only protection you need to consider when you take your office home. Your occupation, office space, and the tools of your trade all call for scrutiny. Let's begin with the space itself.

Coverage for Increasing Your Home's Value

When I reviewed my homeowner's coverage with my insurance agent I was shocked to find that my home was underinsured, even without including my newly finished attic office. Improvements we had made increased the home's value substantially since we bought it in 1984, but we had never upgraded the insurance to cover the current replacement cost. My insurance agent stressed that because the cost of replacing a home changes constantly, homeowners need to review coverage every few years even if they do nothing to the house. If you make changes, the review becomes imperative.

Your homeowner's policy also doesn't likely cover your needs when you run a business out of your home. Liability, business property, and disability are types of coverage you'll need to consider adding. You may be able to attach a rider to your homeowner's policy to extend your coverage for any or all of these. Or buy a separate policy. Let's look at some typical types of insurance you may need.

Liability in Three Flavors

Various policies cover some kinds of liability related to your occupation or location. Here are three types and where to get them:

Professional liability insurance. This kind protects certain professionals for actions brought against them in the course of conducting their specialty. The coverage, obtained through specialty insurers, can cost you in the tens of thousands of dollars if you are involved in a highly vulnerable occupation such as certain kinds of engineering.

General liability insurance. This type can cover you for events that occur outside of your office. It would cover me in my work as an architect, for example, if I damaged part of a client's home while measuring it for redesign. You can buy this type of coverage as a separate policy or as part of a small-business insurance package.

Liability to customers and other visitors. Protection for individuals who come to your home office isn't automatically included in your homeowner's policy—it is more likely specifically excluded—but you may be able to expand your policy to include this coverage at reasonable cost.

Business Property

Even if your homeowner's coverage is current for the value of your home, it probably doesn't cover your computers and other business equipment. Rather than seeking specific insurance for these items, look into a rider tacked onto your homeowner's policy. You can expect to pay $200 or more for a special policy, but you can tack on an endorsement to your homeowner's policy for $20 or $30 a year.

Once you obtain coverage, it's a good idea to document your business property, including date of purchase, serial numbers, prices, and receipts. My agent, Tom Hamon, advises his clients to record all business equipment with a video camera, with a card placed next to each item bearing the serial number, date of purchase, and cost. However you document your property, update the list periodically and store a copy in a safe-deposit box or with your attorney.

Small-Business Insurance

Business property, general liability, business interruption, and errors-and-omission protection can be combined into a package small-business policy. A policy like this goes further than riders attached to your homeowner's policy to cover such items as loss of business data. Home business writers Paul and Sarah Edwards suggest that you consider a separate policy if more than 20% of your home is used for business or when your business activity poses a high risk of liability.[5]

Alternatives to Insurance

Insurance is something everyone wants but no one wants to pay for. Home office professionals live in morbid fear of an incapacitating accident or illness, getting sued, or losing our ability to make an income—to say nothing of our fear of getting wiped out by a hurricane, fire, or earth-quake. One way to calm yourself in the face of these horrors is to buy the right amount of the right kind of insurance. But it's not the only—or necessarily the best—protection for every kind of possible risk.

Paul and Sarah Edwards say insurance is but one of three approaches to risk management. The other two are avoiding risk in the first place and planning to absorb the risk. Tom Hamon agrees that you should avoid risk, if possible, but you can't avoid all risk. "I haven't been able to find any other kind of protection against the risks—except insurance," he advises. The question should focus not on what type of insurance to carry, but on how much of each type. He advises to start with an agent you can trust who won't overinsure you.

In the meantime, heed the advice of Paul and Sarah Edwards and keep your risk to a minimum by "staying healthy, keeping up your property, doing a quality job, and maintaining valuable equipment."[6] This strikes me as sound advice even if you're insured.

CHAPTER 3

HOW MUCH SPACE DO YOU NEED?

Boxes filled with reader's letters line her living room. The dining room serves as a conference room and work area for her employees: an assistant and a marketing director. Her office is crowded with small-business tomes and a computer, for which she battles her husband, Joe, who's also a writer. Her son's closet doubles as a filing cabinet. The only room in the house that's off-limits to the business: 10-year-old daughter Jeanne's bedroom.
Judith Schroer[1]

Jane Applegate's home office was at the crisis point just before she moved into bigger quarters in the remodeled garage. Ironically, Applegate is an expert on small business, the author of a weekly newspaper column, and consultant.

Why didn't she know better? My guess is that, like many other home-based entrepreneurs, Jane Applegate's business began small enough to easily fit into the most obvious spare space. In time, the room that seemed so generous with only a desk, filing cabinet, and a few shelves, soon filled up, leaving no room to grow.

GET IT RIGHT AT THE BEGINNING

In these uncertain times of rapid change you will be hard pressed to chart a precise course for your home-based business. Will it grow, shrink, or move sideways? Each of these directions affects how much office space you will need and the part of the house best suited for it. Take it from the many home office workers who have traveled the road of Jane Applegate—it's better to get it right at the beginning.

This chapter will show you how to come up with a preliminary idea of how many square feet of floor area to look for before you start plugging your computer into the spare bedroom. Designers call this process programming and wouldn't think of designing a building without going through it. An idea of the square feet of space you need will help you identify the best office site and guarantee that you can lay out the space to work.

Because the home office movement has caught us off guard, there are few guidelines available to help us size a home office. And all offices are not alike. Imagine how your home office differs from an office you may have worked in.

Like a symphony orchestra, your former office probably accommodated a number of players, each working in a specially designed task area. Other common areas housed the copy machine, central files, mailing, conference, and reception facilities.

But your home office is more like a one-man band. To work well, it has to be big enough for the necessary functions, but small enough and well organized to allow one person to operate everything with ease and efficiency. This is a tall order.

It's tempting to spot the first underused space in your home, then jump in and try to make it work as an office. It can. With enough creative cramming, you can fit equipment into almost any size space. Some books on home offices go to great lengths to show how to stuff an

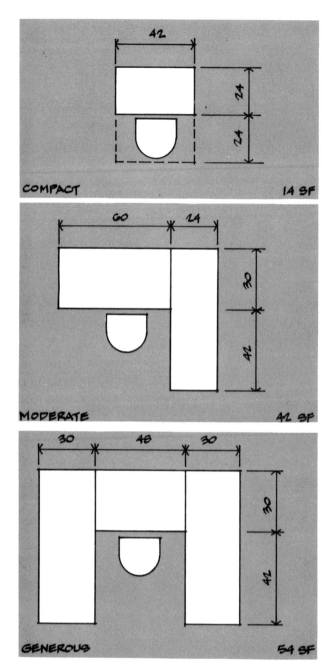

up varying amounts of floor area, depending on how they are laid out, so coming up with a reliable figure is as much art as science. The method described here will give you a range of the floor space required (in square feet) for three levels of amenity: compact, moderate, and generous.

The lowest (*compact*) figure will satisfy your functional requirements if every item is carefully planned. You will have to get the most out of vertical spaces, such as shelves above and below the primary work surfaces. This size office won't allow for much clutter, flexibility, or expansion, but it may suit you if you always have an immaculate desk or if the office is for occasional or temporary use.

The middle figure (*moderate*) will provide more space for a bit of spread and flexibility, but still limit growth.

The high number (*generous*) will yield a space large enough for flexibility with some room to spread out without worrying about displacing some piece of equipment or encroaching into space you need for storage.

The total of all of your separate office functions and items of equipment, plus an amount added for circulation, should give you an idea of the space you need. A summary worksheet is included at the end of this chapter to allow you to total your space needs. The floor space required for individual functions and pieces of equipment is described in the next section. Where dimensions are given, they are in inches.

BASIC WORKSTATIONS
Desk Spaces

Everyone needs some kind of horizontal surface to serve as the focus of operations. Think of it as a home base where you sit, write, talk over the phone, and ponder decisions. A desk or table are the most frequent answers. The floor space required for a basic sit-down work station is the same whether or not you use a computer. At the compact level, a 42" × 24" surface will accommodate a writing surface with just a little space left

Figure 3-1: Basic Workstations. *The compact level represents the smallest desk or space for a computer keyboard and monitor. Increasing the work surface and adding a side table yields a more practical (moderate) arrangement. A U-shaped arrangement makes the most generous work surface and allows the greatest flexibility of organization.*

office under stairs, into a nook, or even a hallway. Choosing these locations not only slights you of necessary space, but of privacy (more about that in the next chapter).

Your working areas and equipment can take

over for phone and desktop clutter. Underneath the work surface, you can fit your knees and one two-drawer file cabinet.

Widening the desktop by just 4″ allows enough space at one side for an L-shaped side return, a very useful surface for a keyboard, reference materials, or just more spread-out space.

Standard office desks are both wider and longer than the compact 24″×42″ desk. Their larger size (30″×60″), combined with a slightly lower side return adds space and flexibility. Standard double-pedestal desks come with storage drawers on two sides (the pedestals) and a shallow drawer above the center knee section. An 18″×42″ return may contain shelves, drawers, or be open to house a separate file cabinet.

Computer Workstations

If computers and their accessories are the driving force behind the home office trend, then it pays to plan carefully to accommodate them. Yet, planning for them is like shooting a moving target. Technology is changing so fast that the most careful planning may be obsolete in a year or so, as new devices make your present equipment obsolete. You've got to stay flexible.

Flexibility is made easier by the way computer equipment is sold. You can buy computer components separately, rather than in one all-purpose unit. This makes it possible to continuously upgrade, mix, match, and add peripherals.

Unless you rely on a portable laptop computer, you need a task area at desk height for a keyboard (and perhaps a mouse) and display monitor. Everything else can be located in other places above, below, beside, or even remote from your task area. You can integrate your computer equipment into your desk area if space is tight or if your desk area is fairly large, but this isn't a terrific idea for lighting and functional reasons (I'll cover these in chapter 7). You're better off with a separate computer station with enough space to house at least the computer (CPU), monitor, keyboard, and a printer.

The most compact arrangement I've seen is a rack on castors, measuring just 24″×18″×33″ (Global Computer Supplies). The monitor perches above the CPU, on the top shelf. A shelf below this pulls out to reveal the keyboard. Below, another shelf houses a printer. The little cabinet needs only 3 sq. ft. of floor space, but the leg room seems limited.

In addition, it's nice to have space beside the computer for reference material, disks, and maybe a cup of coffee. A 30″×44″ surface will suffice, if the printer perches on a shelf above or below the work surface (moderate). But printers can be messy. Continuous (tractor-feed) printers gobble paper from a stack below or behind the printer. Paper often jams, requiring you to open up the machine and put things right. Laser and ink-jet printers need a tray at the front for feed stock. And, if you are running more than one computer unit into a printer, you need to be able to get to the plug terminal in the rear to switch cables back and forth (or get a switching device).

Access to the printer is much improved if you don't assign it a place on a shelf, but put it at task level on the work surface where you can get to all sides of it. This is possible by widening the moderate computer surface from 44″ to 60″, to get a generous arrangement.

Drawing Surfaces

Architects, designers, engineers, and graphic designers rely heavily on drawing board work surfaces in addition to, or in place of, desk surfaces. Though graphic design is increasingly done on a computer, some hand drawing is usually required. A portable drawing board may serve your needs if you draw infrequently. When not in use, the board can store on end in a slot somewhere else. If this arrangement is too inconvenient to serve your needs, consider a free-standing drawing surface.

At the compact level, the surface can be a small 30″×42″ table with shallow hutch at the side for materials. This arrangement might work

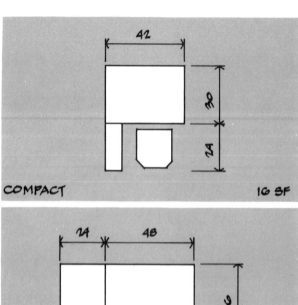

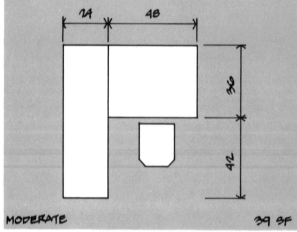

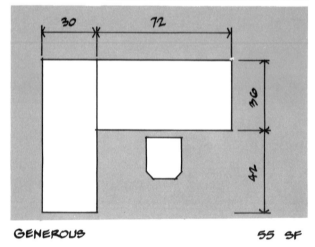

Figure 3-2: Drawing Surfaces. *A compact arrangement of a drawing board with a utility stand for drawing instruments will service graphic design or paste-up work. A moderate arrangement adds a side table, which is indispensable for interior designers, architects, and engineers. The generous level can accommodate the large-format media common to site planning.*

adequately for paste-up work, graphic design, or cartooning. Increasing the table size to 48″ × 36″ and adding a side table (moderate) should suit most design professionals. The generous arrangement will suit people who deal with large format graphics or who spend most of their time at the board.

Telephones and Answering Machines

The Dictaphone I bought back in 1977 consumed 4 sq. ft. of workspace. My present answering machine is no bigger than the phone base itself, because it's part of the phone. You probably don't need to allow a separate space for a phone plus an answering machine. Even separate machines can be small enough to fit on a shelf, thereby consuming no additional floor space.

Copiers

Always locate copy machines at work-height level so you can easily get to both ends and the guts of the machine (they are always jamming). Compact arrangements, just large enough for a small copier, measure about 36″ × 18″ (with feed and receiving trays extended), but allow no space for papers going into or coming out of the copier.

Anyone who uses copiers much knows that you can never have enough space around the machine. For a moderate arrangement, add paper stacking space to each end of the machine space, widening it to 60″. Deepening the surface to 30″ (generous) gives you additional space in front of the machine for papers.

Fax Machines

Because fax machines also take paper in one end and churn it out the other, they, too are better deployed at the work surface height, particularly if the fax machine doubles as a copier. But fax technology is changing rapidly. At this time, there are stand-alone fax machines and units integrated into copiers as well as hardware and software that allow your computer to function as a fax. Who knows what tomorrow will bring?

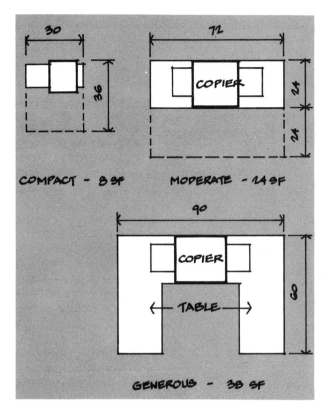

Figure 3-3: Copy Machines and Printers. *The compact level is the minimum required space for a table supporting a small copier, dot-matrix printer, or laser printer. A moderate arrangement adds work space on each side of the machine for queing and sorting. The generous arrangement increases the space at both sides of the machine.*

Like computer printers, fax machines can be placed on shelves, at no cost in floor space (compact).

Allow a space of at least 12″ × 18″ for a countertop fax machine (moderate). For a very useful space on one side for papers to be faxed, increase the width to 24″ (generous).

AMENITIES

Reception, Waiting, and Conference Areas

If you expect regular visitors, you'll need a space to receive them and confer. A minimal waiting area for one client consumes about 10 sq. ft. of floor space, just adequate for a chair and small table (compact).

A better arrangement, containing two chairs, needs 20 sq. ft. (moderate), and you can accommodate four clients in 35 sq. ft. (generous).

Before figuring conference space, think of how you work with clients. If you are a tax consultant, the best location for the client may be a chair in front of or beside your desk, in a space of about 4 sq. ft. (compact). A more intimate and less formal arrangement is a separate table that allows you and your client to sit across from each other as equals. The same amount of space will accommodate two lounge chairs and a small coffee table. For a separate two-person conference table, figure at least 14 sq. ft. (moderate).

If you need to display large graphic materials, figure on a table of at least 36″ × 60″, for a total area of 48 sq. ft. (generous). A table this large seats six persons. If you need a table for more than six, allow 4 sq. ft. for each additional person.

Will you be able to receive clients immediately or will they have to wait? Because waiting and conference functions occur only occasionally but consume a lot of floor space, they are expensive inclusions. Your waiting clients probably end up at your conference area anyway, so why not combine waiting and conference functions into one space for greater economy? You can do this by making the conference furniture a bit more comfortable than hard chairs and providing some magazines and a place to hang coats.

Rest Rooms and Refreshment Centers

An office that ends up outside the main house may make access to bathroom and kitchen facilities inconvenient. When planning to remodel a garage or other outbuilding for an office, or to add onto the main house, it may be worthwhile considering a separate toilet facility and refreshment center (these issues are explored more deeply in the next chapter, along with possible layouts).

STORAGE

Regardless of your occupation, you're sure to need storage space, and there never seems to be enough. Seriously consider what you need to store, and in what priority. Can "dead" storage

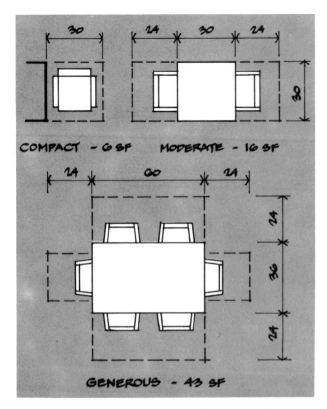

Figure 3-4: Conference and Waiting Space. *If you rarely receive outside visitors, a chair at the side of your desk might suffice (compact). The moderate arrangement provides a writing or display space between you and your visitor. On the more generous level, a 3 × 5 table seats up to six people and can be used for other purposes as well.*

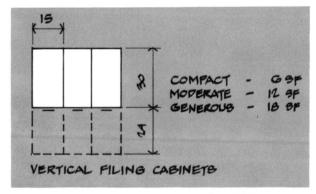

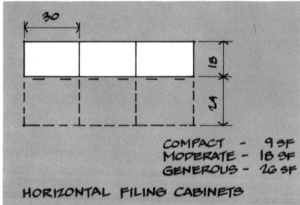

Figure 3-5: File Storage. *You can store files in containers on shelves above or below a work surface or in tubs on casters. The numbers here represent the floor space you'll need for vertical or horizontal filing cabinets in one-, two- or three-unit combinations.*

be relegated to a space outside the office entirely? Once again, flexibility is the best guide.

Data Files

The trusty vertical metal filing cabinet is only one option for storing files. Very active files can also be put in tubs, vertical organizers atop your desk, or stacked trays. I use all of these methods, as well as three-ring binders, depending on how active the file is. When I am working on a project that requires keeping many files at hand, I remove the metal file support rack from the file cabinet and put it on top of an accessible work surface. The rack returns to its permanent location when the project is complete.

The most compact space for files is under a work surface. You can even use them as supports for your work surface by laying wood doors over

two-drawer file cabinets (though this is too high for a keyboard). For files higher than two drawers, treat them as free-standing (moderate). Standard letter-size metal file cabinets are 15″ wide and vary between 18″ and 28″ deep. Legal-size units are 18″ wide in the same depths.

Lateral file cabinets make for easier retrieval but use more floor space because they have to be placed with full access to the long side. Most cabinets are 18″ deep and 36″ or 42″ wide. Because of the additional access space, they fall into the generous category.

Drawing Files

Many systems in a variety of modular sizes are available for storing drawings. Plan racks hang sets of drawings vertically, flat files store drawings in shallow drawers, pigeonholes house

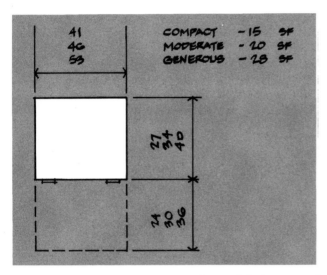

Figure 3-6: Drawing Storage. *Artists and designers need flat storage for drawings. Flat files come in the approximate sizes given, with a space in front for the drawers when open. Modular flat files can be stacked or stored under a work surface.*

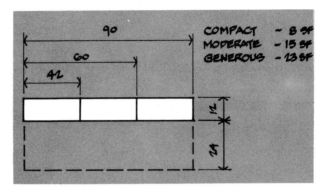

Figure 3-7: Shelves. *Free-standing shelves consume about 1' for width and 2' for access. If you have enough unused wall space above work surfaces, you may not need to allow extra floor space for shelving.*

rolled drawings. Artists may opt for vertical slots to store work mounted on board stock. I'll mention only the typical sizes of flat files here. If you need another type, you'll find a wide assortment in graphics supply catalogs.

A compact flat file storage drawer unit for 36″ × 24″ sheets measures 41″ × 27″. The next larger sheets, which are 42″ × 30″, require a moderate drawer, measuring 46″ × 34″. Generous files, big enough to house 48″ × 36″ drawings, come in at 53″ × 40″.

Shelves

Shelves house books, files, and supplies, as well as equipment. To work best, shelves should be ample in number and allow for flexibility of arrangement. If you deal with graphics, consider combining shallow shelves for books and supplies with deep shelves for drawings.

The most space-conserving arrangement employs shelves above or below work surfaces, thereby requiring no additional floor space of their own. Free-standing shelf units come in standard widths of 24″, 30″, and 36″. We'll consider a compact layout to be a single 12″ × 30″

unit. If it is 6′ tall and fitted with six shelves, it results in 15′ (lineal) of storage space. Two of these units, side by side, make up a moderate arrangement; three make a generous one.

SPECIAL EQUIPMENT
Reproduction Machines

Architects and designers often find it more economical to make their own prints than to have them done outside. Diazo process machines, the old standby, copy by exposing photosensitive paper to mercury-vapor lamps, then passing the paper through ammonia gas to develop it. Drawings are fed into the front of the machine and emerge at the rear.

Large format copiers that use electrostatic technology similar to copy machines are now available. They can copy opaque, as well as translucent, media, producing crisp, black-on-white images without the fumes of ammonia. However, they do cost substantially more than diazo printers.

Don't expect the new machines to save on floor space, though. The size of the machine is set by the width of the drawing. A compact layout would include a small 42″ wide printer that could be mounted on top of a side table or work surface. A moderate arrangement accommodates a wider machine and a side table. Better, still, is a

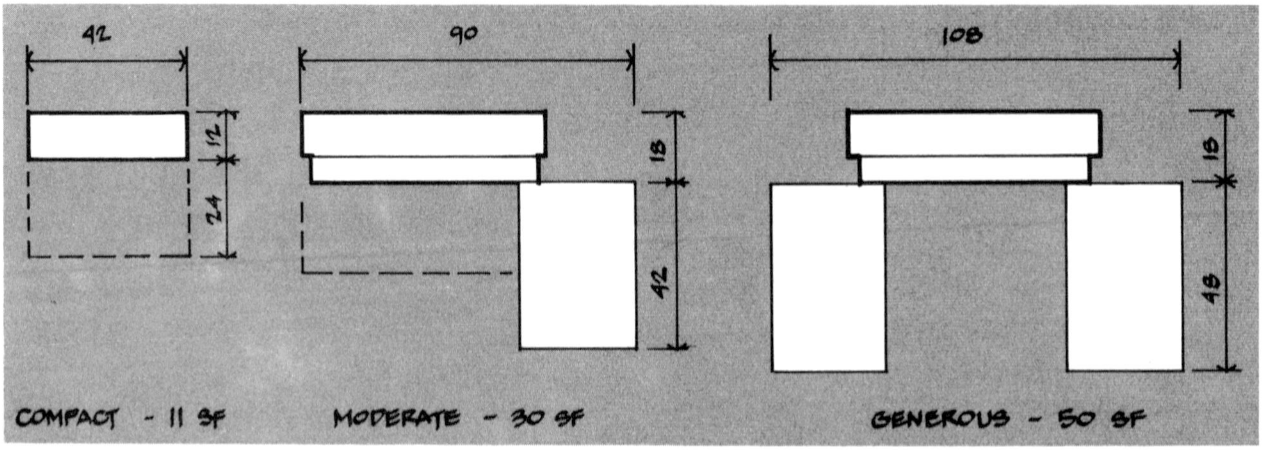

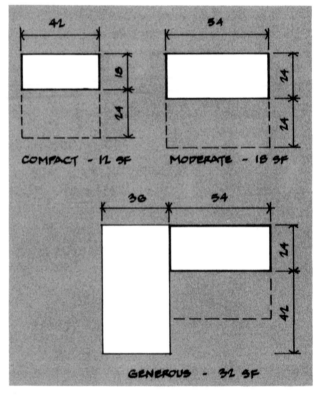

Figure 3-8: Diazo Printers. *Diazo printers (also called blueprint machines) reproduce drawings up to 42" wide. One or two side tables will come in very handy for drawings and prints. Space below the side tables can serve as storage for print paper and supplies.*

side table on both sides of the machine in a U-shaped arrangement (generous).

Plotters

As the graphic capabilities of computers continue to evolve, we can expect to see change in graphic output devices. Thermal, ink jet, and electrostatic plotters now join the popular pen plotters as faster ways to translate electronic images created on the computer directly to hard copy. Pen plotters mechanically apply an ink or pencil image by zigzagging back and forth over the paper as it rolls past the nib.

Regardless of the type, all free-standing plotters require an access space in front of and behind the unit because they accept paper in the front and release it at the rear. Most have castors that permit adjustments in location. A compact plotter handles up to 34" wide (D-size) sheets. For larger than D-size sheets, figure on a larger machine (moderate). This plotter arranged with a side table to hold sheets yields a generous arrangement. If your plotter is other than a pen plotter, adjust the dimensions to reflect its exact size.

Other Special Equipment

The equipment described so far covers only some of the items you may need. The revolution in

Figure 3-9: Plotters. *As with any large-format printing device, an adjunct space at the side adds utility.*

computers and electronic communications has spawned a dizzying array of gadgets to complicate your planning. Because the selection is so diverse and changing so rapidly, specific information risks becoming obsolete by the time you read about it. But there is a way you can quickly

Worksheet 3-1

SPACE SUMMARY

Each function or piece of equipment that occupies floor space is listed with the square footage of floor space required for a **compact, moderate,** or **generous** arrangement. Circle each of the three figures for every line-item that applies to your operation. Write in below any additional items that apply to your office space. Multiply the subtotal of each column by the appropriate circulation factor to get a total square footage for each column.

Function/Equipment	Compact	Moderate	Generous
Primary workstation	14	42	54
Computer workstation (if separate)	14	42	54
Drawing surfaces	16	39	55
Copiers	5	8	13
Large sheet (blueprint) printers	11	30	50
Computer plotters	12	18	32
Conference/waiting area	6	16	43
Waiting areas (if separate)	6	16	43
Filing cabinets, vertical	6	12	18
Filing cabinets, lateral	9	18	26
Flat file (drawing) cabinets	12	21	28
Shelves (12" deep)	8	15	23
Rest room (if separate from house)	16	24	32
Refreshment center (if other than house kitchen)	6	10	16
Other:			
....			
....			
....			
....			
Subtotals	___	___	___
Circulation Factor	x 1.2	x 1.3	x 1.4
Total Space Required	___	___	___

determine the floor area needed for any piece of equipment.

First, decide whether the item consumes floor space of its own or uses space you have already accounted for. Your phone, for example, will probably inhabit the top of your primary workstation and even be moved around. So, having allowed for its surface already, you don't need to add extra space. Similarly, include separate space for a free-standing filing cabinet; this isn't necessary if it will be stashed under a table or other work surface.

For items that need space of their own, start with the overall horizontal dimensions. Get these from catalogs or take a measuring tape to an office-supply store. If you typically sit at the item to operate it, add a clearance of at least 18" in front of the item (increasing its depth). This space, necessary for access to the device, is simply considered as part of its dimensions. Be sure to include any clearances required at the rear or sides to get to switches or plugs. Multiply the width and depth (including clearances) to get the minimum (compact) square foot area required

for the item.

To get numbers for the next two levels of amenity, moderate and generous, think how you use the equipment and where it would be helpful to have additional space (recall how we added space at the sides of the copier for papers going into and coming out of the machine). If you don't want to get that specific, multiply the compact number by 1.5 for moderate, and by 2 for generous.

THE SUMMARY

The Space Summary Worksheet is designed to help you summarize the space you'll need for a *compact*, *moderate*, or *generous* arrangement. Besides the floor space consumed by the footprint of each item of equipment and furniture, you'll need to add an amount to enable you to circulate within the layout. Multiplying the subtotals by the three "circulation factors" at the bottom of the worksheet should suffice.

The total figures will give you a yardstick for comparing various parts of your house, as we'll explore in greater detail in chapter 5.

CHAPTER 4

THE BEST FIT BETWEEN HOME AND OFFICE

When I left the corporate world of marketing to start my own advertising and marketing business, I set up shop in several existing rooms of my house and finally decided to add office space. I learned the importance of making the home office a professional environment the hard way.
Carol Russo[1]

Carol Russo followed the path taken by many home office workers. Most of them eventually agree that home and office mix about as well as oil and water. Carol's first office, a guest bedroom, met with snags each time guests occupied the room. So she moved her desk and equipment to a long wall of the master bedroom—an even bigger mistake. Twenty hours in the same room each day is stressful enough. It also got downright awkward when clients visited. She remembers having to use the bed as a conference table to show clients graphics she was preparing for a trade show. During another meeting—this one in the living room—she went back to the bedroom to retrieve some artwork from her drafting table. When her client unwittingly followed her in, Carol was embarrassed by the unmade bed, a baby swing and bottles, and print type strewn over the floor.

HOME AND OFFICE: KEEP 'EM SEPARATE

Repeated conflicts of this sort convinced Carol that she needed an office convenient to—but separate from—the house. "I needed a place to think, be creative, and focus on the day's project. And it *had* to be a place where tiny hands and paws would not disturb my paperwork or computer keyboard," she noted.[2] Carol solved her space dilemma by building a new addition onto the rear of her house.

Family Responsibilities vs. Your Need for Privacy

The need to oversee small children is the main reason many people choose to work out of a home office in the first place. They soon discover that keeping one eye on the little darlings and the other on their work causes more than eyestrain. When their productivity sags they may take their frustration out on the easiest target, the kids.

Work-at-home gurus Paul and Sarah Edwards offer sound advice in their book, *Working from Home*: "Keep your home a home and your office an office." They advise hiring a babysitter for a few hours each day or finding another child-care arrangement that will allow you a valuable chunk of unbroken time to work. Doing so enables you to locate the office in a remote part of the house that is free from the distractions of the rest of the house. This arrangement also clues other family members as to when you are "at work" and not to be disturbed. It might even help you shift mental gears into the "work" mode when you enter the office space.

If you have no other choice but to share space with another room, the need for separation still holds. If your only options are taking over space from a dining room, living room, or bedroom, try to find a workable way to create privacy. Bookshelves, curtains, even a demountable partition might at least isolate you from sights, if not sounds and smells, of the household. If the room must revert to the house at night, find a way to close off your equipment. It may be hard to close off a bay or hutch without compromising the adjacent room, and you may have to make do with a dividing screen, such as a free-standing row of bookshelves.

Even the most elegant designs for sharing office space with another part of the house should be viewed as temporary, or to serve as secondary offices. Beyond the conflicts inherent in sharing space, you'll probably come up short for room to work. Some of the more compact arrangements, such as closet spaces, require you to sit out in the adjacent room when the office is in use. Like submarines, every square inch of space is so dear that you'll have few choices in the way you organize it, no potential for expansion, and no place to stash the usual clutter that accompanies even the most fastidious professionals. And even if you don't see clients in your office, it's hard to feel professional while staring into a closet with your back to a bedroom.

Which brings up another point. Could you work efficiently in a room that suggests strong psychological associations with another use? Or, like me, do you need physical separation from "home" to allow you to center on your work? I read about one consultant whose need for separation between work and home life was so strong that he made sure his home office had a separate entrance. He avoided slipping into the comfortable habits that attract others to working at home by dressing for work each morning, then walking out the front door to enter his office through its own door.

If you can work in any space, anywhere, disregard the previous advice. But, in the interest of efficiency, you owe it to yourself to know your own work habits before you choose your workspace.

Sounds and Smells

Sounds and smells are also compelling reasons to physically isolate your office. Shutting out the household din is next to impossible in a shared space. It's easier in a separate space, and best in a remote space, such as a garage or outbuilding (specific tips for soundproofing floors, walls, and ceilings follow in part 3).

Physically separating your office is also the easiest way to keep household smells at bay. You don't want food aromas wafting through the air during a client conference. The closer your office is to the kitchen or bath, the more likely the problem. Keep odors out with doors that close your office off completely. Exhaust fans in kitchens and baths—a good idea in any case—help by removing the odors at their source.

The Flow of People

To minimize conflicts with household traffic and accommodate visitors in a professional manner, you need to attend to two types of circulation: the way(s) into and out of your office, and flow patterns inside the office. Only the first pattern is important at the early stage, while you are thinking of an office location. We'll deal with internal circulation later on.

Siting your office for easy access is a simple matter if you're the only one who travels the path, but it gets challenging if you expect to receive visitors. If you do, and making a favorable impression counts, use visitor access as one factor in deciding where to locate your office (the subject of the next chapter).

Imagine, for example, that you own the typical ranch-style house shown in Figure 4-1 on page 27. You are trying to find a site for the office where you can receive occasional clients. With one of the kids now off to college, your first thought is to take over one of the three bedrooms. But getting to any of these rooms from

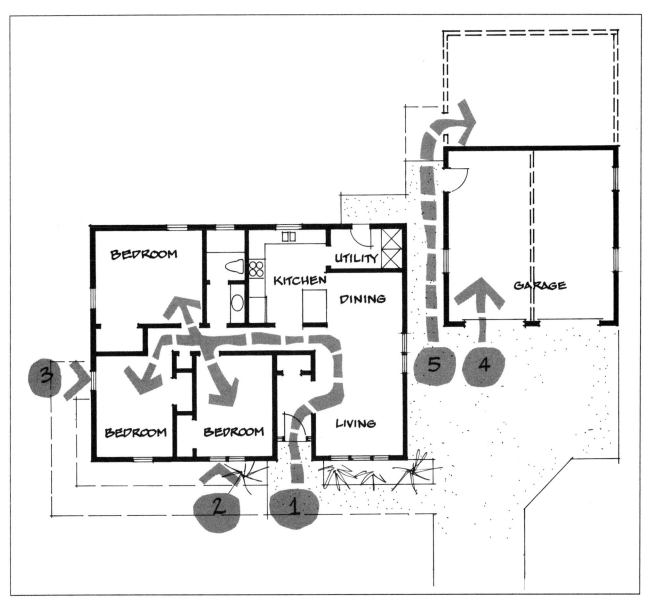

Figure 4-1: Using Entry Paths to Assess the Best Site for an Office. *Using a spare bedroom without a separate entrance* **(1)** *requires clients to pass through the bedroom hallway. Replacing the window of the front-center bedroom* **(2)** *with a door provides an accessible outside office door, easily visible from the street, but it may compromise the residential character of the house. Extending the front walkway around the side of the house to access the rear corner bedroom* **(3)** *avoids this dilemma and is only slightly less convenient. Converting half of the garage* **(4)**, *or adding onto the rear of the garage* **(5)**, *offers the best solution, if a heavier stream of visitors needs to be accommodated.*

inside the house requires clients to pass through the bedroom hallway, which is a sure way to risk running into other family members.

How about an outside entrance? Each of the three bedrooms has windows at ground level that could be converted to doors. A doorway to the bedroom at the front of the house would be most convenient. Would it make your house look too much like an office, though? Maybe extending the front walkway around the side of the house to enter through the rear corner bedroom might be a better compromise.

If you expect many visitors, converting half of the garage to office space offers the most direct route in, as well as the best separation from the house. If you need the garage space for the second car, then how about adding onto the rear of the garage? Visitors can then pass through the breezeway to get there—in fact, you could extend the breezeway roof to keep them dry en route. But this option would cost a lot more.

OFFICES FOR TWO: VARIATIONS ON A THEME

Our discussion of the home-to-office fit thus far has assumed a single office to accommodate one full-time worker. While this model includes an impressive 12 million home-based professionals, just as many operate part-time businesses from home[3] and 13.7 million more keep an office there for convenience[4]. Within this milieu, there are numerous variations:

- Offices for couples who work together in one business
- Offices for couples who manage two separate businesses out of a shared space
- Offices for one full-time partner and one part-time partner
- Two separate offices in the same house

Each arrangement calls for the right kind of emotional and physical space. Emotional space is deftly handled in the books listed under "Spouse and Family" in the appendix. The focus of this book is the physical space.

Even if two people can work compatibly, how they arrange their physical space can enhance or disrupt their harmony. Consider how two couples have created quite different fits between business, office space, and home.

Two Businesses, One Office

Can a large table with a couple of filing cabinets below, a single computer, and a few bookshelves serve the needs of two people working at two unrelated businesses? They can and do for Robert Monteaux and Elaine de Greck. Fitted into a corner of the kitchen-dining area of their Portland, Maine, apartment, this minimal home office is the base of operations for Robert's interna-

tional trading business and Elaine's fitness and yoga venture.

The key to making it work is as much time as space management, according to Robert. He works full-time in the office, whereas Elaine uses it occasionally for administrative tasks, spending most of her professional time teaching classes at health clubs. "If we were both at home working at the same time, we would need more space," says Robert, who adds that his business is a perfect one for running out of a home office equipped with the latest tools of electronic communications. "I'm dealing with people in Russia, in Yemen, in Australia, in Georgia—I'm not dealing with anybody in Maine." So he intends to remain in a home office, even if the day comes when the couple has one in a separate room in their own home.

Two Businesses, Two Offices

Wayne and Barbara Kings' businesses couldn't differ more. Barbara is a potter, and Wayne is a structural engineer. Both wanted to work out of their Ipswich, Massachusetts, home, but to separate their work life from their home life. They found the perfect architectural solution by remodeling a three-story barn that had been used only for storage since they bought the place 20 years earlier.

Except for wiring the radiant heating system and painting, Wayne did all of the work himself. The basement level became Barbara's pottery studio, equipped with kilns both inside and out in the yard. The floor above, opening to the ground level at the front, houses a sales gallery and public entrance from the street. Wayne's engineering office occupies the former hayloft on the third floor. Wayne built a glass-enclosed porch to connect the barn to the house to shelter their way during the long New England winters.

Barbara's business receives the most public visitors, so it made sense to locate it on the main floor. The visitors that come to Wayne's office enter via the same entrance, are then greeted by

Barbara or one of her staff, and directed upstairs. The arrangement suits everyone. The couple rarely see each other during the workday, except for Wayne's occasional trip downstairs for coffee.

ACCOMMODATING VISITORS

For regular visitors, you should aim for a separate entrance, or at least a pathway leading in that circumvents household traffic. Adequate off-street parking is also a must, and probably required by your zoning board to establish a home office. Once visitors are inside, there are other needs to be met: reception/waiting, rest room facilities, and possibly refreshments.

Reception/Waiting

Waiting areas of three sizes were suggested in the last chapter to enable you to arrive at a total square footage for your office. But maybe you won't need a separate waiting area at all. Most home office workers get by without one. They usually know in advance when to expect the occasional visitor and seldom get more than one at a time. Of course, they may arrive when you are on the phone or in the middle of something else. The solution is to provide a place where visitors can sit down and regroup from the trip without having to mill about inside your work area.

One or two comfortable chairs between the entrance and your work area may serve nicely, or you can do as I do: make the conference table serve double duty as a waiting area. And don't forget to provide a place—other than a chair—to hang your visitors' coats.

Rest Rooms

Offices in garages and outbuildings are ideally sited for separation from household traffic, noise, and smells. These advantages are offset, however, by the greater distance to bathrooms. If the distance is too far or you expect many visitors, look into the feasibility of separate toilet facilities in the office building. First make sure your zoning ordinance allows plumbing (of any sort) in

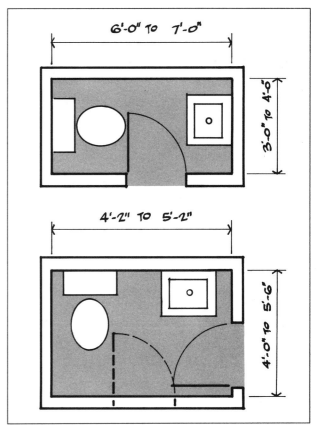

Figure 4-2: Toilet Room Layouts. *A toilet and lavatory (sink) will fit into a 3' wide space. The top layout requires from 18 to 28 sq. ft. The bottom layout, which allows entry from either of two sides, requires from 17 to 28 sq. ft.*

an outbuilding. Many ordinances prohibit plumbing outbuildings in order to prevent the owners from converting them to apartments, thereby changing the occupancy classification of the lot.

If you can legally plumb your office, call in a plumber. The individual can tell you if hot and cold piping and a waste line can be run from the house; ask for a cost quote. Ripping concrete garage floors up can be expensive. The new piping and fixtures are sure to make a separate rest room the most expensive part of your office, so bear this in mind when you compare location options in the next chapter.

Coffee, Tea, or Milk?

Your guests will appreciate being offered refreshments, whether or not they accept. A re-

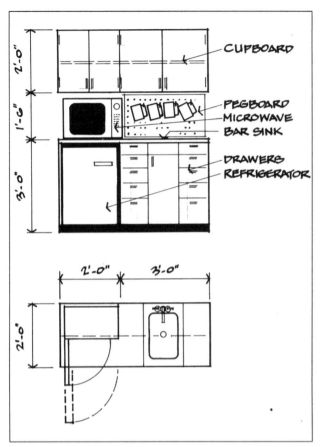

Figure 4-3: Refreshment Center. *An unused corner measuring 2' × 5' can become a handy area for warming up lunch, making coffee, and storing cold drinks. Cupboards and drawers keep dishes and utensils out of sight when not in use.*

freshment center in or adjacent to the office is the most convenient location. An ideal refreshment center consists of a 3' or 4' length of counter with a single-compartment sink (bar sink). A small refrigerator tucked below stores cold drinks, ice, and milk. Cups, saucers, and drinks can nicely fit in shelves or cupboards above.

If you do build a separate rest room, the additional plumbing for a small refreshment-counter sink will add little to the cost. If plumbing is not in the cards, the center will still serve this purpose. Just remember to have enough water on hand for the coffee machine (or make coffee in

the kitchen and keep it in an insulated dispenser), and be sure to have enough cups on hand so that you don't have to constantly bus them back and forth between the refreshment area and the house kitchen.

What About Disabled Visitors?

Since the 1970s, certain public buildings have had to comply with design standards aimed to accommodate persons with handicaps. As of January, 1992, the Americans with Disabilities Act (ADA), broadens the scope to include any public facility where more than fifteen people are employed. Your home office most likely falls beyond the reach of the ADA, at least for now. But there are two cases where your remodeling should conform to handicap standards: if you expect visitors with disabilities, and if you, yourself, are handicapped. In either case, get expert design help from a consultant or from one of the books listed in the appendix.

Certain provisions aimed at the disabled make good sense for any home office. If your entrance is only a foot or so above grade, consider a ramp, rather than two steps. It's just as easy to walk up and much easier to negotiate for anything on rollers. Similarly, 36" wide doors will be much easier to get furniture and equipment through. Lever handles are easier to operate than round knobs.

We've looked at several heady issues you may face in fitting your home office to your home: the need to oversee children yet establish privacy, how offices can suit two people working full or part time on the same or different businesses, and accommodating visitors. Thinking through each of these at an early stage—before you commit to a particular location—will ensure that the time, money, and effort you spend creating your office space will be well spent.

CHAPTER 5

THE BEST LOCATION

If you followed the guidelines and completed the worksheet in chapter 3, you have a fair idea of how much office space you need. Chapter 4 suggested some things to think about in situating the office with respect to the rest of the house. Unless you have only one choice for location, you must now decide where to put the office. Let's put seven likely candidates under the microscope to see what each offers — and where the alligators lurk.

THE CANDIDATES

Spare Rooms

Spare rooms are undoubtedly the most favored site for most home offices. Already finished, they are about the right size for most single-person businesses and require the least remodeling. If you keep your alterations to a minimum, you can easily reconvert the room to its former use when you move on or no longer need a home office.

On the downside, spare rooms may be poorly situated for traffic. A remote bedroom may not be easily accessible to visitors. Passing by the bathroom and other bedrooms may be no problem to you, but it may be embarrassing if you need to present a professional image to visitors.

Separation from household noises and smells may also be a problem. A room too close to a kitchen or bath is particularly vulnerable to migrating odors. A room near a living or recreation room or below a teenager's bedroom is vulnerable to noise. There are ways to isolate sounds and smells, as we'll see later, but the fewer you have to isolate, the better.

Lofty Opportunities

The sloping ceilings that intersect at odd angles and cramp headroom make attics challenging prospects, but I bet those very features are what makes an attic the site of choice for artists, architects, and designers. Just imagine sitting up there above the fray of the household with the sunlight streaming in through dormer windows or skylights. During work breaks you can get up and look out the windows at the best view from anywhere in the house.

If the attic is unfinished, you face the cost of insulating and finishing the walls and ceiling, as well as maybe the floor. Windows may have to be added or upgraded, and heating, cooling, and electrical work installed. The tab for all this work could easily approach that of building an addition. But the lack of finishes also allows much greater freedom to tailor the space to your needs; in a spare room you pretty much have to take things as they are. You'll appreciate these advan-

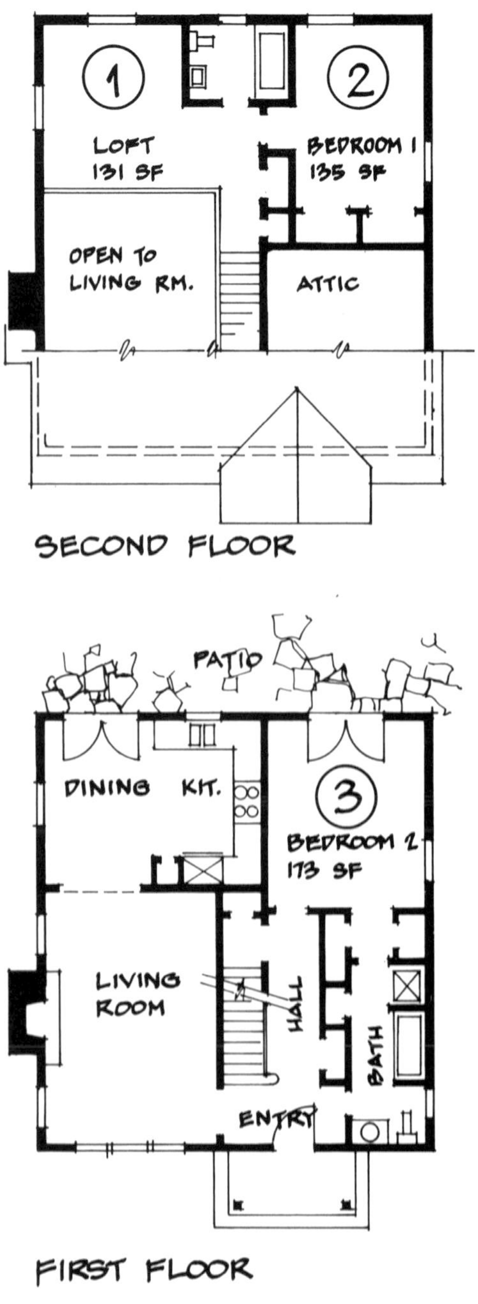

Figure 5-1: Sizing Up Candidate Rooms. *Three rooms of this two-story home offer potential office sites, but their assets and liabilities must be compared to make the best decision. The loft on the second floor* **(1)** *overlooks an open railing to the living room below. One bedroom* **(2)** *offers acoustic privacy, is slightly larger, and comes with some built-in storage. The second bedroom* **(3)** *is larger still and separated from the house. It is the best choice because the separate entrance, the French doors to the patio, are easily reached from the side of the house.*

tages when it's time to install lighting and wiring or to decide on the best type of windows or skylights.

But before you rush up to clear out the treasures that have accumulated over the years, be aware of the problems you may encounter in converting your attic to an office, and whether they can be solved without breaking your budget.

Naturally, the first requirement is to be able to get to and from the space. Like finished rooms, getting to the attic may entail a tour through parts of the house you would be just as happy to have visitors skip. The stairs may be too narrow or steep for safe and easy passage. Can you get office equipment in and out of the space?

Perhaps there is no way up at all. Many unfinished attics can be reached only via a hatch in the ceiling of a room below. If this is the case, you will need to determine whether it is feasible to extend an existing stairway or even build a new one outside.

Lack of headroom plagues many attics. If the attic space is a triangle with two corners at the floor and the third at the roof ridge, the width of floor near the center with adequate headroom may be as little as a third of the total width, if the roof is steep. If the roof pitch is low, there may be no adequate headroom. Before you commit to converting the attic, measure the space, then draw an accurate cross section to see how much is usable without raising the roof.

Most codes require at least 7'6" over 50% of the floor space in main rooms. If your attic meets this test, don't worry about the low spaces at the sides. Use it for storage and erect a 4' high kneewall along the sides to provide a vertical surface to back up desks and furniture to. Even if you don't have enough headroom, don't rule out the attic completely; explore the options to gain more headroom described in chapter 11.

Another problem in many attics is the floor. If the attic floor was designed to support only the ceiling below, it is probably too flimsy to support office equipment. If in doubt, ask an architect or builder for advice. There are several ways floors can be beefed up, as we'll see in chapter 11, along with ways to light, heat, and cool the space.

Down, But Not Out

Sloping ceilings with quirky windows offering wonderful views to the outside make solving the problems of converting attics worth the effort. Basements come with some of the same problems — lack of headroom and difficult access — but without the perks.

Or do they? If you live in a split-level home, the basement windows may look out over the yard. Because this type of house wasn't common until the later 1940s, your basement probably does have adequate headroom. You may also be blessed with a firm, level floor that stays dry, and modern, workable wiring and piping that fits neatly between solid, evenly spaced joists overhead.

The basement that underpinned my New England farmhouse lacked these advantages, to say the least. The walls consisted of rubble stone cobbed together without the benefit of mortar. The gaps between stones offered no resistance to cold air and moisture, or to a seasonal migration of small creatures from the field out back. When temperatures dived outside, it got cold enough inside to freeze water pipes, despite the heat emanating from the old boiler.

Overhead, confusion reigned in the amazing jumble of wiring and piping, cobbed together by succeeding generations of owners. A section of garden hose joined the water supply piping in one area. Electrical circuits and wiring added haphazardly over the years resulted in a mess that was unsafe and hard to figure out.

Part of the sloping floor was crumbling concrete. The rest was dirt. When the heavy rains came in the spring of our first year, a foot of standing water covered the entire surface.

If your basement resembles the first type, you are lucky indeed. Your main problems will be iso-

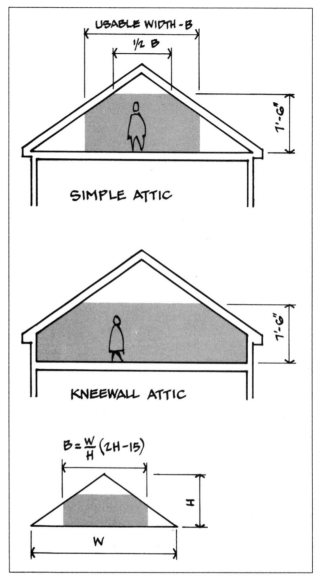

Figure 5-2: Attic Headroom. *Major building codes require a minimum of 7'6" of headroom over one half of the area. The shaded portion shows the net usable space permitted by this criterion. A simple, triangular attic yields far less usable width than one with kneewalls at the sides. You can determine your own attic's potential by measuring its total inside width (W) and clear height at the center (H) and drawing a cross section to scale, or by plugging the numbers into the formula at the bottom.*

lating the noise of the floor above, creating a thermal and moisture barrier in the walls, and maybe leveling the floor. If your basement comes closer to mine, your battle is an uphill one. But take heart. Except for intractable problems (such as a ceiling that is simply too low), most problems can be solved. I took on the obstacles one at a time and today have a warm, dry basement with up-to-date wiring and a TV room at one end.

The new basement room could have served as my office, but I decided on the attic because of the potential for views and daylight. But you may not want the distraction of windows, particularly if you will only be working in your office a few hours at a time, or at night. In that case, take a second look at that basement. You can probably remodel it much more economically than an unfinished attic.

Porch Perches

Because they are outside the house, porches are often overlooked as candidates for office space. Too bad. The potentially great views and chance for a separate outside entrance make them appealing choices. What's more, they are probably the easiest areas to separate from household noises and smells.

But converting a porch into a workable office isn't always easy or cheap. The first thing to look for is width. If the porch is less than 5'4" (the dimension from the house wall to the edge) and there is no way to expand outward, you are probably kidding yourself. You should have at least 8' clear in the other direction (the net width after deducting any space needed to maintain an entry passage into the house).

If the porch lies in the path to the main entrance door you may have to find an alternate route into the house or endure foot traffic through your office space. This arrangement also lets in too much cold air.

The floor is another thing to size up at this time. Does it slope away from the house to allow water to drain? If so, you'll need to level it and probably insulate it from the ground below.

Count on adding new walls, windows, a ceiling, heating, and electrical wiring. All these things explain why porches may not be the most economical office space candidates.

Moving the Mazda Out

Garages offer much potential for office space, if you can free up the space. A wall down the middle of a two-car garage can mark off a separate, 230 sq. ft. area, which is a sufficient size for most one-person offices. If detached, the location provides excellent isolation from household smells and noise. The possibility for a separate entry makes them compelling to anyone expecting many visitors.

If you can't sacrifice car space, don't give up. Detached garages often come with attic spaces. These spaces may not be high enough to use as is, but can often be modified by adding shed roof dormers or raising whole sections of the main roof, as we'll see later on.

If the garage is out, how about converting the potting shed out back? Converting any outbuilding into finished space ought to be cheap, because the structure is already built. But if it is no more than a shell, you will have to insulate, wire, add heat, as well as new finishes for walls, floors, and ceilings. In garages, if there is to be a door connecting the car bay with the office portion, you will need to heed fire separation provisions of the prevailing codes, as we'll see in chapter 14.

Before proceeding, make sure your zoning ordinance allows offices in an outbuilding. If it doesn't allow them, you may be able to sneak your office into the garage or potting shed if you don't change the exterior. But doing so will make you vulnerable to legal recrimination if the municipality finds out. And keep in mind that action can be instigated on nothing more than a tipoff from an unfriendly neighbor.

The cost of converting a garage or outbuilding to finished office space will almost always exceed that of doing a spare room. But it will be less than an addition. In any case, it will be worth the expense because of the advantages of its complete separation from the household. Don't overlook the fact that the remodeling will probably be the least disruptive to your household, as well.

You can even tear the roof apart without worrying about the mess.

Adding On

An addition to your house offers opportunities unmatched by converting existing spaces, but at a cost exceeding conversion of existing space, finished or unfinished. If you can afford it, you'll have the chance to create an area unencumbered by a previous use, well separated from the house, and with its own entrance.

As with outbuildings, first check the legality of adding on. When you determine what zone you are in, you can look up the corresponding chapter of the ordinance to find out the required setbacks on the front, sides, and rear of your house. Then measure the distance between the house and each property line to compute additional buildable area.

Expect an addition to cost about the same as a new, separate structure, even though one wall may be common to the house.

A Separate New Structure

If an addition appeals to you but you lack a common wall from which to add on, a separate structure may be your answer. How better to lay out the space exactly as you want with its own entry and unexcelled physical separation from the house?

You'll naturally need to ensure that your lot has an area you can build on and one that will pass legal muster. A zoning ordinance that allows you to take over your garage for office space won't necessarily allow you to build a separate office structure on a residential property.

The cost of a new structure built specifically for your office will be the most expensive option yet, because you will probably want to include a toilet.

RATING THE OPTIONS

Many factors may affect your choice of the best office site. Worksheet 5-1 can help you compare various candidate sites in terms of various factors.

Feasibility begins with determining whether or not using the space for an office is possible in terms of legality and accessibility. Then consider such factors as enough headroom and usable floor area. Another feature that may be desirable is isolation from home noise and smells. Finally, consider whether you can convert the space without ruining your marriage.

You should be able to come up with a preliminary idea for each of the factors on the worksheet by visually inspecting the area, armed with a measuring tape. If you feel insecure about things such as cracks in a basement wall or whether an attic floor could be rebuilt for office use, get opinions from one or more of the outside experts described in the next chapter.

The cost weighs into feasibility for most of us. But estimating the total cost of converting each site is more of a head scratcher. You can't put a reliable number on the construction until you know exactly what has to be done, and you won't know that until you have completed the planning and design phases. For that reason, I have left a detailed discussion of costs to the next-to-last chapter.

For now it might suffice to get a general idea of the relative magnitude of converting each site. Without including equipment or furniture, the construction cost of your home office will be least for a finished spare room and most for a new separate structure. All other options will probably fall somewhere between, in line with the table on page 37. These very approximate numbers are based on 1994 costs per square foot of a total area of around 180 sq. ft. (about a standard bedroom). They assume you will have someone else do the work. Deduct about one half if you do the work yourself.

Combining the preliminary costs of each of your options with the worksheet should steer you toward the ideal office site. I say "steer" rather than "decide" because some factors spe-

Worksheet 5-1

COMPARING CANDIDATE SPACES

Put a number for each of the following factors in the column that applies to candidate spaces. Write a "2" for good, a "1" for adequate, a "1" for okay/some, and "0" for inadequate/no. If the factor is irrelevant or unimportant to you, don't rate it at all.

Identification of spaces:

SR1	Spare room #1	B	Basement/cellar
SR2	Spare room #2	P	Porch
SR3	Spare room #3	G	Garage
A	Attic	AD	Addition
		NS	New structure

FACTOR

CANDIDATE SPACE

	SR1	SR2	SR3	A	B	P	G	AD	NS

Legality
Allowed by zoning ordinance
Have adequate parking for office
Building permit not required

Accessibility
Can reach space as is
Can reach if new stairway
Easy to add new stairway
Path to office is adequate for visitors

Separation
Kitchen/bath odors are not a problem
No noise is likely from space above
No noise likely through walls

Size and Shape
Enough area (as determined in chapter 3)
Headroom is adequate
Space is not too narrow

Other
Water or dampness is not a problem
Remodeling can be done without
   disturbing family or neighbors

Total Scores:

COMPARATIVE COST RANGES FOR VARIOUS OFFICE SITES

Site/Extent of Work	Costs per Square Foot of Floor Area ($)
Spare Rooms	
Basic (walls, ceiling and floor unaltered)	$0 to $5
Add for altering floor or wall for sound control	$3 to $5
Basements	
Basic (finish ceiling and 2 exterior walls, add two new interior partitions, carpet floor)	$15 to $20
Add for new wood floor	$5 to $7
Attics	
Basic (insulate and finish walls, roof, and floor)	$20 to $35
Add if floor has to be rebuilt	$5 to $8
Add if new windows/skylights (2) needed	$9 to $12
Add if new interior stairs needed	$6 to $8
Add if unit heater needed	$8 to $12
Add if new exterior stairs needed	$15 to $30
Garages and Outbuildings	
Basic (convert half of two-car garage)	$30 to $60
Add if unit heater needed	$8 to $12
Porches	
Basic (enclose walls and ceiling, level floor)	$40 to $80
Add if unit heater needed	$8 to $12
Additions	
Basic (one common wall with house, crawl space below)	$60 to $120
Add for full basement below addition	$10 to $20
Add if unit heater needed	$8 to $12
New Separate Structures	
Basic (new structure without basement)	$70 to $130
Add for full basement	$15 to $30

cific to your situation undoubtedly play a bigger role than others. Raising the roof above the garage or attic, for example, might put your office just where you want it, damn the costs. It's your office, after all, so why not get what you want?

PART TWO

THE PLANNING PHASE

CHAPTER 6

HELP: WHERE TO GET IT WHEN YOU NEED IT

A professional home office should be planned and executed with the same care and foresight as a professional office anywhere. Modern office projects draw on the contributions of many specialists—architects, interior designers, efficiency experts, equipment consultants, human resource planners, engineers, and so on. You may think you won't need any of these high-priced outsiders for a simple one-person office. You may think you can do everything yourself. And maybe you can. But there may be tasks you either can't do yourself or just don't want to. Or, you may realize that even if you can do it yourself, it may take just too much time to be cost effective.

Most homeowners, only vaguely aware of the range of specialists and the services they provide, have even less idea of what these services cost. I no longer wince when educated people ask me "How much do you charge to draw up a set of house plans?" The question is sort of like asking a surgeon about the charge for an operation. Yes, I do "draw plans." But this is the final step in a design process. It begins with determining needs, setting goals, exploring alternative solutions, presenting options for interaction with the client, revising, and finally describing the decisions in a set of plans that communicate all of this to a builder.

Yet I don't blame folks for not understanding my profession. Architects as a group haven't done a very good job of communicating with the public. And most people never really need an architect anyway. But when they do, they get the most out of the relationship if they understand how the architect can help them realize their goals and at what cost, and what kind of working arrangement to expect. This chapter will help you choose specialists when you need outside help. But, let's first decide what tasks you can and should do yourself.

WHEN TO DO IT YOURSELF, WHEN NOT TO

Before biting off more than you can chew, be sure you are the best person for the job and—even if you are—that doing it yourself is in your best interest. How can you tell? Here are five questions you should be able to answer in the affirmative before proceeding.

Do I Truly Want to Do This Task Myself?

If you can't answer this one with a yes, stop right here. You probably have good personal reasons for wanting to avoid certain tasks, even if you know how to do them. Digging in your heels to do a chore you don't like just to save money will probably not result in a good job and will turn the challenge into drudgery—a terrible beginning for your home-based business.

Do I Have Enough Time to Complete This Task?

I'd wager that your nonsleeping time has to be meted out carefully between making a living and keeping up with family obligations, with seldom enough left over for things you want to do for yourself. To determine whether you will have enough time to do specific items of work necessary to get your home office up and running, you first need to know how much time they will take. If you have done similar projects in the past—built a bookshelf, remodeled part of the house, painted—you have a basis for estimating. If you are undertaking a task for the first time, you can only make your best guess. For example, if you have never installed drywall, ask a friend who has done it how long it took, then add another 30% to 50%, depending on the difficulty you expect in learning how to do it.

Do I Have the Ability to Complete the Work Successfully?

As in the previous example of hanging drywall, you will know if you have the necessary skills if you have done it before. If not, don't beg off without exploring what's required. Maybe hanging drywall is something you would like to learn and, having mastered, find satisfying. Even if you can hang drywall yourself, it's faster and easier if you have a helper to hold panels in position while you drive the first screw or nail. So part of answering this question may come down to whether you have a family member or friend who can help you.

Do I Have, or Can I Get, the Necessary Tools?

You can hang drywall armed with nothing more than a utility knife, measuring tape, a straight edge, and wide putty knife, though a swivel-base sander is a back saver in the finishing stage. You probably have some of these tools already. If not, you could probably buy the whole set for less than $50. Even plumbing requires few specialized tools today, now that plastic and copper have replaced cast iron and steel piping. When you find out which tools are necessary, or just helpful, see if you have them or can borrow them from a friend. Some tools are necessary but too expensive to invest in for the limited amount of use you will put them to—floor sanders, for example. Check if there is a rental agency nearby. You'll be surprised at what you can rent these days.

On the other hand, if you plan to do much major construction yourself, you should have a reasonably good set of carpentry tools including a good power saw and drill. But don't invest in these tools if you don't foresee using them again.

Can I Save Enough Money to Justify Doing It Myself?

The final test is economics. If the time you spend doing this task would otherwise be spent in earning money, you have to decide whether the 10% to 20% you might save over a contractor's fee is a real savings or if you would actually save by working at your job and paying a contractor. This is, of course, the most simplistic approach. In the real world, there may be other factors to consider. If the time you spend is after work, you can count it as nonbillable. You may even see it as recreation, if you consider banging down shingles therapeutic stress relief.

If you answered the previous five questions in the affirmative, bear in mind a few other factors. Your municipality may permit you to do your own plumbing or electrical work without a license, but be sure you can do it safely and to meet codes; otherwise, you're better off hiring a licensed professional. Laws that limit the installation of plumbing and electrical work to certified specialists are in the interest of public safety, so it's best to find out your area's requirements before trying to circumvent them. And, if you have to get a building permit, you'll also be inspected.

Worksheet 6-1 (shown on page 42) helps you to rate various tasks in terms of the five criteria. A quick scan of the completed worksheet should give you a good idea of the tasks you can or should do, and those where you may be better off calling in outside help.

IF NOT YOU, WHO?

It's one thing to recognize the areas where you need help, and it's quite another to know who to call on and how much the service will cost. In our world of increasing specialization it's almost impossible to keep abreast of who does what and how they go about it. Here's a thumbnail profile of several of the most likely outside specialists who can help you.

LICENSED PROFESSIONALS

Before they can offer their services to the public, many professionals are required to obtain a license from the state, ostensibly to protect the public health or welfare. Because the road to licensing is usually long and arduous, requiring a professional degree, internship, and passing a state exam, the number of licensed practitioners stays lower than the number of unlicensed specialists who offer the same services. Hiring a licensed professional guarantees the consumer that the provider has satisfied the objective requirements to legally provide the service. It tells you nothing about certain other important, subjective qualities — such as the person's design approach and personality — and fees. You'll have to find these out through interviews and talking to past clients.

Architects

Architects are trained to give physical form to a client's space needs and objectives. Full architectural services for a project begin at the idea stage and end when the last piece of trim is painted; they usually include programming, schematic design, detailed design, preparing construction drawings and specifications, selecting a contractor, and interpreting the plans during the construction. Fees are a percentage of the construction cost (usually 5% to 15%), an hourly rate, or a lump sum.

Unless you are building from scratch, it is unlikely that you will need the full range of an architect's services for your home office project. You might, however, engage one on an hourly basis to help you with such things as planning the layout, designing an addition, or evaluating the structural capacity of an attic floor or roof structure.

Structural Engineers

Structural engineers can also analyze floors and roofs, as well as other parts of the home's structure. If you want to finish off part of your basement for an office but wonder if those cracks in the foundation spell trouble, an engineer can prepare a plan if corrective action is warranted. An engineer can also advise on how to correct water leaks, if that is the cause of the problem. For consulting on specific problems, engineers bill at an hourly rate.

Electrical Engineers

An electrical engineer can help you solve any or all of the problems you may encounter with additional power circuits, switching, communications wiring, security and alarm systems, and lighting (engineers do not install the work they design). If you can describe the full extent of your requirements, you may get these services for a fixed amount; otherwise, the engineer will bill you by the hour.

Mechanical Engineers

Consider asking a mechanical engineer for advice on heating, cooling, or ventilating your office; for either a fixed fee or hourly rate. You can get these services for free from heating contractors, but don't expect them to consider equipment other than their own line.

Worksheet 6-1

TO DO OR NOT TO DO IT YOURSELF

Scan the list of tasks for those that apply to your office conversion. Check each task that you can, should, and want to do yourself. To help you decide, you should be able to answer the following questions in the affirmative:

1. Do I want to do this task?
2. Do I have enough time to complete it?
3. Can I do this alone, or, if not, is there a mentor/helper available to help me?
4. Do I have or can I get the necessary tools?
5. Can I do this task more economically than hiring it done?

Planning/Design

_____ Measure area to be used for home office and draw to scale
_____ Lay out floor plan of office
_____ Draw cross sections or elevations
_____ Design exterior modifications to blend with house
_____ Prepare application documents for approval
_____ Plan changes to electrical circuits
_____ Plan how space will be heated or cooled
_____ Design changes in yard required for office
_____ Determine colors and finishes

Evaluation

_____ Evaluate cracks in building foundation
_____ Evaluate insect damage or dry rot in wood beams and joists in basement
_____ Evaluate extending existing heating system to home office area
_____ Evaluate bringing additional circuits to home office area
_____ Determine whether attic floor is adequate to support home office use

Construction/Installation

_____ Lay out lines to locate new addition on site
_____ Excavate foundation trenches
_____ Form and install concrete work
_____ Do rough carpentry work
_____ Do finish carpentry
_____ Install roofing
_____ Install windows and doors
_____ Make office furniture and shelving
_____ Paint, install wall covering or carpeting
_____ Install electrical power wiring
_____ Install plumbing
_____ Install heating ducts, pipes, and equipment

Other

_____ _____
_____ _____
_____ _____

General Contractors

General contractors manage the construction of an entire project, including any trade/subcontractors who may install specific parts of the work. General contractors tend to specialize in projects according to size and type, so seek out only those who do residential work under "Contractors—General," "Home Builders," or "Builders" in the yellow pages. They can give you preliminary advice on things such as replacing damaged beams, foundations, floors, and the likely cost of construction. Some even offer design services, though be aware that contractors probably lack formal design training. You may get a preliminary consultation for nothing if the contractor believes it will lead to a contract for construction. Or, you may be asked to pay an hourly fee. We'll talk about the various fee arrangements for the actual construction in chapter 17.

Trade/Subcontractors

You can hire any of a number of trade contractors separately if their service is not to be included as a subcontracted portion of a general contract for construction and managed by a general contractor. Following is a list of a few trade contractors who can help you with work you can't or don't want to do. Only plumbers and electricians are required to be professionally licensed.

Carpenters. Rough carpenters or framers specialize in erecting the floors, walls, and roofs of wood-framed structures. Call on finish carpenters for trim, cabinetry, and detail work.

Concrete contractors. These individuals form, pour, and finish concrete for floor slabs, foundation walls, and other concrete structures, a service that you might use for building an addition.

Drywall installers. These individuals hang and finish drywall, a messy job most amateurs can do themselves, but don't enjoy.

Electricians. These individuals not only install wiring and lighting, but can configure circuits and locate outlets. If your needs are more complicated than extending wiring or adding a circuit or two, you should probably call in an engineer and entrust only the installation to an electrician.

Excavation contractors. These individuals can dig a hole big enough for the foundation of your addition or small enough for new utility lines you may need to run to a garage or outbuilding. They usually work on a firm price with a unit price for work required due to unexpected subsurface conditions, such as stone.

Foundation contractors (see Concrete contractors).

Heating contractors (see Plumbing and heating contractors).

Insulation contractors. Stuffing fiberglass into walls or rafters makes your eyes run and your skin itch, even when you wear protective gear. If this prospect bothers you, entrust your insulating to an installer.

Lighting (see Electricians).

Masons. These persons install stone, brickwork, and ceramic tile in walls, floors, and paving. Doing decent masonry yourself is possible if you have the time, interest, and patience to learn how (you might start by building a barbecue in the backyard).

Painters. These workers not only paint, but also install wall coverings. Painting is one of the tasks you can likely do yourself, however, and the increasing variety of water-based paints eliminates objectionable odors and health risks of solvent-based paints.

Plumbing and heating contractors. Do-it-yourself plumbing is more accessible today than ever. Still, plumbing is unforgiving—the smallest leak spells failure. You should have the desire to learn how and the patience to do a thorough job; and make sure your municipality allows plumbing done by unlicensed persons. You may have to call in a licensed plumber.

Extending heating ducts or lines and installing additional cooling or heating equipment (other than a window-mounted package unit) is better left to a heating contractor. If your job is simple and straightforward, the contractor can do any design required. If it's complicated or you want to explore alternative approaches, call on a mechanical engineer to design the system, then entrust the contractor to do the installation.

Roofers. You can probably install unit roofing (shingles, shakes) yourself if you don't mind perching on high places. Flat roofs call for membrane roofing—a specialty better left to a qualified installer.

Wallcovering installers (see Painters).

PROFESSIONS LICENSED IN SOME STATES, NOT IN OTHERS

Some professions are moving toward licensing but are as yet not required to be licensed in all states.

Landscape Architects

A separate entrance for a home office, or a garage converted to an office, may call for landscape improvements to send the right message to visitors. Landscape architects can suggest planting arrangements and paving options to enhance an entrance or create a sense of privacy. Most landscape architects do not install the work they design, so expect to pay a fixed fee or hourly rate.

Interior Designers

Interior designers can help you organize the interior layout, pick color schemes, furnishings, and finishes. For their service, they may charge a flat fee, an hourly rate, or a percentage of the cost of items they specify, such as furniture, carpets, and draperies.

UNLICENSED PROFESSIONALS

Many very capable specialists provide services equal to their licensed counterparts, though you as a consumer face the added risk of not knowing the extent of their technical expertise.

Design and Drafting Services

Home designers and drafting services also do interior layout work, as well as basic planning and design services in connection with residences, for which they charge a flat fee or hourly rate. Drafting services may or may not design. Call on them if you know exactly what you want and only need someone to draw it to scale.

Landscape Services

Landscapers may include design within the overall cost of installation. But be aware that they are primarily contractors, not designers, so unless you know exactly what you want, you stand to get a better project by having a landscape architect do the design, then bid it out to a landscaper for installation.

Equipment Vendors

When you acquire phones, faxes, computer peripherals, and any of the other high-tech stuff that makes today's home offices possible, you may require assistance getting them configured and operating, as well as a source of servicing when they break down. Competent local suppliers often send a technician out to help get the item hooked up and running as part of the purchase price. Mail order suppliers can't provide this service—a point to consider before buying through them.

Some basic data about each of the professionals mentioned are summarized in the "Outside Experts Comparison Chart" (shown on page 45) to give you a quick idea of the kind of service each offers and the most likely fee arrangement.

FINDING THE RIGHT PRO FOR THE JOB

Knowing which jobs you will do yourself and those you will entrust to outsiders is only the first step. Next comes the chore of finding specialists who have a good track record and are easy to work with. Where do you begin?

Let me illustrate with an example with which I am familiar: architects. Say you are considering

OUTSIDE EXPERTS COMPARISON CHART

Outside Experts

Key:

● Always, mainly

○ Sometimes

	Architect	Landscape Architect	Civil/Structural Engineer	Electrical Engineer	Mechanical Engineer	Interior Designer	Home or Building Designer	General Contractor (Builder)	Plumbing/Heating Contractor	Landscape Service	Electrical Contractor/Electrician
Licensing											
License required by state	●	○	●	●	●			○	●		●
Evaluation Services											
Evaluate condition of foundation	○		●				○	○			
Evaluate structure of floors, walls, roof	●		●				○	○			
Evaluate heating/cooling systems					●				●		
Evaluate electric power and lighting systems				●							●
Planning and Design Services											
Plan and design home office addition	●						●	○			
Consult on structural members	●		●				○				
Plan and design interior	●					●	●				
Plan and design heating and cooling systems					●				●		
Plan electrical circuiting and lighting				●							○
Design landscaping and improvements to site		●								○	
Build and Install											
General building and remodeling								●			
Install plumbing and heating work									●		
Install electrical work											●
Install landscaping										●	
Possible Fee Arrangements											
Hourly rate	●	●	●	●	●	●	●				
Fixed fee (lump sum) for stipulated work	●	●	●	●	●	●	●	●	●	●	●
Cost-Plus-Fee (see Chapter 19)											
Percent of cost of construction work	●		○	○	○						
Percent of cost of items furnished						○					
Fee included in total cost of work											
Fee included in that of another provider		○	○	○	○	○			○	○	○

a home addition to situate your office. You have a good idea how you want the room layed out, but you're at a loss when it comes to designing the structure. You would like to have an architect's help, but fear it will cost too much and that the architect will try to dictate the design.

Your network of friends and business associates is a good place to begin. Do you know anyone who has worked with an architect for a new home, home addition, or in connection with their business? If so, ask them for details—not just how much it costs and if they were pleased with the results, but how the planning process actually worked. Did the architect keep an open ear to desires and an open mind to possible solutions? Would they hire this person again?

If you can't locate leads through your network, try the yellow pages. When you phone candidates, ask them first if they do residential work (larger firms may not), ask about how they approach a project such as yours, their fee and method of payment, how soon they can get to your project and how long it will take, and anything else you would like to know. Be sure to ask for the names and phone numbers of a few client references.

The personality of the professional is naturally a bigger factor with architects and interior designers than with drywall installers or roofers, unless it bothers you that they are up on your roof grumbling. With tradespersons such as these, though, you will still need to know if they can do a good job and if they are financially solvent (more about working with contractors in chapter 17).

With a good idea of which parts of your project you can do yourself and where to get capable outside help, your project planning is off to a good start. Now, it's on to the heart of the matter (and the fun part): planning the space itself.

CHAPTER 7

ORGANIZING THE SPACE

"It's a nice office," he said. "Not showy, maybe, but that's all front anyway. You've seen my place. Serves fine. Desk, file cabinet, what the hell else do you need?"
Raymond Chandler and Robert B. Parker, *Poodle Springs*[1]

You'll need probably little else if your needs are as simple as those of the private eye quoted above. But I suspect the electronic cottage is a more apt model of your home office. It may be so complex that you should consider getting planning and design help from one of the professionals mentioned in the previous chapter. But if you intend to be your own architect, you can plan it by computer, using graphic-based space planning software or more advanced CADD software, or the simpler low-tech method outlined later. Even the simplest computer methods entail an investment of time and money not likely cost effective unless you will be using them for more than one shot. Professional CADD software is so costly and difficult to learn that you should rule it out unless you are in a business where you will use it continuously.

SPACE PLANNING TOOLS

For the simple method, you'll need the following materials:

1. A clipboard and pad of paper.
2. Sheets of 18″ × 24″ (or larger) gridded translucent media, with grids spaced at ¼″ intervals.
3. Steel measuring tape, preferably 25′ long, but you can make do with a shorter one.
4. Soft lead pencil, eraser.
5. A roll of drafting tape (masking tape will also do).

The previous list is the most basic set of tools. To move up from a Chevy to a Rolls—and make your planning task a lot easier—add the following items to your list:

6. A T square.
7. A triangle (30/60 or 45/45).
8. A drawing board, 24″ × 36″ (you can make do with a table or desk that has a straight edge).
9. An architect's scale (triangular one or flat one) with scales of ¼″ = 1'0″ and ½″ = 1'0″.

Graphic supply stores and office equipment stores carry most of this stuff. You can buy measuring tapes at lumberyards or hardware stores.

I envision nine steps in your office planning process:

1. Prepare a space summary (as in chapter 3).
2. Document the existing space.
3. Draw a base plan.
4. Draw cross sections.
5. Make copies of your base drawings.
6. Make cutouts of equipment and furniture.
7. Explore alternative layouts.
8. Select one scheme as your final plan.
9. Plan the vertical use of the space.

To illustrate how the nine-step planning process works, I have contrived an example. Your own operation and candidate office area will no doubt differ in details, but the process is similar.

Ken Jones, the hero of my example, got inter-

ested in the commercial applications potential of videos when he was asked to produce some safety training films as a personnel officer for his former corporate employer. In time he gained

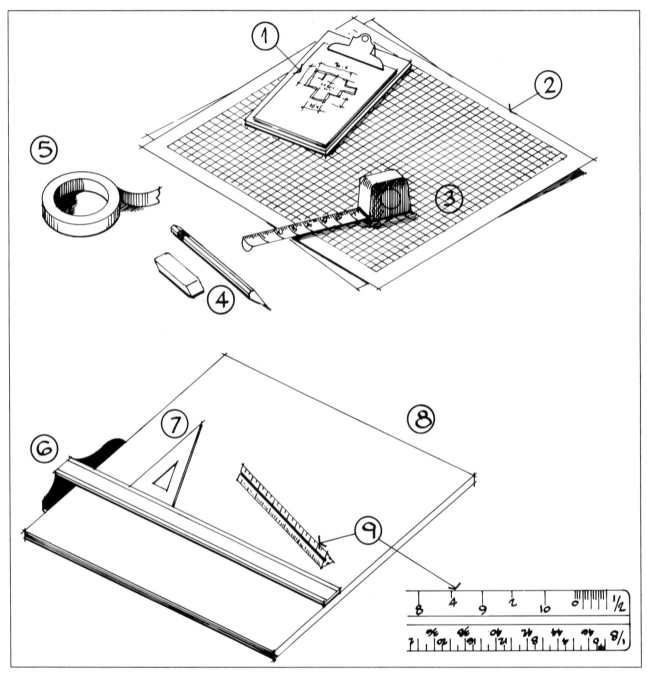

Figure 7-1: Space Planning Tools. *The five items at the top are indispensable for measuring and recording the dimensions of your office space and planning the final layout:* **(1)** *a clipboard and pad of paper;* **(2)** *sheets of plain tracing paper or tracing paper with grids drawn at ¼" intervals;* **(3)** *a steel measuring tape, 25' long;* **(4)** *pencils and erasers;* **(5)** *drafting or masking tape. The items shown below will make drawing up and laying out your space easier and more exact:* **(6)** *A T square or parallel rule;* **(7)** *a triangle, 30/60, 45/45, or adjustable;* **(8)** *a drawing board, 24" × 36" or larger;* **(9)** *an architect's scale.*

Worksheet 3-1

SPACE SUMMARY

Each function or piece of equipment that occupies floor space is listed with the square footage of floor space required for a **compact, moderate,** or **generous** arrangement. Circle each of the three figures for every line-item that applies to your operation. Write in below any additional items that apply to your office space. Multiply the subtotal of each column by the appropriate circulation factor to get a total square footage for each column.

Function/equipment	Compact	Moderate	Generous
Primary Work Station (FOR ADMINISTRATION)	(14)	(42)	(54)
Computer work station (if separate)	14	42	54
Drawing surfaces	16	39	55
Copiers	(5)	(8)	(13)
Large sheet (blueprint) printers	11	30	50
Computer plotters	12	18	32
Conference/waiting area	6	16	43
Waiting areas (if separate)	(6)	(16)	(43)
Filing cabinets, vertical	(6)	(12)	(18)
Filing cabinets, lateral	9	18	26
Flat file (drawing) cabinets	12	21	28
Shelves (12" deep)	(8)	(15)	(23)
Other:			
VIDEO PRODUCTION CONSOLE	(35)	(53)	(60)
CLIENT SEATING	(8)	(12)	(21)
PHOTOGRAPHY	(16)	(25)	(30)
Subtotals	98	183	262
Circulation Factor	x 1.2	x 1.3	x 1.4
Total space required	118	240	367

Figure 7-2: Worksheet 3-1, Space Summary for Ken's Video Production Studio. *The three totals at the bottom give Ken a good idea of what level of convenience he can expect from his candidate attic office/studio.*

enough expertise to launch his own video editing and production firm. Ken realizes that the heavy initial investment in equipment will strain his financial resources, so rather than rent office space, he would like to convert two small unused attic bedrooms into an office/studio. Here's how Ken used the nine-step planning process:

PREPARE A SPACE SUMMARY

Architects begin planning space layouts with a program of space needs. Worksheet 3-1 from chapter 3 is a version of a space program modified to suit your home office planning needs. In Figure 7-2 (shown on page 49) you can see how Ken Jones used this sheet to arrive at three different totals, representing a compact, moderate, and generous layout.

The first item, "Primary Workstation," will not be Ken's primary workstation. He'll use this item as a desk and side table for his administrative work. Because his computer will occupy this area, he doesn't list any additional space under "Computer Workstation."

The heart of Ken's operation is a specially designed workstation where he edits video media. The configuration, listed under "other," consists of a cluster of electronic monitors, control boards, and recording equipment, carefully organized so that each device works efficiently within the system and is easy to operate from a single seated position. To get an idea of what the configuration should look like and how much space it would need, Ken did some research—reading all he could find on the state of the art, talking with others in the field, and poring through equipment catalogs. The instructor in the film production department of a nearby college helped him prepare an equipment list and three possible layouts, as shown in Figure 7-3 (at right). The basic furniture consists of a desk with a shelf above, into which modular electronic components can be plugged. A clear space of 1'8" behind the console allows Ken to access the various plugs, jacks, and wires. You can similarly determine the space

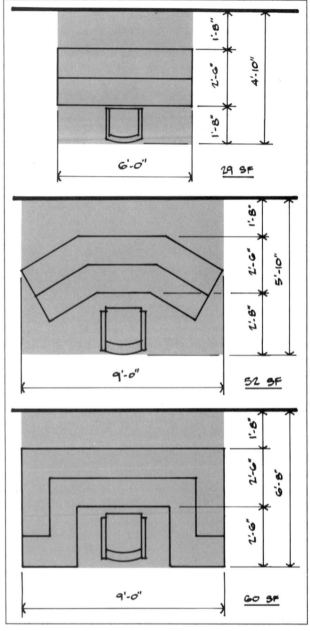

Figure 7-3: Ken's Video Production Console Options.
Ken's basic workstation includes various components for editing and producing video media in a bilevel console for easy access. Using his master list of equipment and sizes, Ken came up with three possible console arrangements, requiring from 29 to 60 sq. ft. of floor space. He decided on the middle unit of 52 sq. ft.

requirements for your own special equipment or furniture specific to your operation.

Ken envisions an interactive working relationship with clients. To enable clients to interact during the editing/production process, he wants

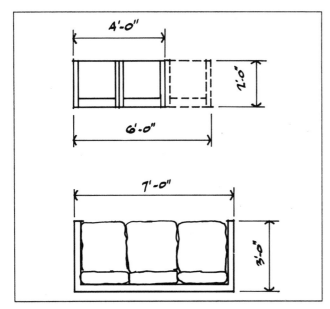

Figure 7-4: Ken's Client Seating Options. *Ken needs at least two chairs positioned in back of his production console. In an 8-sq. ft. space Ken can provide two small armchairs for minimum requirements. A third chair can be added with 12 sq. ft. The lower arrangement accommodates a three-person sofa within 21 sq. ft.*

to provide a seating area behind the console and his own chair, as he indicated under "client seating" on his space summary worksheet.

Ken's last item, the photography area, is a place with a simple backdrop that he can use for shooting subjects used in his films.

After totaling his space needs and multiplying the subtotal by the appropriate circulation factor, Ken determined that he could squeeze his entire operation into 118 sq. ft., in the most compact organization, 240 sq. ft. for a moderate one, and 367 sq. ft. for a generous layout. From a quick preliminary measurement of his attic, he found that the available area, 371 sq. ft., would afford him a generous layout, although he knows the floor space is not entirely accessible when standing upright, due to a sloping ceiling (more about this later).

DOCUMENT THE EXISTING SPACE

Before you start organizing a plan for your space, you need an accurate base plan of the area as it

now exists. Take your clipboard, measuring tape, and a helper (to hold the "dumb" end of the tape) to the part of the house to be converted to your office.

Begin by making a rough freehand sketch of the floor plan on a clipboard. Don't worry about aesthetics or proportions at this point, your goal is simply to record the locations of walls, windows, doors, and built-in items such as chimneys, stairs, and storage cabinets. After drawing in all of the architectural features, go back and sketch in the location of secondary features, such as electrical outlets, heating vents, and light fixtures.

Begin by measuring the overall room dimensions, wall to wall, then go back to the corners to measure off features such as windows, doors, and projections from the wall. Figure 7-5 (page 52) shows Ken's rough plan, along with some of the common architectural plan symbols you can use to denote various features.

DRAW A BASE PLAN

Now you're ready to transfer the rough data from your notepad to create a more refined plan drawn to scale. Copies of the new "base plan" will serve as a beginning point for evaluating potential layout schemes. When you arrive at a final scheme, you can draw it directly on the base plan.

If you do intend to add to the base plan for the final drawing, you should use a good-quality reproducible medium—a translucent sheet that can be copied by diazo (blueprint) or electrostatic (Xerox™) means. Translucent media includes any of a number of various tracing papers, vellums, and mylar available from graphic and office suppliers.

Here are two ways to draw your base plan to scale:

1. Draw freehand or with instruments (triangle and T square) on a gridded sheet, using the gridlines to measure off dimensions.

2. Draw freehand or with instruments on a gridded sheet, using an architect's scale to measure off dimensions.

Using Grid Lines for a Scale

Tape a sheet of the gridded paper to your drawing board or table with the drafting tape. You

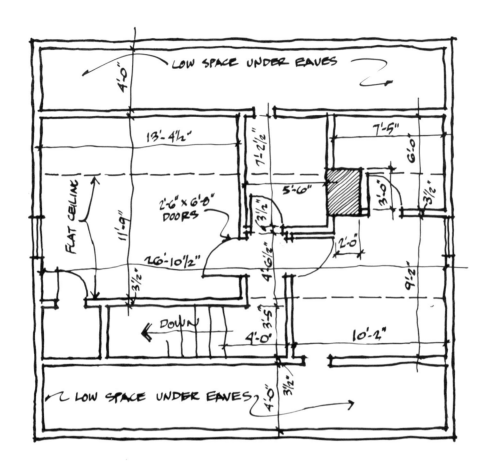

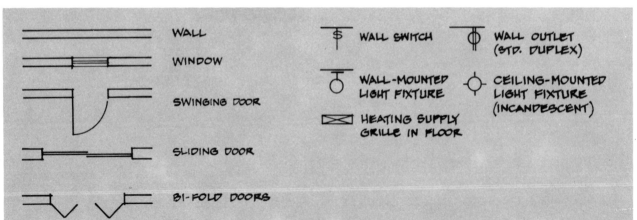

Figure 7-5: The Rough Floor Plan. *After you have picked a candidate space, the next step is to measure it and record your data. The example shown at top is Ken's future office/ studio, an attic presently containing two small bedrooms, a storage space, and shallow 4' margins under the eaves.*

The data shown, so far, includes walls, doors, windows, chimney, stairs, and dimensions. Other information—such as lighting fixtures, outlets, and heating appurtenances— can be added as necessary. The standard symbols used on floor plans are indicated below.

can assign any scale you want to the grids, but I suggest letting each square represent a dimension measuring 6" × 6". This is drawn to a scale of ½" equals 1'. The grids on the sheet will give you accurate markers at each 6" interval, but you will have to guess at dimensions less than 6" and the location of lines that don't fall exactly on a 6" interval.

Using an Architect's Scale

With an architect's scale you can accurately place any dimension if you are willing to take a few minutes to learn how to use the tool. Don't be overwhelmed by the apparent confusion of numbers on the odd-looking device; it's not a ruler and there's a logic to the madness. Find the side that says "1" at the left side and "½" at the right. Because 1 is a multiple of ½, this is actually two scales—one reading from the left and the other reading from the right. Look at the right end, for a moment. The "feet" measure begins at the 0 point (the first foot actually reads "10," because this is the 10' measure from the other end of the scale).

The finely subdivided portion to the right of the 0 represents a full foot, marked in inches. So if you want to mark off 6'3", simply find 3" to the right of the 0, as your starting point, then move left on the scale until you find the 6' mark. When you have practiced on a few dimensions, you will find that using the scale is much faster and more accurate than relying on grid lines.

Drawing the Base Plan

Whether you choose to transfer the information from your notepad sheets freehand or more accurately with straightedges (triangle and T square), you use the same sequence. First draw the inside face of all outside walls. If you like, you can add the outer face of the walls, using the appropriate thickness. Then draw in the windows, doors, and other features from your notes. Take the "as is" plan to a copy center and have a copy made on a reproducible medium—such as vellum, mylar, or sepia—for use as your final plan. Have one or more additional copies made on any medium to use for scheming various layout alternatives. Figure 7-6 (page 54) shows Ken's plan drawn freehand with grids to measure scale and keep lines straight (method 1), and drawn by instruments on unlined paper (method 2). Plain paper could be substituted in the second method, but the grids will come in handy for positioning furniture and equipment, as we'll see later on.

DRAW CROSS SECTIONS

If your candidate space is, say, a bedroom with vertical walls, you might get by with just a floor plan, though a cross section would be helpful for planning the vertical use of the space. But if your space changes with height, as does Ken's attic, you should draw one or more accurate cross sections to avoid fooling yourself into believing you can use space where the overhead clearance is too low. In Ken's case, there is a 7' wide strip of ceiling running through the length of the attic, below which the clear height is 7'6", the code minimum. The ceiling slopes down with the roof to either side of this strip, ending in a corner that is 4'6" high at the side walls. Ken can still use this low space for cabinets and storage, but not for walking around in.

How to Draw Cross Sections

Use another gridded sheet and the dimensions on your finished base plan sheet as a starting point for one or more cross sections. If you are drawing a cross section through an attic that has a roof sloping symmetrically down from a center point, locate the center point, measure up from the floor to the underside of the roof and mark the point. Then locate the height where the roof begins to slope upward at the outer walls. Connecting the ridge with these points will describe your ceiling.

Cross sections also give you the opportunity to draw in existing or planned windows, so that you can coordinate them with cabinetry and

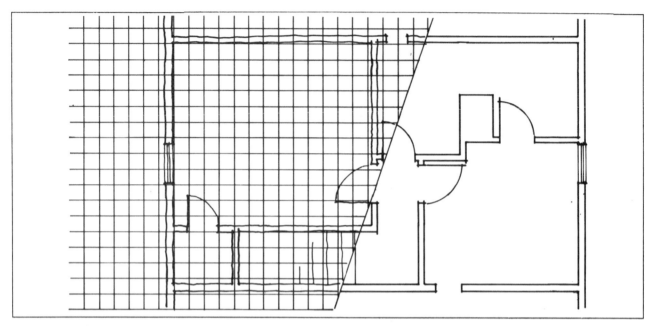

Figure 7-6: The Base Plan. *After you have measured your space and recorded the data on a rough plan, draw it to scale to serve as the base plan for your layout schemes. You can draw freehand on a sheet of gridded media, as shown at left, or aided by drawing instruments on plain media, as shown at right. This drawing is the base plan of Ken's attic space as it now exists.*

equipment. Because Ken's attic varied from one end to the other, he drew two sections, one through each end (Figure 7-7 on page 55).

MAKE COPIES OF YOUR BASE DRAWINGS

Steps 4 and 5 yield base drawings you can use to scheme various design alternatives and, later, complete to create the final product. Think of them as akin to the stock you get when you boil meat with flavorings and put aside to be recombined at the finishing stage of the dish. Here's how you can get the greatest mileage out of your base drawings:

• Make one copy each of your base drawing plan and cross sections on reproducible media, to serve as record copies of the existing space for future use.

• Make several copies of your base drawings on any media. Use these to scratch around on and develop alternative schemes.

• Add the final layout of furniture, equipment, electrical, lighting, and heating/cooling vents—and any wall changes—to your original base drawings, to create final plans and sections.

You can get electrostatic (Xerox™) copies made at a copy center or on your own copy machine. Specialized copy centers can make opaque (blueprint) copies or translucent copies that can be used to make other copies.

MAKE CUTOUTS

Cutouts are useful tools for studying alternative layouts. Moving them around on the base plan can be a lot of fun and lead to the most workable floor plan layout. Make three or four copies of the appropriate templates shown in Figure 7-8 (pages 56 and 57) (all drawn to the scale of ½" = 1'0"), then cut out the ones that apply to your office. Any specialized items not shown, such as Ken Jones's video production console, you'll have to create yourself, using dimensions from equipment catalogs and configurations you know will work. Note that the cutouts shown include the clearances necessary to get to and from the item—this will prove very handy when you are shuffling them around on a plan.

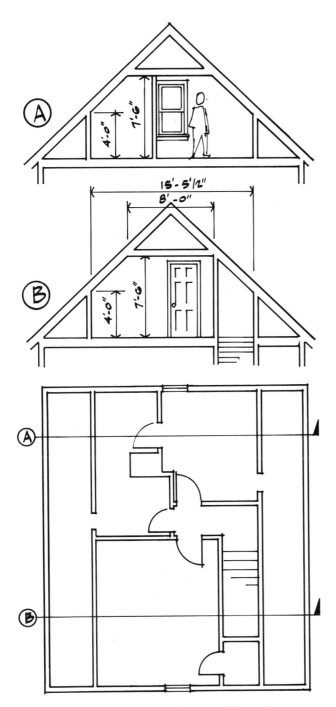

Figure 7-7: Cross Sections. *These are helpful in planning the vertical use of your space. They are absolutely necessary if the ceiling slopes, as it does in Ken's attic, shown above. Ken used his base plan (lower drawing) to project two sections,* **A** *and* **B.** *In both sections, the 4' knee walls at the low end are too low for walking, but can be used for furniture. From these sections, Ken determined that he had a 7'6" ceiling for just over half of his total space (average 15'5½" width), as required by codes.*

EXPLORE ALTERNATIVE LAYOUTS

Finally we get to the fun part, the actual planning. Move the cutouts around on the copies of the base plan. When you get a layout that seems to work, tape or glue down the cutouts and put it aside, then take another plan copy and try a different arrangement. Try to generate at least two alternatives for comparison.

If possible, locate your main working desk near a window. This aids natural lighting and gives you a chance to look outdoors to rest your eyes. Locate your computer so that direct sunlight from the windows never strikes the screen. If this is impossible, you can rely on blinds or shades to control the glare.

If you are planning for clients, try to create a flow pattern where they can move into and out of your office without disrupting your own activity. Locate the reception/waiting point near the entrance with the conference room abutting so that visitors won't have to cross through your work area to get to the conference table. Of course, you may want them to do this, if selling them on your services or product will be helped by exposing them to your work in progress. Plan your layout, if possible, so that public areas are also contiguous to amenities, such as refreshments and rest rooms.

Professional designers arrive at the best layout by exploring several alternatives. You can, too, even if your options are limited by existing conditions, as they were for Ken.

Figure 7-9 (page 58) shows Ken's two most promising schemes. In scheme 1, Ken's workstation is placed in the larger of the two former bedrooms, and the second, smaller room is used for client reception and his administrative desk. The two former closets have sloping ceilings, but can serve as a photography room and general storage, respectively.

In scheme 2, Ken reversed the arrangement, gaining a larger client/administrative room at the sacrifice of some space for the workstation. Note

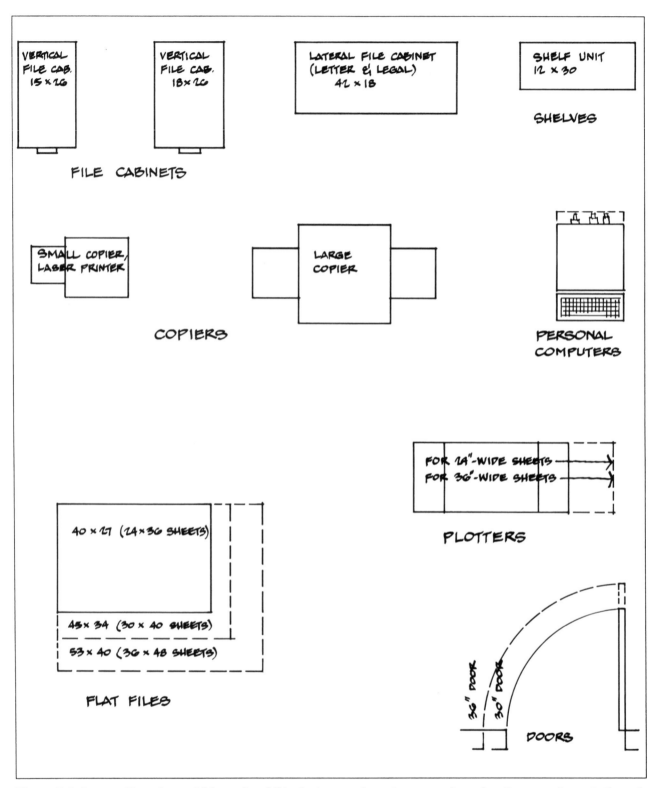

Figure 7-8: Layout Templates. *Make copies of this sheet and the following one, then cut out any items applicable to your office. Use the cutout templates to organize the space you have drawn on a base plan. Items are drawn to the scale of ½" = 1'0". You can use a sheet of gridded paper or the scale shown here.*

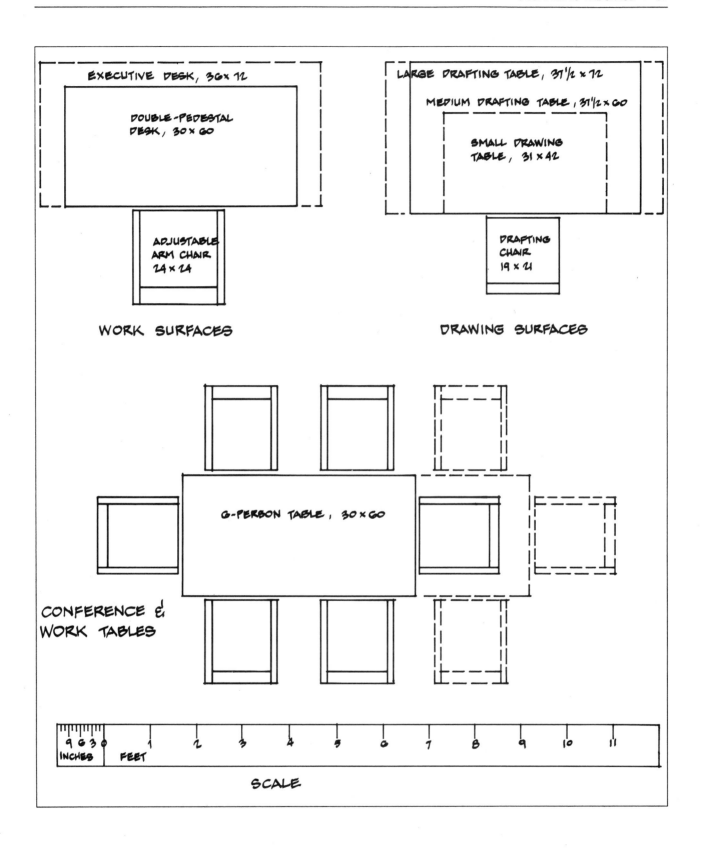

EXECUTIVE DESK, 36 × 72

DOUBLE-PEDESTAL DESK, 30 × 60

ADJUSTABLE ARM CHAIR 24 × 24

WORK SURFACES

LARGE DRAFTING TABLE, 37 1/2 × 72

MEDIUM DRAFTING TABLE, 37 1/2 × 60

SMALL DRAWING TABLE, 31 × 42

DRAFTING CHAIR 19 × 21

DRAWING SURFACES

6-PERSON TABLE, 30 × 60

CONFERENCE & WORK TABLES

9 6 3 0
INCHES
FEET
1 2 3 4 5 6 7 8 9 10 11

SCALE

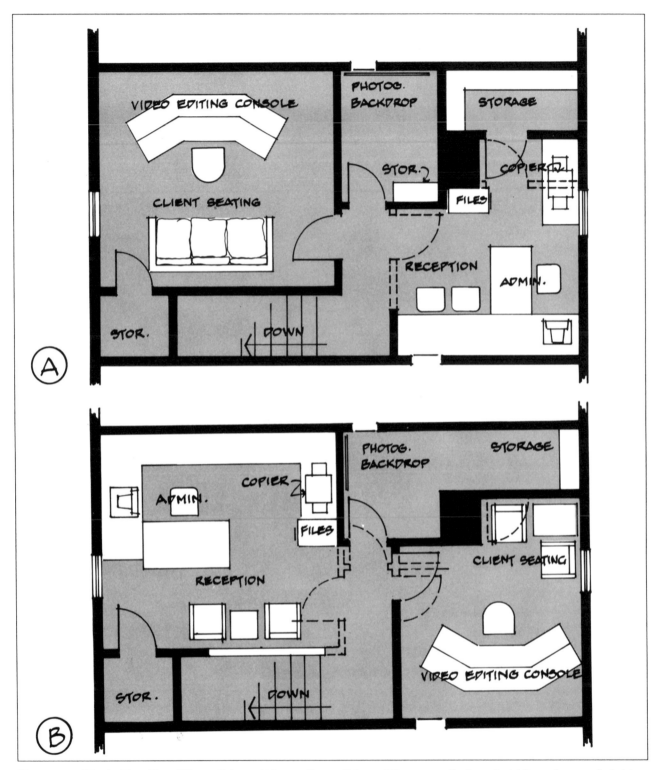

Figure 7-9: Ken's Two Best Plans. *Scheme (A) uses the larger room for his production room, and the smaller one serves as the administrative and reception area.*

Scheme (B) reverses the layout yielding a larger administrative and reception area. Which layout would you choose, if you were Ken?

that he has created a more pleasant entry, though, by removing the top of the wall between the stairs and reception room.

SELECT ONE SCHEME AS YOUR FINAL PLAN

The larger work area and better view from the window were, in the end, the factors that made Ken decide in favor of scheme 1. Because he expects to spend most of his office time at the production console, it made sense to favor the larger room for this function.

You will, similarly, have overriding criteria—a favored view, a direction you like to face, or perhaps the way sunlight permeates the space. When you decide, you can draw your final plan.

Tape the copy with cutouts onto your drawing board; tape a blank sheet of translucent paper or vellum (either gridded or unlined) over it. Trace the final layout, including all equipment and furniture. Show any changes in partitions, windows, or doors. Finally, indicate lighting fixtures and electrical outlets (more about electrical systems in chapter 9). You may, as an option, make a separate tracing for electrical systems, omitting the equipment and furniture.

Use diazo prints or electrostatic copies of this drawing if you do the construction yourself, or if you use any outside professionals.

PLAN THE VERTICAL USE OF THE SPACE

You have noticed by now that planning the space involves thinking in three, not two, dimensions. Things happen under, on top of, and above, other things—particularly with electronic office equipment. For simple items that sit atop desks and work surfaces—phones, faxes, and copy machines—a floor plan alone suffices. Configurations that contain more vertical layers, such as Ken's production console, bookshelves, and the like, should be described as seen head on. And if you are using a space such as Ken's attic, you will want to make sure the equipment layout has adequate vertical clearances.

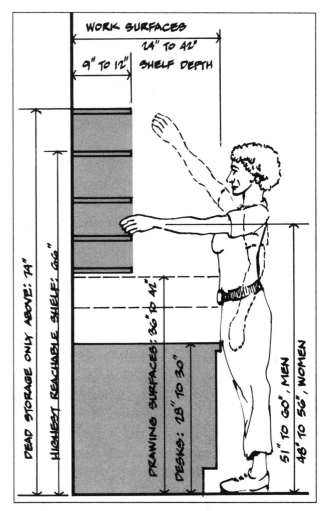

Figure 7-10: Reference Heights. *These dimensions show the usual range of average adults. But because you can plan your furniture to suit yourself, use a tape to measure your own dimensions.*

Use the base cross sections to study vertical space use. You can make cutouts of equipment in much the same manner as you did in your plan, then follow the same steps, 7 and 8, to move from idea to final drawing. Figure 7-10 (above) shows some useful heights for planning your vertical space.

With your interior layout firmed up, you can turn your attention to any changes to the exterior walls that will enhance your comfort or utility, as we'll see in the next chapter.

CHAPTER 8

SHELL GAMES

How do you want your office to feel inside? I'd guess that you would like it to feel snug in winter and cool in summer. Unless it's in a basement, you probably want to use the sun's light and warmth. If you're like me, you want it to be reasonably quiet, at least when you are working. You can achieve these goals through thoughtful planning. This chapter will help you make informed decisions about the design of the floor, walls, and roof. The following one will focus on the equipment that heats, cools, and lights the space inside.

CREATING GOOD WEATHER AND NOISE BARRIERS

To create the kind of interior environment just described, your office shell needs to keep water, wind, and noise out; keep the heat inside in winter but outside in summer; and bar moisture from entering the walls from the inside, but let any entrapped moisture escape through the outer skin. Fortunately, a thoughtfully designed, well-constructed shell can do all of the above.

Keeping Water and Wind Out

Your office shell's outer skin—the roofing, siding, or masonry—keeps water and wind at bay in two ways: redundancy of materials and atten-

tion to sealing. Redundancy in roofs results when a layer of roofing felt underlies the shingles. The sealing takes place when the asphalt tabs on the bottoms of the shingles melt in the sun and seal each shingle to the one below, and through proper flashing and caulking of joints where the roof meets a vertical projection such as a wall, chimney, or pipe.

Wrapping the outer wall sheathing with an air barrier such as Tyvek™ or Typar™ creates a redundant layer between the sheathing and the siding or masonry veneer. Good detailing of siding and trimwork, combined with caulking of all joints, ensures that the skin will shed water but allow moist air to escape from inside the wall.

Controlling Moisture

The inner skin should keep moist inside air from penetrating into walls, floors, and ceilings, where it can condense and damage the structure or degrade the insulation. Even though your office probably won't generate moisture on the scale of a bath or kitchen, the moisture level is high enough in winter to warrant a moisture barrier on the heated side of the wall and ceiling.

For new construction, the surest moisture barrier is a layer of polyethylene sheeting, 4 or 6 mils thick, laid just below the wall finish material, with attention to taping the seams and sealing any cracks with caulking. The wall surface itself can become a moisture barrier (airtight drywall approach) if all penetrations are sealed and a moisture-resisting coating such as shellac or oil-base primer is used on the wallboard or plaster. Sealing the penetrations requires thorough caulking around baseboards and window trim and caulking around the insides of electrical boxes with a nonhardening sealant such as silicone.

Keeping Heat Inside in Winter, Outside in Summer

Enough insulation of the right kind can help you stay comfortable year-round. The amount depends on your climate. Insulation resists heat flow because of a multitude of tiny air spaces encapsulated within its matrix, or by a reflective foil, or both. Figure 8-1 (below) lets you match your location to the minimum level of R-value

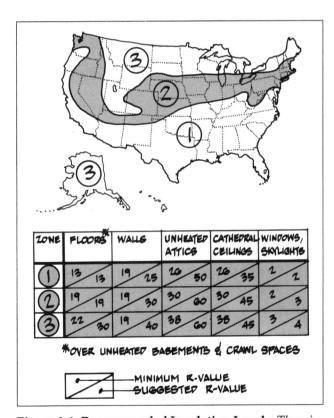

Figure 8-1: Recommended Insulation Levels. *The minimum R-values listed represent current standards of well-insulated homes. Increasing R-values to the suggested levels will pay back in greater energy savings and better comfort.*

(unit of heat resistance) and to the R-value I recommend for better comfort and lower energy bills.

When choosing insulation you have to consider the cost and type, as well as its R-value. The table on page 62 compares the R-values per inch and relative cost per unit of R-value for the most likely options.

Blankets and batts are best suited to installing between studs and joists. Rigid boards nailed over the studs or joists are a good way to increase the R-value when space is tight. You can also use them to increase the R-value of an existing wall by nailing them right over the old wall surface and following with a new layer of wallboard. Loose fill insulation is an economical way to insulate an unheated attic and the main way to add insulation to the cavities of existing walls without first ripping the finish off.

Keeping Noise Out

You'll be happy to learn that if you adequately insulate and seal your walls and roof against weather, you also create an excellent barrier to outside noise. Your weakest link will be the windows and doors. We'll talk about how to upgrade their noise defenses further on.

FLOORS

The underfoot portion of your office shell should not chill your feet as you sit at your desk and should be soft enough to walk on with ease. Cavities, such as in wood floors, make convenient places for running electrical wiring.

None of these qualities are inherent in concrete floor slabs, which are common to garages or basements. You can make them feel softer and warmer simply by laying down carpet, if the slab is level and smooth, though this won't give you a place to run wiring. In very cold climates—and if a wiring chase is necessary—I suggest you build a wood floor above the slab, as described in chapter 12.

Insulation Type	R-Value per Inch	Relative Cost per Unit R-Value
Blanket and Batt:		
Fiberglass	3.3	Lowest
Mineral wool batts	3.6	Lowest
Rigid Sheets:		
Phenolic foam	8.5	Highest
Polyurethane/Isocyanurate	7.2	Medium
Polystyrene (extruded)	5.0	Medium
Polystyrene (beadboard)	4.0	Medium
Fiberglass board	4.0	Highest
Loose Fill:		
Cellulose (blown in)	3.7	*
Perlite (pellets)	2.7	*
Fiberglass (blown in)	2.2	*
Mineral wool (blown in)	2.9	*

*Medium if blown in by a contractor, lowest if you install yourself.

Wood-Framed Floors Above Crawl Spaces and Basements

A wood-framed floor at the ground level perches above a shallow crawl space or full basement. The insulation can go either in the foundation wall (keeping the space below the floor warm) or in the floor itself (allowing the space below to be the same temperature as the outside). Cold basements and crawl spaces risk frozen pipes when temperatures plummet. Strangely, many homeowners seem more drawn to band-aid remedies—such as heat tapes, keeping the water running in the pipes, or perhaps keeping a wood stove going in the basement—rather than insulating the basement.

Figures 8-2, 8-3, 8-4 and 8-5 (pages 63 and 64) show four ways to insulate a wood floor. In Figure 8-2, the insulation between the floor joists leaves water piping below exposed to the cold where it can freeze, even if wrapped separately with insulation. This approach makes sense only in warm humid climates that may require ventilation to prevent rot due to moisture.

Figure 8-3 shows how to insulate a crawl space floor from below. Begin by laying down a layer of poly sheeting over the exposed earth. Extend the sheeting up to the sill plate and staple to the plate. Overlap joints in the sheeting by 6" or more to get a good moisture seal. If you want a better barrier against insects and rodents, have an unfinished concrete "rat" slab poured over the sheeting. When the sheeting is positioned, lay batts or blankets over the top, beginning by stapling them between the band joists, then running them down the inside of the foundation wall and out into the floor to a distance of 3 feet or so.

The same method works for wood floors above unheated basements. Insulate the basement walls by one of the methods described in chapter 12 instead of insulating the floor from the basement.

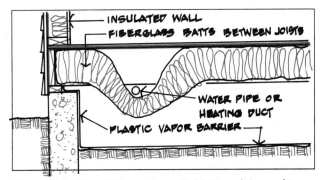

Figure 8-2: Wood Floor Over Cold Crawl Space/Basement. *If you insulate the floor rather than the foundation, take care to enclose all heating ducts and water piping on the warm side of the insulation.*

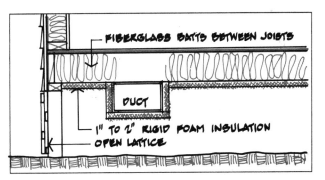

Figure 8-4: Wood Porch Floor Over Open Space. *Insulate the floor of a converted porch, as shown here, or the foundation, as shown in Figure 8-5. As with cold crawl spaces, you'll need to insulate any heating ducts or water piping.*

Floors Open Below

If you are enclosing an office space above a floor whose underside is open to the elements, such as a porch, this demands not only insulating the floor, but also keeping the wind out, as cold wind wafting through unprotected insulation renders it almost worthless. You can keep the underfloor space open (Figure 8-4) or close it off (Figure 8-5).

For an open floor, nail an inch or so of rigid insulation below the floor joists. The board will keep cold winds at bay and provide part of your total insulation requirement. You can then insulate the floor by pouring loose-fill insulation, such as perlite or fiberglass strands, directly into the joist cavities, or by fitting batt or blanket insu-

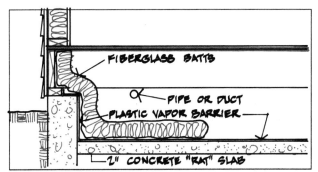

Figure 8-3: Wood Floor Over Warm Crawl Space/Basement. *Insulating the foundation of a crawl space or basement allows you to leave ducts and piping uninsulated. In crawl spaces, extend the insulation out into the space a few feet. Because the crawl space is kept warm, moisture can migrate up through the soil. To prevent this, cover the ground completely with a vapor barrier of 4-mil plastic (polyethylene) extended up the walls. An optional "rat" slab will keep rodents from burrowing into the space.*

lation between the joists before installing the floor. If the floor is already in place and can't be removed, you'll have to install the insulation from below—a task I don't envy you.

Closing off the space below the porch, as shown in Figure 8-5, can be done by extending the wall sheathing down to grade and finishing it off with siding to match your house. If you want to maintain the appearance of lattice, paint the sheathing a dark color and install the lattice an inch or so in front of it. Where wall meets ground, nail in a rot-resistant (redwood, cedar, or pressure-treated fir) 2″ × 10″. If you go this route, be sure to lay a plastic moisture barrier over the ground, because moisture wicking up through the soil won't have an escape route.

If heating ducts are to run through a cold crawl space, wrap them with insulation as shown in Figure 8-2 or 8-4.

WALLS

To fulfill the goals listed earlier, your office walls should have a watertight but breathable outer skin, heat-resisting core, and moisture-resistant inner surface. Start by selecting the right R-val-

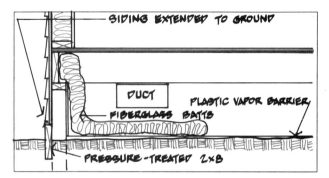

Figure 8-5: Wood Porch Floor Over Enclosed Space. *You can insulate the foundation of a wood floor porch in much the same way as you would a warm foundation. Extend the house siding down to grade on the outside. Be sure to cover the ground with a plastic vapor barrier to keep moisture out.*

ues for your climate from Figure 8-1, then pick a wall design from one of the wall types shown in Figures 8-7, 8-8, or 8-9 (page 65). The R-values apply to insulation only; a standard 2″ × 4″ stud-wall insulated with R-11 batts actually yields a total value closer to R-16, but still below the minimum recommended value of R-19.

If you are modifying an existing wall, you will likely start out with a wood-framed wall similar to Figure 8-6 or a solid masonry wall. You can add insulation to the wall without removing the existing finish material by applying rigid-board insulation between strapping (Figure 8-7), and, in the process, gain a cavity to run new wiring. Figure 8-8 shows how to build a new, insulated, inner wall to a wood-frame or masonry wall. Figure 8-9 shows a way to insulate a wood-frame wall by combining batts/blankets and rigid insulation. This method also works for any new walls you may build. With 2″ × 6″ studs and 1″ of rigid insulation, the wall yields an R-value of between 15 and 27½, depending on the type and thickness of rigid insulation. Taping the joints of the rigid insulation obviates the need for a separate poly vapor barrier.

Each of these methods creates spaces in which to run new wiring, though the National Electrical Code requires at least 1¼″ of cover over plastic-sheathed cables. If your wiring comes

closer to the finish surface than that, you can still meet code by nailing a metal strap over each place the cable passes through a stud. Get the straps at any building supply outlet.

ROOFS

A minor roof leak can ruin electronic office equipment. Fortunately, proper selection and installation of roofing can prevent this disaster. You can probably install asphalt shingles or roll roofing yourself if you take the appropriate safety measures and don't mind working in high places. I'd leave the installation of other types to qualified roofers.

Selecting the Right Roofing

You will probably want to match the roofing of the house if your office is in a new addition. That's no problem if the addition is an extension to the gable end or an intersecting gable form. A shed-roof added to the main roof is invariably of shallower pitch than the main roof, so be sure the roofing you choose is suited to the actual pitch. Say your addition lands on the side of an asphalt-shingled roof with a 3/12 pitch (3″ rise for each 12″ of horizontal dimension, or run). The pitch of the addition is closer to 1/12, which is below the minimum for asphalt shingles. One solution would be to match the color and texture of the shingles with asphalt roll roofing.

The table on page 66 can serve as a preliminary roofing selector, based on the pitch of your roof and budget.

Insulating Roofs and Ceilings

As with walls, select an insulation appropriate to your climate. Use Figure 8-1 as a guide. Installing the recommended level of insulation overhead is a simple matter if you end up with a flat ceiling with an unoccupied space above. Batts, blankets, or loose fill all fit neatly between the ceiling joists, leaving the space above ventilated to the outside.

Cathedral ceilings may be necessary if headroom is tight or desirable if you want a more in-

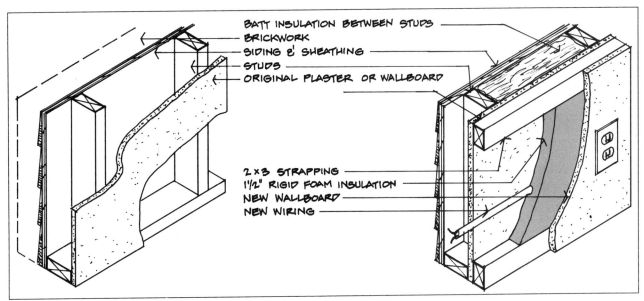

Figure 8-6: Uninsulated Exterior Wall. *Old houses are often underinsulated; sometimes uninsulated. If you are unsure about the wall insulation in your new office space, remove enough of the wall finish to find out how much insulation it contains and whether there are gaps.*

Figure 8-7: Adding Insulation Without Tearing Into the Wall. *You can add insulation to an existing wall and leave the plaster intact by nailing 2" × 3"s or 2" × 4"s horizontally, spaced 16" apart, and filling the space between with rigid foam insulation. You can even use the space as a chase for new wiring, but run the cable away from the strapping to prevent puncturing by nails or screws. Make sure the cable stays 1¼" behind the face of the new wall surface.*

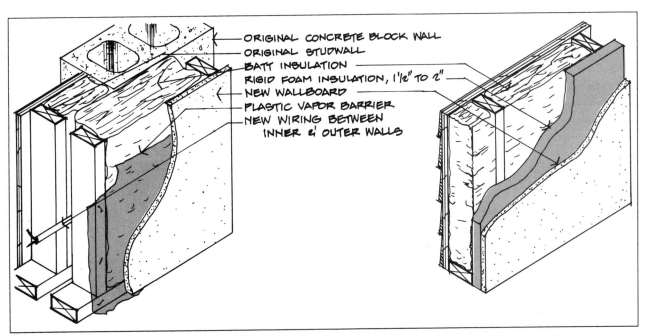

Figure 8-8: New Inner Wall. *If you start with a studwall too shallow to accommodate the desired level of insulation (as in a garage) or an uninsulated masonry wall, a new inner studwall will create a space for insulation and new wiring, and provide a base for a new interior wall finish.*

Figure 8-9: Adding Rigid Foam Directly. *You can add R-value to a new or existing wall by applying up to an inch of rigid foam insulation directly over studs (as shown here) or existing wall finish. Attach new wallboard with screws matched to the total thickness of cover over the studs.*

Roofing Type	Minimum Pitch*	Relative Cost
Membrane roofing	Up to ?	High
Metal panel	2.5″ and up	High
Roof rolling	1″ to 3″	Low
Composition shingles (asphalt, fiberglass)	3″ and up	Medium
Wood shingles	4″ and up	Medium
Slate	4″ and up	High

*Rise in inches per each foot of horizontal surface.

teresting space than one defined by a flat, level ceiling. The natural space for insulation—between the rafters—is often not deep enough for the desired thickness of batt/blanket insulation plus a necessary 2″ gap above the insulation for air to circulate under the roof deck. One solution is to install additional rigid board insulation below the rafters.

Both roof approaches are shown in Figure 8-10 (page 67), which could be a typical attic ceiling. Four features are fundamental to any roof/ceiling system:

1. Vents in the eaves to take in air
2. A space between the insulation and the roof deck for air to circulate
3. A vent at the roof ridge to allow air to escape
4. A vapor barrier on the heated side (below the ceiling)

The vapor barrier can be plastic (poly) sheet, taped joints of foil-faced rigid insulation, or wallboard ceiling coated and sealed as in the "airtight drywall approach" mentioned for walls on page 61.

WINDOWS

To make sure you get the most in the way of light, ventilation, solar heat, and view, you need to decide on appropriate window types, glazings, and the best locations for windows.

Window Types

Designers and builders classify windows according to the ways in which they operate (open and close). Here are the most common types of residential windows:

Fixed windows. As the name implies, fixed windows do not open. They come as glass sheets to be installed into a finished opening or as units preglazed into wood, metal, or plastic frames. Fixed windows are cheaper than operable ones, so they make sense if you know they will never be opened, or where they can't be reached, or in combination with operable units.

Double-hung windows. Likely the most common type of window in homes, double-hung windows have an upper portion (lite) hung in a separate channel from the lower portion, leaving each lite free to slide up or down. Newer types allow each lite to be tilted in for easier cleaning. Double-hung windows are natural openings for gable dormers.

Single-hung windows. These are the same as double-hung windows, but only the lower lite moves. The upper lite stays fixed in place.

Casement windows. Like double- and single-hung windows, casements are vertical—longer than they are wide. Rather than slide, they hinge into their frame and open outward. Because the whole opening is exposed, this type is the best window to encourage natural ventilation. The

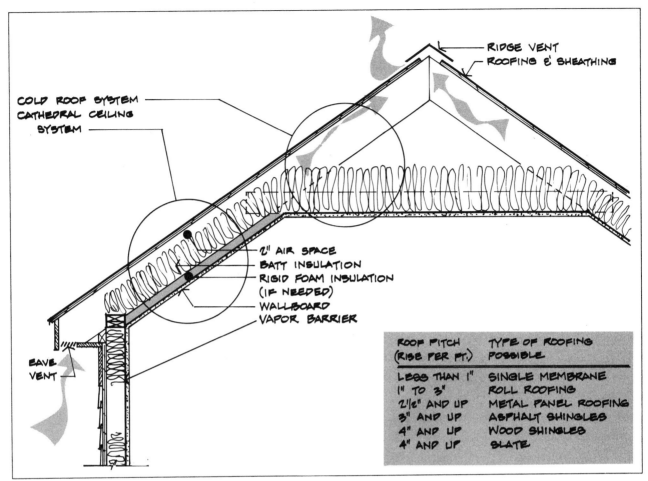

Figure 8-10: Roof Systems. *Finishing an attic for an office will likely require a cathedral ceiling (as shown at the left) for all or part of the roof in order to gain the necessary headroom. Make sure to ventilate above the insulation with vents in the eave and roof ridge and maintain a 2" air space above the insulation. Apply additional rigid foam insulation below the rafters, if necessary, to increase R-value without increasing the depth of the rafters.*

open leaf helps direct breezes into the room.

Awning windows. Imagine a casement turned on its side and you have an awning window. When open (with the bottom extended up and out) they deflect rain better than other types. Awnings can be easily incorporated into shed dormers. As horizontal windows, they fit nicely above desks and work surfaces, allowing daylight and view at standing height, leaving a few feet of free wall space between the sill and your work surface.

Sliding windows. Sliders resemble double-hung windows turned sideways. They offer the same advantages of other horizontally shaped units, as far as leaving more wall space below the sill. But where awning windows open out to shed rain, sliders leave one half of the opening exposed.

Each of the above window types is available in wood, metal, and plastic (PVC) frames. Wood windows come primed for painting or with the exterior encased in vinyl covering. Aluminum-framed windows are available unfinished (satin-sheen natural silver color), anodized (electrolytically coated), or prefinished with baked enamel in various colors.

Your next window decision is the type of glazing. Until the last decade, the only choice was between single- or double-glazing. Single-glazing offered poor resistance to heat loss, which meant high energy bills and discomfort if you were sitting next to a window. Double-glazing cut the heat loss by half, doubling the R-value from R-1 to R-2.

Advances in glazing technology in the 1980s yielded additional choices that not only further reduce heat loss, but improve your comfort and working efficiency, as well. The biggest gain was a special coating on the inside surface of a double-glazed window that manages the light and heat properties of the glass to your advantage. The coating, a metallic oxide with low emissivity (low-E), allows the sun's visible light inside while barring ultraviolet rays that fade fabrics. Get the advice of your window distributor to select a type of low-E coating tuned to your climate. The type most suitable to areas with cold winters allows solar heat in and keeps it from escaping back out. For southern climates, you'll want a type of low-E that minimizes solar heat gain.

Low-E coatings improve the R-value of double-glazed windows from R-2 to around R-3. Filling the space between the panes with an inert gas such as argon boosts this to around R-4. Greater efficiency still is possible in windows that encapsulate one or two layers of polyester film with a low-E coating between the glass. The Insol-8™, manufactured by Hurd Millwork Co., boasts an R-8.

Naturally, the more energy saving the glazing, the higher the cost, but you'll eventually recoup the additional 10% to 20% premium through lower heating and cooling costs. More importantly to anyone who works for hours at a time near a window is the greater comfort.

Locating Window Openings

Where you place openings in the walls and roof of your office is as important as the type of window or skylight. Their placement affects where and how you place furniture and equipment, control of heat gain and loss, and glare.

Your work surfaces are likely to be between 29″ (desk) and 42″ (drafting table) high, so a win-

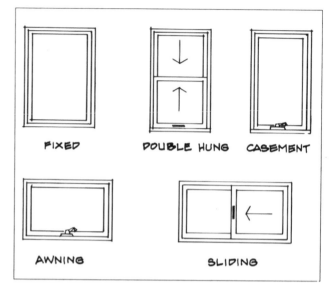

Figure 8-11: Window Types. *Five of the most common residential window types are shown here, as seen from the inside. Casement windows open out from the side, either left or right, whereas awning windows open out from the bottom. Both are operated by cranks at the base. Insect screens go on the outside of double hung and sliding windows, and on the inside of casements and awnings.*

dow with a sill too low is a place where you can't place furniture without obscuring part of the window. Even if the sill is just above desk height, say at 36″, it can cause you grief if you place a computer terminal next to it. The contrast between the bright light outside and the screen can strain your eyes.

A good sill height in an office is 48″—well above the desk, but low enough to permit you to look out and see the view while standing. Horizontal windows such as sliders or awnings are well suited to this height. If you are locked into vertical windows, such as double hung or casements, to blend with the house, there may be other answers. How about a mix of high, horizontal windows, with an occasional vertical window thrown in for view (without eating up too much wall space)?

Solar heat gain, heat loss, and glare are affected, for better or worse, by which direction the opening faces. While each orientation has its own quirks, south is probably the best overall compromise. Consider the pros and cons of each

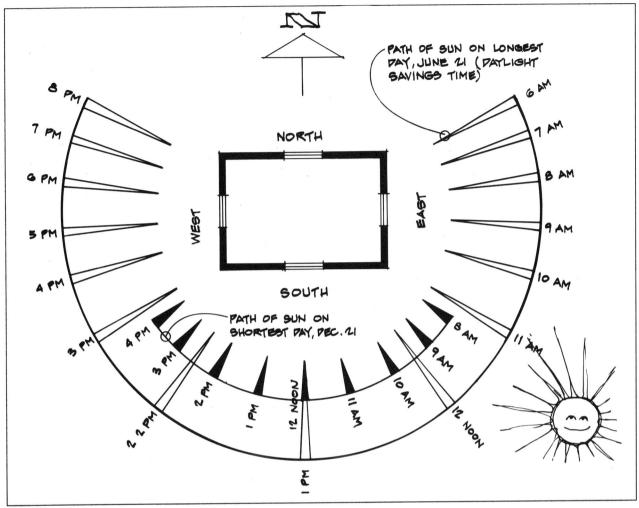

Figure 8-12: Locating Windows by the Sun. *Because the position of windows affects the room's solar heat gain and lighting, it pays to know how the sun's path will affect them at each time of the year. Two solar paths are shown for a latitude of 40 degrees north (the approximate location of Salt Lake City, Denver, Kansas City, Indianapolis, Columbus, and Philadelphia). On the longest day (June 21) the sun (adjusted for daylight savings time) rises to the north of due east, to cast its rays on the east, south, and west sides of the example office. During late afternoon, the hottest part of the day, the sun is at a low angle, which makes west-facing windows hard to shield from the unwanted heat gain. On the shortest day (December 21), most of the sun's energy falls on the south, making this the preferred side to locate windows for solar heat collection.*

orientation to get the best out of your windows.

North. This is the worst side for heat loss in cold climates, though high-performance glazings (R-4 or better) make this less important. Best side for glare-free natural lighting, and avoidance of solar heat in hot climates. Also the preferred location for windows in artists' studios.

East. This is a good choice for early morning natural lighting. Too much glazing on this side in cold climates wastes heat at other times of the day, though.

South. This is the best side for winter solar heat gain in cold climates. Glare and heat gain are easy to control through overhangs, because the sun is highest when it is least wanted, lowest when most needed.

West. This location is probably the worst choice for all climates. Solar gain comes only in the late afternoon, when the sun is too low to do much good in the winter. In the summer, the afternoon is the hottest part of the day and the sun striking west-facing glass at low angles can turn your office into an oven. If you must have west-facing windows or skylights, consider tinted glass and vertical blinds to block the low-angle summer sun.

Glare control, difficult for all types of windows, is more of a problem today with computer display screens than in the days when the typewriter was the office workhorse. Here are some things you can do to minimize glare, while ensuring a good supply of natural daylight:

• Aim for a total glass area at around 10% of the floor area you want to receive daylight.

• Opt for more, smaller windows/skylights rather than fewer, larger ones (if you need 40 sq. ft. of glazing, you'll get better light distribution from eight openings of 5 sq. ft. each than four openings of 10 sq. ft.).

• Favor south-facing glass in cold climates, north-facing glass in hot climates. Avoid or minimize west-facing glass.

• Provide the right type of window treatment for east-, south-, and west-facing windows, as described in chapter 16.

• Choose light, rather than dark, wall and ceiling finishes, to minimize contrast between the bright exterior and darker interior.

Windows or skylights that open can help cool your attic office for part of the year. As with lighting, you'll get the best ventilation from more, smaller, openings, than with fewer, larger ones. Try to place openings on opposite walls to allow breezes to circulate completely through the space. Combining low windows in the walls with operable skylights near the roof ridge is a good way to keep air moving in attics during warm months.

DOORS

The downside of forcing visitors to pass through the private parts of your house to reach your of-

fice might persuade you to install a separate entry to the outside. If so, you'll want to make sure you understand your options, beginning with the best location.

Figure 8-13: Exterior Doors. *Choose a new door with a solid or insulated core and weathertight frame. Flush doors that come unglazed or with a few small panes near the top suit modern-style homes. Panel doors blend well with many traditional-style homes. The top two panels are often glazed. French doors, fully glazed, blend well into almost any style and allow full vision and light. If you are converting a room that has sliding aluminum doors, replacing them with a pair of French doors gives more conventional operation and a better weather barrier.*

Locating Exterior Doors

The door location may be determined by the floor plan of the office space, or an existing window that can be replaced by a door, saving you the headache of digging into the wall and installing a new header. If you are relatively free to locate the door where you want, follow the guidelines suggested in chapter 4 to get a workable relationship between the office and the home. Aim for a location near an abutting sidewall where the door can swing inward against the wall. The door swing will be out of the way and traffic will flow around the perimeter of the room, rather than through the middle, where it could get in the way of your work.

Exterior Door Sizes and Types

Standard entry doors for homes measure 36" × 80", but you can still move furniture and equipment through a 32" × 80" door. You will probably want your office door to blend with the style of your house and land on one of three types: flush, panel, or French. Glazed panels (lites) often enhance flush and panel doors and occur in many small panes in French doors.

Each of these three types comes in various species of solid-core wood and insulated core doors faced with steel or fiberglass. Steel doors are primed, but require a final coat of enamel. Make sure you use oil-based enamel; the primer may not accept a water-based topcoat. Fiberglass-faced doors are available in fairly convincing imitations of natural wood, but they can also be painted.

Your other big door decision is whether to buy only the door — to be installed in a separate frame — or as a complete, prehung unit. Whether you have a carpenter install the work or do it yourself, the second way is better. Prehung doors come factory weatherstripped, ready to pop into place and trim out. After the lockset is installed, they operate with ease and seal tightly when shut.

CHAPTER 9

THE WELL-TEMPERED OFFICE

You may spend a third or more of your waking hours in your home office, if it is your primary base. A comfortable, workable environment can make this easier. The key is planning your mechanical and electrical systems early on, before finished walls and ceilings can no longer be breached for ducts, wiring, or lighting fixtures. Whether you install the systems yourself or entrust them to suppliers or contractors, an informed knowledge of your options will help you create an environment to your personal needs and the requirements of your business.

Modern mechanical devices alone can create almost any office environment. But if your office shell is poorly insulated or you use mechanical and electrical devices excessively, you waste energy and deplete nonrenewable resources and harm the environment.

You can do much to promote wise use of energy and resources by planning your heating, cooling, ventilating, and lighting to make the most of conservation and passive forces. Starting out with a weather-tight shell (as described in the last chapter) and using the sun, shade, and wind intelligently will not only cut your energy bills and save resources, but make for a more comfortable, cheerful place to work in.

STAYING WARM

Heating takes the back seat to cooling in large office buildings. Even the environmentally sensitive ones generate so much heat from lighting, equipment, and people that they may never require additional heat. Not so with home offices, at least those located in areas with cold winters. Even with a computer running constantly and one or two lights blazing, your office will need about the same amount of heat as the household. You'll get the greatest warmth for the least cost if you follow these steps:

1. Insulate the outer shell to the levels described in the previous chapter.
2. Locate most of the windows or skylights on the south side to collect solar heat. Choose high-performance windows (see chapter 8).
3. Extend your home's heating system to heat your office, if possible.
4. Install a wall-mounted unit heater (if step 3 is not feasible).
5. Install a small ducted furnace (if step 4 is not feasible and your office will have several rooms).

How Much Heat?

If you take steps 1 and 2 seriously, your office will need the minimum amount of auxiliary heat.

But it still needs some, and someone will have to determine how much if your auxiliary heat source is sized to keep you comfortable. Oversizing can be just as bad as undersizing. With too much capacity, the heater will cycle on and off less frequently and leave you cold toward the end of each "off" cycle.

We measure heat in British thermal units (BTUs) and heat transferred in how many BTUs pass through a material in an hour (BTUH). Your heating equipment distributor or mechanical engineer will size your heating (or cooling) equipment by first estimating the heat loss through the outer shell. Your home's furnace probably puts out from 80,000 to 120,000 BTUH. Your office, if well insulated, may need, at most, from 8,000 to 15,000 BTUH—keep these capacities in mind when selecting separate heating devices.

Tapping House Heat

In spaces converted from areas in the house presently without heat—such as attics, basements, and porches, or even additions—the most economical source of heat will probably be an extension of your home's heating system. How can you tell? Phone the company that regularly services your home furnace or heating system. They may send someone over to determine if the furnace has unused capacity and if it is feasible to extend ducts or piping into your office space (a mechanical engineer can also provide this service, but you'll have to pay for it).

Air systems can be altered to deliver heated air by extending branch ducts to the new space, if the space is not too far from the existing ducts and there is a place to run extension ducts. A furnace in the basement should be capable of heating any space on the first floor (even an outside porch) without too much trouble, but finding a way to run ducts from the basement to an attic office might be tricky.

Getting the right amount of heat can be an even greater hassle than finding a place to run the supply duct and provision for returning air

to the source. The amount of hot air delivered to the rest of your house is likely controlled by a central thermostat that senses the average conditions. You can adjust the amount in each room only by partially closing the heating registers (though well-designed systems have dampers in the supply ducts for balancing). But an attic or porch office is sure to have different heating demand than the rest of your house, particularly if you operate it as a completely separate entity, so be sure to ask your advisor about the control issue.

Hot water (hydronic) heating systems can also be extended, often more easily than air systems, because the copper piping is much smaller than air ducts. Heat delivered to spaces like attics and porches can be supplied according to need, by a separate circulating pump controlled by a thermostat in the office space. You can even run piping buried in the ground between the boiler in the basement and a garage office. Ask your heating advisor to compare the cost of doing this against installing one of the separate heating systems discussed in the following section.

Unit Heaters

A small heater that supplies only heating makes good sense if you don't need mechanical cooling. Even though my own attic office gets a bit warm in July and August, I stay comfortably cool the rest of the summer by opening windows on the east and south for cross ventilation. Since I didn't need air conditioning, I chose a unit heater mounted in an outside wall to warm my office in winter. The direct-vent Empire gas unit in my east wall puts out a maximum 35,000 BTUH. Combustion air comes into the heating chamber through a sleeve in the outside wall. Mounted inside the sleeve, a smaller-diameter tube exhausts burned gasses directly to the outside (hence the tag, "direct vent"). The device is fueled by propane from tanks mounted in my backyard, but could just as easily hook up to a natural

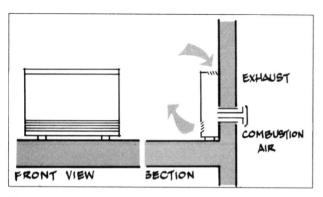

Figure 9-1: Direct-Vent Heaters. *These are fueled by natural gas or propane and can be mounted next to any outside wall. Combustion air enters a tube through the outside wall and exits through a sleeve around the same tube, never mixing with the air inside the room.*

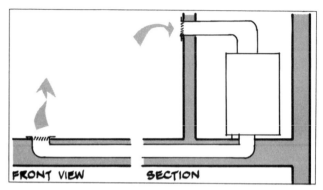

Figure 9-2: Small Gas Furnaces. *These units can be installed in a closet-size room next to your office or located on the floor below. Pulse furnaces need only two 2" diameter PVC pipes for intake and exhaust to the outside, whereas conventional units require a flue through the roof.*

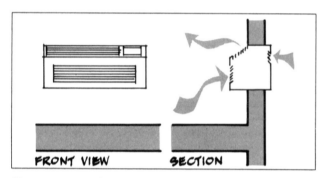

Figure 9-3: Package Unit Heat Pumps. *These devices mount conveniently in an outside wall, and deliver heating, cooling, and fresh outside air all in one unit.*

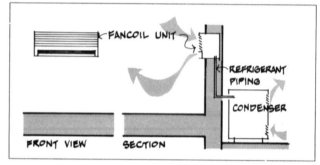

Figure 9-4: Split-System Heat Pumps. *These deliver heating and cooling through fancoil units mounted in each room served. Each fancoil is connected to the central condenser unit outside by refrigerant piping in the walls or floors.*

gas supply line, if one were available. Kerosene-fueled direct vent heaters are also available.

Small Furnaces

Whereas small unit heaters work fine for a single-room office, you may need an additional heat source if your office comprises more than one room. Incidental and infrequently used spaces such as toilet rooms can easily be heated with small adjunct devices (more about combination units later on). An office containing more than one separate main room can be heated by a separate unit heater in each room or a centrally located furnace with ducts or distribution piping to diffusers in each room. Small furnaces that deliver around 40,000 BTUH fit nicely into closets or small furnace rooms. Some, such as gas pulse

furnaces, don't even need chimney flues; they need only two 2" diameter plastic pipes for exhaust and for combustion air.

Electric Resistance Heaters

The easiest way to heat a separate office, regardless of the number of rooms, is with electric resistance heat. It is, unfortunately, the most expensive to operate in many parts of the country, because electricity is the highest priced fuel. For this reason, it makes economic sense only if your office needs very little heating, your electric rates are low, or both.

Baseboard units located near the floor of outer walls are the easiest and most economical way to deliver electrical resistance heat. Though they radiate heat, they heat the room mostly by warming the adjacent air, which circulates upward by natural convection.

Resistance heating wires can also be imbedded in a ceiling, as in the converted barn of structural engineer, Wayne King. He installed the system himself by stapling a mylar film containing resistance wires to the ceiling framing prior to installing the wallboard. Wayne reports that the system works well and doesn't cost too much to operate in his Connecticut location, thanks to high levels of ceiling and wall insulation.

Wood Stoves

Wood stoves are a tradition in rural New England where my home office is located, for good reasons. The region abounds in firewood, lacks natural gas, and is cursed with the highest electric rates in the United States. Even so, a wood stove wouldn't be my first choice for an office. Controlling the heat is difficult; keeping it stoked with fuel consumes time and creates mess. And stoves hog valuable space—not just for themselves and any provisions for firewood storage, but for the required clearances between the stove and combustible materials.

COOLING YOUR OFFICE

As with heating, you can trim your cooling costs to the bone by first reducing your demand through passive alternatives. A well-insulated shell works just as well to keep unwanted heat out as to keep winter heat in. Because windows are the weakest link between the climate outside and the one you want inside, they merit your first attention when thinking of cooling.

Well-situated, high-performance windows help keep your office cool by blocking unwanted solar heat in summer and providing free cooling in the form of natural ventilation.

As you'll remember from the last chapter, west-facing windows create the biggest heat-gain problem on summer afternoons. If you are stuck with them, try first to shade them from the outside. A trellis planted with vines will do the trick naturally, or you can use vertical louvers (more about this in chapter 16). Horizontal louvers that block the higher early afternoon sun don't block the lower sun of late afternoon, unless closed. The same shading strategies also apply to east-facing windows, but because solar heat from the east comes in the early morning, which is the coolest part of the day, it's welcome most of the year.

To get the most natural cooling out of your windows, locate them on opposite walls and combine low windows in walls with operable skylights in attic spaces. Casement windows are the best window type for natural ventilation.

Natural ventilation can cool your office when the outside temperature is lower than inside, and cool you even when it's warmer outside by evaporating sweat from your skin. On the muggiest days a fan will cool you if the speed is high enough. Unfortunately, it's hard to get enough air moving past your skin without blowing your papers around like confetti. Which brings us to the hard realization that passive cooling—though desirable—has limits.

In most of the United States, there are times of the year when soft approaches—insulation, shading, ventilation—meet their match in extreme outside temperatures, humidity, or a combination. A fan, the least energy-intensive mechanical cooling device, will work up to a point. If you live in a dry climate, such as the Southwest, you can cool your space for much of the year with an evaporative or "swamp" cooler, which uses a fan blowing over water.

When these low-energy approaches reach their limit of effectiveness, we enter the world of higher priced refrigeration cooling.

How to Size Air Conditioners

The amount of mechanical cooling your space will need each hour is measured in BTUHs, similar to heating (though specialists also use "tons"—where one ton of cooling equals 12,000 BTUH). If your office is below another occupied floor or below a well-insulated roof you can figure around 20 to 40 BTUH for every square foot of space to be cooled. Using this rule of thumb, at 426 sq. ft., my office would require a unit of $426 \times 30 = 12,780$ BTUH (a one-ton air-conditioning unit).

Room Air Conditioners

Air conditioners that pack everything in one box that fits into a window opening have been around for years. Installing one in a window blocks off all or part of the window, however, and always looks like an afterthought. A better solution is to decide the best place to locate a unit, based on your floor plan and equipment layout, then punch a hole in the wall and install a through-wall type of unit. If possible, pick a spot remote from your workstation so you're not in the path of a constant cold draft. Through-wall units slide in and out of metal sleeves for service and replacement, so you won't be stuck with the same brand forever.

Window or through-wall air conditioners deliver from 5,000 BTUH to 29,000 BTUH of cooling. Most home offices will probably get by nicely on a unit in the 5,000 to 8,000 BTUH range. Because all refrigeration devices are heavy energy consumers (an 8,000 BTUH room air conditioner uses more than ten times as much electricity as your personal computer), it's wise to check the energy efficiency rating (EER) of any unit before buying it. EER measures cooling output per electrical power consumed (the higher the number, the better the efficiency). These values ranged from 7.1 to 10.5 in models I checked in one appliance store.

Split-System Air Conditioners

You can get a room air conditioner capable of cooling any single-room home office up to 2,000 sq. ft. It can even cool more than one room if you leave the connecting doors open most of the time. But if you need constant privacy in other rooms of a multiroom office, a separate cooling source is a better choice. You could simply install additional room air conditioners, but a split system will be quieter.

Like refrigerators, room air conditioners contain compressor motors as well as fans. Even quality units make noise when both motors are operating. The noisy part of a split system—the compressor—sits outside on a concrete pad. Small-diameter copper piping supplies refrigerant to fan coils in the walls or ceiling of each room to be cooled. Separate thermostats control the temperature in each room. The advantages of quieter operation and separate controls mean that these systems naturally cost more than window or wall-mounted units.

HEATING AND COOLING IN ONE UNIT

If you need equipment to both heat and cool your office, consider an all-in-one package unit. Some wall-mounted air conditioners can reverse their cooling cycle to heat the interior, rather than outdoors, as they do when cooling. These "heat pumps" cool just as a cooling-only unit and heat efficiently when outside temperatures are above about 45° F. When temperatures drop lower, they shift to heating through an electric resistance coil. If you are located in an area with long winters, this option is an expensive way to heat.

A better choice is a wall-mounted package unit that backs up its heat pump with gas-powered heating or one that heats entirely by gas. This type of unit, common in motel rooms, is also available for home offices. They require both a separate electrical power circuit as well as a gas supply—either a connection to the natural gas main in the street or a propane tank located in the yard.

The various options for heating and cooling your office can bewilder. You may get some help from Figure 9-5 (shown on page 77), which compares the various options at a glance.

Type of Equipment	Cost Range, Installed Equipment, $, 1994	Fuel Source	Heats or Cools More Than 1 Room	Supplies Fresh Air	Noise	Operation Required
HEATING ONLY						
Direct Vent Heaters	1400-1800	Nat. Gas, Propane			Fan Noise	
Small Gas Furnaces	2500-3000	Nat. Gas, Propane			Fan Noise	
Electric Baseboard Heaters	600-800	Electricity	●		None	
Wood Stoves	1200-3100	Wood			None	●
COOLING ONLY						
Room Air Conditioners	700-1000	Electricity		●	Fan, Compress.	
Split-System Air Conditioners	2500-3200	Electricity	●		Fan Noise	
HEATING AND COOLING						
Package Unit Heat Pumps	1500-2000	Electricity			Fan, Compress.	
Split-System Heat Pumps	2500-3200	Electricity	●	●	Fan Noise	

Figure 9-5: Heating and Cooling Equipment Comparison Chart.

HEATING AND COOLING SECONDARY ROOMS

Toilet rooms, darkrooms, copier rooms, and blue-printing rooms may be heated and cooled by simply leaving the door open when they are not in use, or by small adjunct devices in the walls or ceilings. Ventilation is a more pressing demand to remove odors and moisture.

Graphic design offices are exposed to chemical odors. Photographers' darkrooms are rife with developer fumes. Architects and engineers who have their own diazo printers soon learn how a sudden dose of ammonia can wake you up. Even when these are exhausted to the outside, some ammonia escapes into the room. If the print machine dwells in your drafting and design area, it will smell like a cat box in no time flat. The best solution is a separate room with a door and a good exhaust fan in an outside wall. Wire the fan to come on whenever the light switch is turned on. Undercut the door by an inch or so to allow make-up air from the main office to flow into the print room.

You can ventilate toilet rooms through outside windows or by a ceiling exhaust fan. If you install one with a built-in resistance heater, you won't have to worry about heating this room separately in the winter.

POWER AND OUTLETS

If "electronic cottage" is the model for the modern home office, adequate electrical support systems are its foundation. A one-room home office should contain at least three power circuits (110 V or 120 V) for lighting, outlets, and computers, and an additional separate circuit for any separate heating or cooling device. Small air conditioners with a capacity less than around 15,000 BTUH work off of 110 V or 120 V circuits; larger units require 208 V or 230 V circuits (and different kinds of outlets).

You may not jump at the necessity of bringing additional power wiring into a spare room office that already has convenience outlets in the walls. If the office is for less than full-time work or temporary, you might get by with a multi-outlet surge protector for your computer equipment. For serious, full-time office spaces, look into additional outlets, as discussed in the next section. In any case, do provide a separate circuit for any high-amperage appliance, such as an air conditioner or anything with a motor.

Locating Outlets

There are two rules for electrical outlets: there are never enough and they are never in the right place. I thought I had more than enough when I was wiring the tenth outlet in my empty office. After three years I realize that I should have provided for more flexibility. Several outlets remain vacant, while the two within the 3' radius of my main chair must power seven appliances: a printer, tape recorder, answering machine, computer, radio, and a lamp. If I had it to do over, I would have installed outlets spaced no farther apart than 3', or, better still, a continuous strip along the walls containing outlets at every few inches (such as made by Wiremold Corp.). I would have located them above desk height—say at 36" from the floor—for better access.

You can probably wire your office yourself if you have the time and interest to do it correctly and pick up a few specialized tools. Remember, though, you'll be exposed to constant danger. Mistakes can result in injury or even death. If you don't hire an electrician to do the installation, at least start with one of the how-to books on home wiring listed in the appendix, then have your plan and methods reviewed by an electrician. You will probably need expert advice, in any case, for the best way to bring additional circuits off of your main panel.

In already-finished rooms, rather than bust into walls to run wiring, or trying to fish it through walls, consider adding a surface-mounted conduit of the type made by the Wiremold Corp. (listed in the appendix). Low-voltage wiring for phones and sound equipment can also be run on the wall surface near the baseboard, which is just as well, because this wiring is the most likely to change.

LIGHTING

Don't skimp on lighting for your workspace; your eyes and working efficiency are at stake. Your office should have adequate *ambient lighting* for the entire space and *task lighting* focused at specific work areas.

Ambient Lighting

For ambient lighting, first tap the natural sunlight by properly locating windows and skylights (chapter 8). Daylight is cheerful and cheap, but collecting it without glare is tricky. The right type of blinds can redirect sunlight away from your eyes or work surface and onto a light-colored ceiling, which will diffuse it gently and evenly (see chapter 16 for more about various types of blinds). You'll need a backup source of ambient lighting for cloudy days and at night. You can choose between direct lighting coming down from fixtures mounted in the ceiling, or indirect sources, such as wall-mounted fixtures that throw light up onto the ceiling. I installed fluorescent fixtures in my office ceiling, but I use them only at night. Finding a location for them to avoid reflections in a computer screen or reflective drawing medium is difficult, so they make the best sense in offices that require a high level of dispersed lighting. On dark days, I turn on task lights above my other workstation and a spotlight mounted above my conference table at the other end of the room. This combination creates warm pools of concentrated light rather than the evenly lit effect you get with ceiling-mounted fluorescent.

Task Lighting

Good task lighting throws enough light on your work area to let you see your work without glare. Meeting these objectives equally well for a computer monitor screen and the hard copy sitting on the desk at the side can be challenging. Your screen needs little or no lighting, while printed papers at the side require at least 80 ft.-candles of light intensity. Bouncing your eyes back and forth between the two can strain your eyes and cause headaches.

The keys to visual comfort in the computer-screen workstation are control of the light inten-

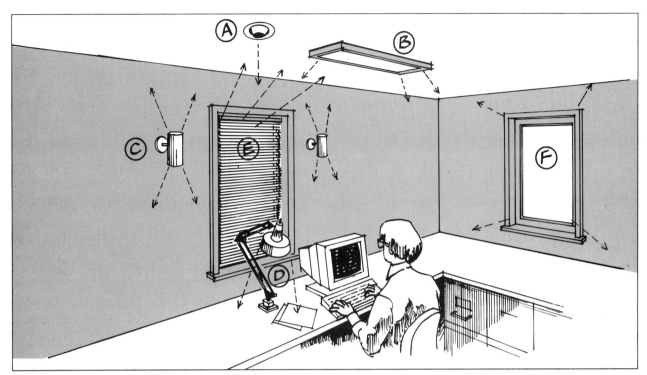

Figure 9-6: Light Sources. (A) *An adjustable ceiling fixture, such as this recessed "eyeball," focuses task lighting on a work surface or, faced toward the wall, delivers indirect (ambient) lighting.* **(B)** *Ceiling-mounted fluorescents deliver a high degree of ambient, or general, lighting at a low cost.* **(C)** *Wall lamps that throw light up, down, or in both directions can provide good sources of ambient lighting.* **(D)** *Swivel-arm desk lamps make the best all-around task lights.*

(E) *Windows located in front of your computer screen, as shown here, are a poor idea. The high contrast between the screen and window causes eyestrain. Horizontal louvered blinds can be adjusted to bounce the sun's rays upward to the ceiling.* **(F)** *A window at the side of your work area can provide a good source of general lighting if it's fitted with a device to redirect direct sunlight.*

sity and flexibility in locating the light source. You can vary the output of any incandescent lamp by up- or down-sizing the bulb or by selecting a lamp fixture with variable controls. To get flexibility of location, rely on portable lamps you can mount near your work surface and that allow you to refocus the beam, move the lamp, or move the entire fixture easily.

My favorite task light is the trusty swivel-arm desk lamp that clamps or screws onto a work surface or shelf. I use the type fitted with a single 60-W bulb. It yields just the right amount of light on hard copy without making it so bright as to contrast too much with the monitor screen. If you need to bounce back and forth between more than one intensity level, choose one of the lamps

that has a secondary fluorescent bulb encircling the primary incandescent one.

Mount task lights at the side of your work surface to keep the direct light out of your eyes and minimize reflections, a particular problem when working with shiny media such as mylar drawing sheets.

SOUND SYSTEMS

There's one more device that can enhance your office environment: a good sound system. Whether you prefer working to Montavani, the Grateful Dead, or talk radio, background sound can make working alone less lonely and help mask noise from outside the office.

You can spend a lot on a unit that comes with

AM/FM radio, plays discs or tapes, and everything else but a back scratcher, or do as I do and get by with a good quality boom box. Whatever system you choose, locate the controls within easy reach of your main workstation so that you can turn down the sound when a hard-to-understand phone call comes in. I leave my sound system tuned to FM public radio for most of the time. After the second hour of harpsichord concerti, though, my nerves clank. I restore my peace of mind by switching to a CD. Could you work to Ravel's *Bolero*?

PART THREE

GETTING THE MOST OUT OF THE LOCATION

CHAPTER 10

CONVERTING SPARE ROOMS

Lucky you if you happen to have a spare bedroom, den, or other finished room sitting vacant. As the candidate space requiring the least amount of remodeling, it was your choice as the obvious and best place for your home office. Right?

Well, maybe. In this chapter we'll look at how you can take the best advantage of your room's assets and overcome its deficits.

THE RECONVERSION QUESTION

With enough effort you can alter any finished room to suit the demands of your office. But whereas superficial changes can easily be reversed, more profound changes make it harder to reconvert the space back to its former use — a valid concern with the home's resale value.

You may think leaving it as an office will actually increase the home's market appeal. Maybe so, if you live in an area where home offices are in demand and if you won't be reducing the minimum number of bedrooms expected in this area. Converting a fourth or fifth bedroom permanently to office space may not undercut your home's resale value; it might even enhance it. But taking one bedroom away from a two- or three-bedroom home is probably unwise.

So in deciding which changes you should make, you need to first determine whether you are permanently dedicating the room to an office. If the space must revert to its former use, each alteration has to be considered in terms of reconversion. Let's begin by sorting out what we mean by *superficial* and *profound* alterations. (See the chart on page 83.)

As you can see, other than ripping walls and ceilings apart to install additional windows and doors, there is a superficial solution to almost every need. Still, you may have compelling reasons to make more profound changes. You may be able to make them and undo them after a few years of use and still save over the cost of rented office space.

WHEN THE SPARE ROOM ISN'T QUITE BIG ENOUGH

With Mike and Sarah off to college, you would like to turn one of their bedrooms into your office. Because you have another bedroom on the main floor and two more on the second floor, you are not worried about losing the space. Unfortunately, Mike's room contains 108 sq. ft.; Sarah's comes in at 132 sq. ft. Neither approaches the 250 sq. ft. you estimate you need. The obvious answer is to knock down the wall between, to make one room out of two.

Removing a stud partition between two rooms is pretty straightforward. First peel off the

Superficial Alterations	Profound Alterations
Walls/Ceilings:	
Paint, wall coverings	New doors or windows
	Alteration for soundproofing
Furniture:	
Portable desks, modular work surfaces	Built-in cabinetry
Storage:	
Shelving on wall-mounted shelf standards	Built-in shelving
Electrical:	
Surface-mounted raceways with outlets	New wiring run through walls/ceilings, new outlets in walls
Lighting:	
Portable desk lamps, floor lamps, table lamps	Ceiling-mounted fixtures, wall-mounted fixtures

finish material; then remove the studs. But before you demolish the partition, make sure you are not removing a bearing wall, or, if you are, that you provide an alternative means of support for the structure above. An hour's worth of advice from an architect, builder, or engineer is valuable at this point. The following suggestions can give you a preliminary idea of whether or not the wall is a bearing wall.

To be a bearing wall, the wall must meet two criteria: (1) support a floor, wall, or roof above; and (2) be itself supported directly below by a beam or solid wall. Consider the three-story house shown in cross section in Figure 10-1 (page 84). Let's say you wanted to know whether wall "A" on the top floor could be removed without the roof caving in. To see if the roof is supported by wall "A" you need to get up into the roof through an attic hatchway. If there is no hatchway, you may have to remove part of the ceiling near the wall. If there are no struts, rafters, or bracing attached to the wall below, you can assume it carries none of the roof's load. In the ex-

ample shown, the roof is supported by a truss that spans the entire width of the house to bear on the outside walls.

To determine whether wall "B" on the second floor is a bearing wall, first check the floor directly below. In this case, there is a beam that runs between steel posts, "C." This looks suspicious enough to warrant checking the floor above wall "B." The only way to do this is by taking off part of the floor itself or removing part of the ceiling, as indicated in the detail. Through the opened ceiling, you note that the floor joists end above the partition, and conclude that the partition carries the floor. Removing a portion of the wall finish reveals a double plate (two 2" × 4"s), a common top for a bearing wall. Non-bearing walls usually terminate in a single horizontal member.

Having determined that wall "B" is a bearing wall, if you still want to tear it down you should call in outside help to design a beam to carry the floor joists over the width of the opening you want to create.

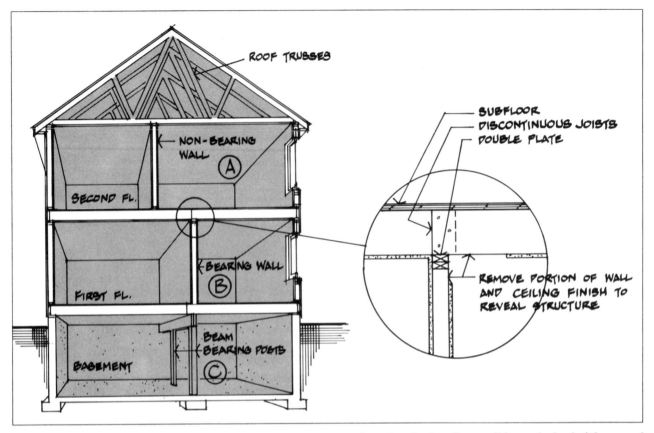

Figure 10-1: Which Walls Are Bearing Walls? *Be sure any wall you dismantle does not carry the weight of floors, walls, or roofs. If you have any doubt, ask a professional. In this three-story house, the second-floor wall does not support the roof, which is trussed to span the full distance between outside walls. A double-plate and joists that overlap are clues that the first floor wall bears the load of the second floor joists. This is revealed when removing portions of the wall and ceiling finishes. More evidence is seen in the basement, where the major post-and-beam supports align with the suspect wall above.*

Another way to create additional square footage is to expand the room to the outside, the subject of chapter 15.

A SEPARATE ENTRANCE

One of the problems that plagues home offices in spare rooms—particularly bedrooms—is the shared path to and from the office. If your office is on the ground floor, you might solve the circulation problem handily by punching a new doorway through to the outside. You can do this at almost any convenient point on the outside wall, but will avoid deep surgery on the wall in order to install new headers if you use an existing window opening. You can compensate for the lost view and light by selecting a door with a glazed panel, such as a French door.

CONTROLLING NOISE

Imagine yourself settled at your workstation in your finished spare room office. Seated, ready to get down to work, you jump at the sound of your teenage son's boom box thundering through the walls. You solve this problem, at least temporarily, by asking him to turn it down. But when you return to work, you can't help being distracted by the sound of pots and pans being shuffled around in the kitchen down the hall, or someone walking on the floor above, or by horns or sirens from the traffic on the street outside.

Any of these or other noises can disrupt your concentration. Here are four ways to attack the problem:

1. Increase your ability to concentrate in the midst of aural distraction.
2. Reduce or eliminate the offending noise.
3. Install a device to play music or "white noise" to mask the distracting sound.
4. Increase the sound isolation of the office space by altering the construction of the shell.

If you can overcome the distraction of noise by increasing your ability to concentrate (measure number 1), lucky you. Measure number 2 may work better with some sounds than others. You may be able to convince your teenager to trim a few decibels of volume, but you'll have no success with a young child or baby.

Many offices use low-level music to mask other sounds and create the mood to extract maximum output from the workers. White noise, as it's euphemistically called, issues forth a steady level of hissing or nature sound, such as a babbling brook. Many commercial offices use Muzak™ to achieve the same end. You can mask many low-level intermittent noises with a white noise machine or by playing music of your own choosing.

If measures 1, 2, and 3 fall short of controlling the noise in your home office, look into things you can do to alter the floor, ceiling, and walls. I listed this approach as the last resort, because total "soundproofing" through architectural means, though possible, is probably not cost effective. Still, there are steps short of creating a sound studio that you can take to cut outside sounds to an acceptable level.

The proper control step depends on how the noise gets into your office. Airborne sound reaches your ears directly or via a wall or floor set in vibration by the airwaves on the other side. Structure-borne sound happens when the wall or floor gets knocked directly, like someone beating a drum. Your noise problem may trace to ei-

ther or both of these paths. Here are some ways to deal with noise based on its source.

Noise From Within the Office

Working by yourself on electronic equipment, you won't likely generate enough noise to be upsetting. If you are bothered by the noise of other people talking or walking on a hard-surfaced floor, you can install sound absorptive finish materials, such as carpeting on the floor and acoustic tiles on the ceiling.

Noise From the Room Above

Except for low-frequency sounds, such as an electric bass in rock music, most of the noise from a room above the office probably comes from people walking on the floor. Figure 10-2 (page 86) shows three ways to reduce this structure-borne noise.

Installing carpet over a pad (A) is the most cost-effective first step. You can improve the sound insulating quality of a standard wood floor from 24% to 65%, depending on how thick the carpet is and the type of pad you install under it.

For more effective isolation of structure-borne sound, adding a separate layer of gypsum wallboard attached to resilient metal channels (B) to the ceiling below the offending floor will improve the floor's impact noise resistance by around 44%. Resilient metal channels come in ½" thick strips and are available from drywall suppliers. Their Z-shape profiles act like springs between layers of the floor or wall assembly to absorb vibration. Space them 24" apart and nail or screw them directly to the existing ceiling, then screw the new layer to their outstanding flange with drywall screws.

Method C combines features of A and B as well as additional insulation to get the best control of airborne sound, doubling the floor's impact noise resistance and increasing its resistance to airborne sound by 35%. Because it requires ripping into the existing ceiling, it is also the most

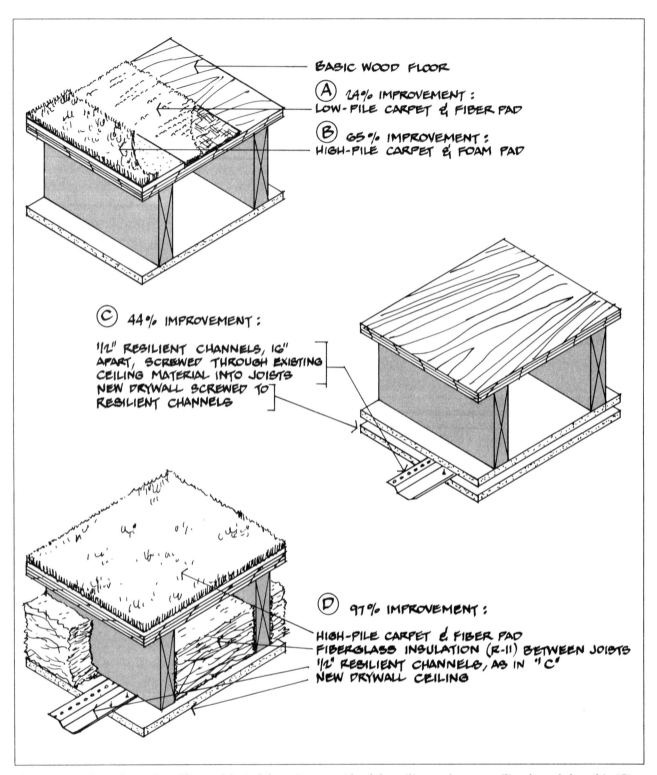

BASIC WOOD FLOOR

(A) 24% IMPROVEMENT:
LOW-PILE CARPET & FIBER PAD

(B) 65% IMPROVEMENT:
HIGH-PILE CARPET & FOAM PAD

(C) 44% IMPROVEMENT:

1/2" RESILIENT CHANNELS, 16"
APART, SCREWED THROUGH EXISTING
CEILING MATERIAL INTO JOISTS
NEW DRYWALL SCREWED TO
RESILIENT CHANNELS

(D) 97% IMPROVEMENT:
HIGH-PILE CARPET & FIBER PAD
FIBERGLASS INSULATION (R-11) BETWEEN JOISTS
1/2" RESILIENT CHANNELS, AS IN "C"
NEW DRYWALL CEILING

Figure 10-2: Soundproofing Floors. *Most of the noise carried through a floor probably stems from the impact of people walking. You can reduce this noise by modifying the floor surface or ceiling below. Simply adding carpet and a pad to a hard floor surface,* **(A)** *and* **(B)***, will cut the noise by up to 65%. Adding resilient metal channels to the under- side of the ceiling and a new ceiling layer below this* **(C)** *reduces impact noise by 44%. Combining all of these mea- sures and adding insulation between the joists* **(D)** *can cut almost all of the impact noise, but requires removing the ceiling material.*

costly. But if there are other reasons to remodel the ceiling, such as the need for surface-mounted lighting, rerouting heat ducts, or the need for a new ceiling finish, it may be justified.

Noise From Other Parts of the House

To control noise you suspect is coming through the walls and doorway, focus your efforts first on airborne sources. The smallest cracks and openings can degrade a room's noise resistance in much the same way that the smallest hole in a balloon wrecks its capacity to hold air. Besides, noise paths through air leaks are the easiest to fix.

Begin with a weatherproofed door. The barrier you get against cold air by weatherstripping an outside door can also block airborne sound from passing through an interior door. Be sure to install a threshold that makes a complete airseal, leaving no crack at the bottom.

Next, seek out other openings between your office and the rest of the house. Is there an electrical outlet in the wall next to a noise-producing adjacent room? Sealing it against sound requires pulling the box out of the wall far enough to allow you to stuff some fiberglass insulation behind it, then sealing around the holes in the box with an elastomeric caulk, such as silicone. Before tackling this messy job, be sure to cut off the power at the panel.

Sound often travels between rooms through shared heating ducts. The best solution is to "unshare" the ducts by running a separate duct to the room from a main duct farther back from the adjacent room's duct. If you can't do this, you may get substantial relief by lining the inside of the duct with acoustic insulation, probably a job for a heating contractor.

Look for any stray cracks in the walls or where the wall meets the floor, and fill them with an elastomeric (nonhardening) sealant such as silicone or polyurethane. If you use silicone, get the "paintable" kind.

When you have plugged all the air leaks and done what you can to stem noise coming through a shared duct, take a reading as to whether or not the noise level coming into the office from other parts of the house has been cut to a tolerable level. If not, your next step is to alter the surface of the walls and doorways by adding mass or adding a layer that is not directly attached to the offending wall. Figure 10-3 (page 88) shows some of the ways you can improve a basic studwall's sound transmitting qualities and how each measure affects the transmission of loud speech in the next room. Note that improvements beyond adding a second layer of wallboard are wasted unless you match the wall's soundproofing by upgrading the door. If you remodel the wall to the extent of insulating the core and installing wallboard on resilient channels (C) you should match the level of soundproofing by replacing a hollow-core door with a solid-core unit and completely weatherstripping the frame.

Sounds From Outside

The steady din of traffic probably won't bother you, but sudden and unexpected sirens wailing, horns honking, children shouting, or dogs barking will. Your outer walls are already fairly sound-resistant, thanks to the multiple layers of materials and thermal insulation. The weakest link is the windows.

The least soundproof window is a single-glazed, operable window. You should replace the window with a better unit in any case to save energy and get better comfort. In doing so, you'll also trim the noise through the window. Aim for a double-glazed, well-sealed window. If you want the best possible isolation from outside noise—as well as the best energy performance—consider multilayer units such as the Insol-8™ window manufactured by Hurd (see the appendix). Two layers of coated plastic sheeting are suspended between the two panes of glass, yielding an R-value of 8 and reducing outside noise by around 40% over a single-glazed window.

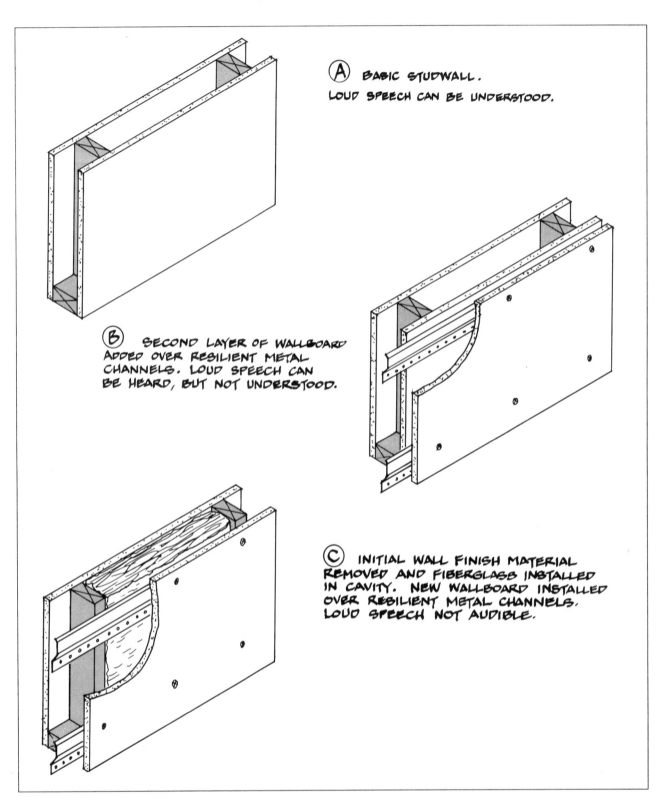

Figure 10-3: Soundproofing Walls. *If speech can be heard from the next room, you can solve the problem by sound-deadening the intervening wall. A second layer of wallboard attached to resilient channels can be added without tearing into the wall. For better sound control, remove the old wallboard and fill the spaces between the studs with R-11 fiberglass, then apply new wallboard over resilient channels. If you take this option, though, make sure any airspaces in and around intervening doors are sealed with weatherstripping.*

MORE OUTLETS

Just as replacing a leaky window with a more energy-efficient one also cuts the decibels of dogs barking outside, removing the wall finish from the inside walls for better noise control also gives you the opportunity to add outlets where you need them, as well as bury any low-voltage wiring you may want for telephones or other equipment.

You might get by quite well by plugging your computer equipment into a multioutlet surge protector that, in turn, is plugged into the nearest electrical outlet. But if the existing outlets are inconveniently located or share a circuit with a surge-generating home appliance, modifications are in order. And, though low-voltage wiring for telephone lines can be run along the top of baseboards, it's much cleaner to have them buried in the walls.

Of course ripping into a finished wall to add wiring probably isn't justified unless you have other reasons, such as adding soundproofing. If you don't, consider installing wiring chases on the wall surface, as described in the previous chapter. Surface-mounted wiring, installed with care, looks handsome enough to leave permanently, but can also be removed in the future, if you want to reconvert the room to its former status.

CHAPTER 11

ATTICS AND LOFTS

I am fortunate enough to look up from my work and see geese flying south for the winter and maple trees turning scarlet because my office is in an attic perched above the garage, with windows on two sides. After 3 years, I can't imagine a better location. The calming sights of nature changing outside are perks I wouldn't have in another part of the house, and highly unlikely in a downtown office.

But turning this sagging structure into a pleasant workspace was not without struggle. It lacked sufficient headroom. I had to figure a way to get a stairway and entry into the space above the garage without eating up too much of the garage. What remained of the old wood floor sagged badly toward the center beam—a round log ready to give up the ghost. Swallows flew in and out through the missing glass panes of the gable-end window.

But I solved these problems and am now enjoying the payoff. You can too, if you take on each challenge in turn, without letting the whole task overwhelm you. To begin with, you need a way into the attic.

VERTICAL ACCESS

Count yourself lucky if you can reach your attic from an existing stairway. Any stairway might work if your needs are flexible, you don't have bulky furniture or equipment to move in and out and you don't expect much visitor traffic. To better serve these needs, your existing stairway should:

• **Not be too steep.** Steps exceeding 8¼" in height (rise) and less than 9" in depth (run) are hard to negotiate.

• **Not be too narrow.** The width should be at least 36". Anything less than 30" is too narrow to move standard furniture through.

• **Should be free of sharp turns.** Each 90-degree turn is an obstacle to moving items up and down.

• **Should have a rail on at least one side and a protective railing at sides open to floors below.**

If your stairway comes up short on any of the above points, see if it can be altered before seeking other means of access (or giving up on the attic). Too-steep steps might be remodeled if there is a long enough landing at the top or bottom of the stairway. Too narrow? You may be stuck if there are walls on both sides. If one side opens to an adjacent room or abuts a closet that can be sacrificed, it may be possible to rebuild the stairway wider. A railing can easily be added to any stairway.

A stairway impossible to alter or no stairway at all is cause to consider building a new stairway—inside if there is space enough; outside if not.

Stairway Basics

For ease in climbing, steps should have the proper rise to run ratio. The more the rise, the less the run should be. Current national building codes would limit you to a maximum rise of 7" and a run of 11" if your office was in a commercial building. Residences are allowed step rises of 8¼" and runs as short as 9". Here are some workable step proportions (in inches) you may use to build a new stairway or rebuild an existing one:

Rise	Run	Rise	Run
6	13½	7¼	10½
6¼	12⅞	7½	10
6½	12¼	7¾	9½
6¾	11⅝	8	9
7	11	8¼	8½

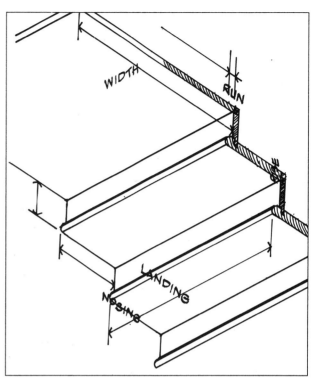

Figure 11-1: Basic Step Dimensions. *These include the rise, run, and width. Nosings typically project about an inch, which makes climbing easier and makes the total stair length a bit more compact.*

Stairs should be at least 36" wide to get furniture through. A width of 42" to 48" is better still.

For safety, landings are desirable (required, if you follow the code) at the top and bottom of each run of stairs and should be at least as wide as the stairway or wide enough to accommodate a door swinging out into the stairway.

New Interior Stairs

Let's say you want to convert all or part of your attic into an office, but the only way in is through a hatchway in the ceiling of a bedroom closet. The closet is obviously too small for a stairway, so you'll have to find another place for it. How much space do you need? It depends on the shape of the stairway and the dimensions of the steps. First determine the number of risers. Here's how:

1. Measure the vertical distance, in inches, from the lower floor to the attic floor (make sure

to use the dimension to the finish floor surface). Let's say it is 108".

2. Divide the total floor-to-floor height by the desired riser height. For a riser height of 7½", the number required would be 108 divided by 7.5, or 14.4. Because you don't want a partial step, this rounds off to 15 (we could reduce the number to 13 by increasing the step to 8¼", if necessary).

Now let's see how much floor space these stairs require if configured into a simple straight run stairway:

1. Determine the actual step rise. If we use 15 steps for the vertical dimension of 108", the rise of each step is 108 divided by 15, or 7.2".

2. Select a tread (run) dimension. The closest tread match for 7.2", from the rise/run table is 10".

3. The number of treads equals the number of risers minus one (15 – 1 = 14).

4. The total length of the steps for a single straight run equals the total number of treads, or

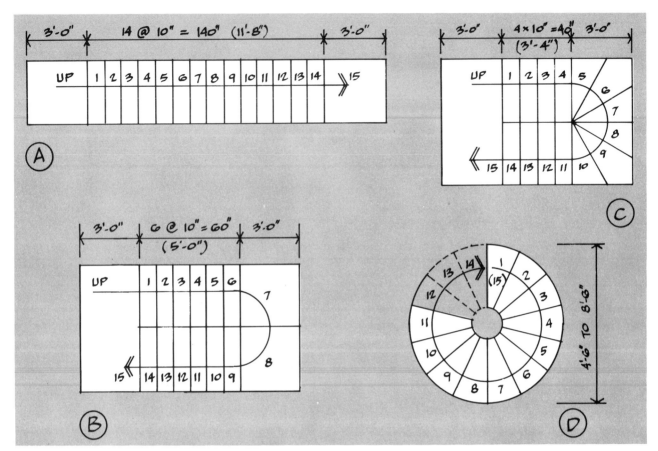

Figure 11-2: Stairway Options. *Here are four ways to get to an attic floor, 8'7" above the floor below, using fifteen risers measuring just short of 7" each. The simplest choice, a straight-run stairway* (**A**), *is also the longest. The scissor stairs* (**B**) *reduces the length but doubles the width. Adding winding stairs to the intermediate landing* (**C**) *trims the length even more. The most compact choice is a circular spiral stairway* (**D**).

14 times 10" equals 140" (11'8").

5. The total stairway length, wall-to-wall, equals the tread length plus landings at the top and bottom, or 140 + 36 + 36 = 212" (17'8").

The stairway is pictured in Figure 11-2, A (above). Do you have a 3' × 17'8" area on the floor below the attic that can serve as a stairway? If not, try another type of stairway, such as two straight-run stairs, as shown in Figure 11-2, B. If the intermediate landing is level, you'll save on the length, but double the width.

So far, we have been considering level landings. If we replace them with winding stairs (11-2, C), we gain 5 additional steps that can now be taken from the straight stairs. The savings in treads are 2 on one run and 3 on the other. Total

stairway length has now been reduced by two treads to 9'. Because the steps that turn the corners ("winders") are wedge shaped rather than rectangular, they are more difficult to negotiate, so make sure the tread width is at least equal to the other treads at a distance of 1' out from the center.

If space is too tight for any kind of straight-run stairway—even with winders at the turn—consider a spiral stairway (11-2, D). Prefabricated out of steel with wood or steel treads, spiral stairways can be squeezed into areas varying in diameter from 42" to 74". You'll have an interesting time moving desks up and down the smallest-diameter ones, but they work fine for foot traffic. Get exact sizes and models from manufacturers listed in the appendix.

Exterior Stairways

Okay, you've searched in vain for a place to build a set of stairs to your attic and the only solution you have come up with is sacrificing half of your kid's bedroom. How about a stairway outside? Other than just providing a way in, it offers you a separate outside entrance for visitors from the ground level. You'll need a spot clear of windows and doors on the floor below, and enough clearance behind the property line to avoid encroaching into the setbacks required by the zoning ordinance.

If the stairs are for regular daily use, they should be protected from weather. An open stairway with a roof overhead might suffice in Florida, but I'd want a weather-tight enclosure in Oregon or Minnesota. Other than walls and roof, the design is pretty much the same as an indoor stairway.

MAKING HEADROOM

If you concluded from chapter 5 that headroom in your attic would be a problem—and it almost always is—you can take one of two approaches to gain additional height:

- Poke the roof up in a few places.
- Raise the entire roof.

The first option is cheaper and more likely to blend with the exterior of your house. And imagine the interesting shapes you can gain inside by contrasting sloping ceilings against higher sections created by shed or gable dormers.

Shed Dormers

Named for the shedlike way they project out from the ridge of the main roof, shed dormers are easier to build than gable dormers. They are also more flexible, because their width isn't limited by the pitch of their own roof. But blending them into the design of the house can be tricky, because of their necessarily shallow slope. And, if your main roof is too shallow, they may not work at all.

Asphalt or wood shingles require a roof pitch of 3 in 12 (3/12) or greater, so adding a shed dormer to a house whose roof is no greater than 3/12 gains no headroom at all at the low end. As a rule of thumb, you won't get much headroom from a shed dormer if your house's roof pitch is less than 6/12, unless the roof begins atop a kneewall (a short wall at the eave end). To evaluate your options, begin with an accurately drawn cross section. To ensure that your revised roof framing is safe, have it reviewed (or designed) by a competent design professional.

Gable Dormers

Gable (or "doghouse") dormers are easier to blend into the roofs of most houses but harder to build. Two, three, or four small gable dormers blend more easily into the design of most homes than a single large one. On the other hand, a single large gable dormer yields a bigger area of higher headroom inside. Figure on a clear minimum width inside of at least 5' to accommodate a standard desk.

To evaluate the headroom you can gain from a gable dormer, you'll need not only a cross section through the attic, but also a perpendicular cross section through the dormer itself.

Raising the Roof

Raising the entire roof above part of your home may be your best choice if you are hell-bent on an attic office but can't squeeze out enough headroom, even with a dormer. This choice is the most costly, but may result in an increase in the resale value of the home.

Raising the roof changes the exterior appearance dramatically, so get accurate drawings made of the proposed change before committing yourself. If you can't do the drawings yourself, ask a building professional to help you with these as well as help design a new roof framing system.

At some time during the construction, the old

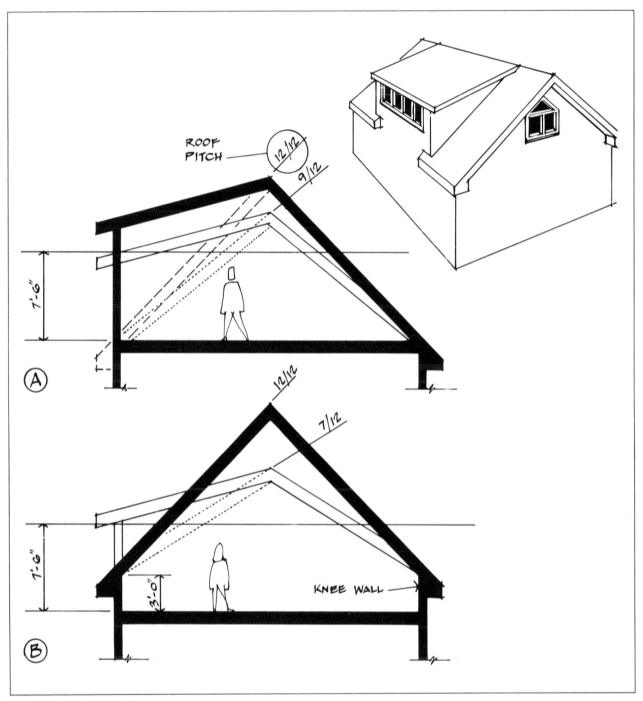

Figure 11-3: Shed Dormer Geometry. *Shed dormers can open up ceiling space, if the roof pitch is steep enough, as shown by the 9/12- and 12/12-pitched roofs in* **(A)**. *Roofs as shallow as 7/12 stand to gain headroom* **(B)** *if the roof begins at a kneewall rather than on the attic floor.*

roof has to be removed, exposing living areas below to water. Careful planning might make it possible to build the new roof with only minor incursions into the lower roof (I did it this way, so I know it can be done). Otherwise, have a large, waterproof tarp fastened to one side of the roof that can be pulled over any exposed areas in the event of a sudden storm.

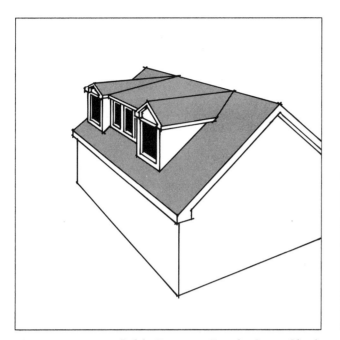

Figure 11-4: Two Gable Dormers Bracketing a Shed Dormer. *This arrangement expands the area inside with high headroom. Small dormers like these, used alone, are too narrow to create useful office space.*

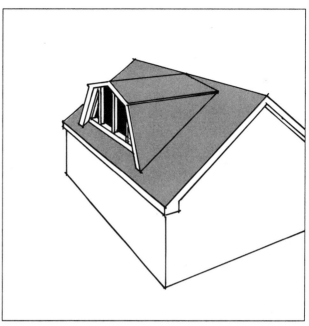

Figure 11-5: A Gambrel Dormer. *This yields a wide area of high headroom, but the gambrel shape may look odd unless it occurs somewhere else on the house.*

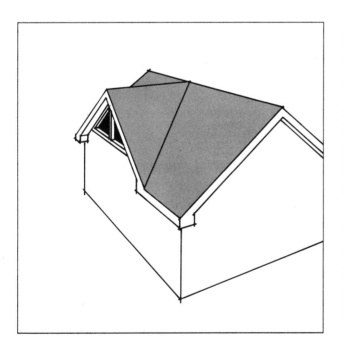

Figure 11-6: A Gable Dormer Extending From Floor to Roof Ridge. *This dormer gains high-ceiling space inside without the narrow vertical sides common to smaller dormer units that perch on the roof.*

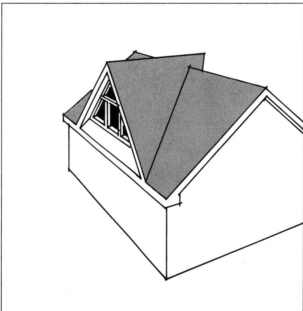

Figure 11-7: Extending the Gable Dormer Past the Roof Ridge. *This structure creates even greater high-ceiling floor space and the possibility of a smaller window in the other end of the gable.*

OPENINGS TO THE OUTSIDE WORLD

If you start with an unfinished attic, it probably has few, if any, windows. This is good, because it leaves you the freedom to select the most suitable types of windows or skylights and put them where they will do the most good. Making the right choice is not simple. Blending in with the rest of the house, sizing and locating openings to accommodate the furniture layout, and the type of glazing all need careful planning.

Dormer and Wall Windows

Attic windows in dormers or vertical walls will be your primary source of views and ventilation.

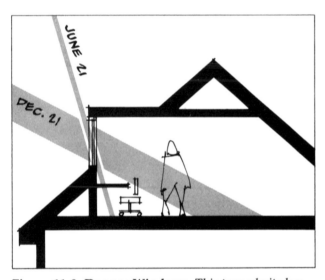

Figure 11-8: Dormer Windows. *This type admits less sunlight than roof windows, but the shape of the window provides a means for automatically shading the window as the hottest part of the year draws near (solar angles for latitude 40 degrees north, such as Denver).*

Because shed dormers span greater wall length, they offer more flexibility for selecting windows — individually or in groups. Choose the appropriate type or mix of types from the window guidelines in chapter 8. Small gable dormers accommodate a single, vertically shaped window such as single- or double-hung and casements. Larger gable dormers and shed dormers offer more possibilities in the types and numbers of window units you can plug into them.

Roof Windows/Skylights

The wonderful thing about an office in the attic is that you aren't limited to vertical windows for light, ventilation and even views. Skylights or roof windows poked right through the surface of the roof make it possible for you to create an opening almost wherever you want to. The basic difference between skylights and roof windows is that all roof windows open by tilting in, allowing the outer pane to be cleaned from the inside. Skylights either hinge outward from the top or are fixed (inoperable). Here are some things to think about when deciding between dormers and roof windows/skylights (RWs):

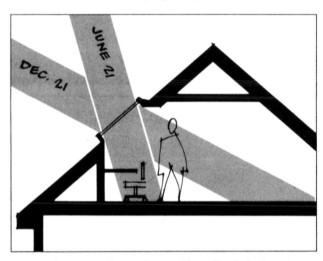

Figure 11-9: Roof Windows. *These flood the interior year-round with much more of the sun's light and heat than do dormers. Without shades or blinds, the solar gain can create unwanted heat in the warm months and glare year-round.*

- **Appearance.** RWs change the overall appearance of the home less than dormers, unless you select "bubble" skylights, which don't blend well with traditional home styles. On the other hand, dormers used sensitively can enhance the home.

- **Cost.** RWs are by far the more economical choice, as well as being easier to install than dormers.

- **Daylight.** Roof windows spread their light more widely inside than dormers, but the light and incipient glare is harder to control. Built-in horizontal blinds, options with some units, make for easier control.

• **Ventilation.** Dormers with casement windows bring in more outside air than operable RWs.

• **View.** My vote goes to dormers. There is something unsettling about looking out through a sloped window surface.

• **Watertightness.** Good RWs, properly installed, are reasonably watertight, as are dormers. But when open, a sudden squall can bring rain inside the sides of RWs—less so with dormers.

Figure 11-10: Locating Roof Windows or Dormers.
Place these to the side of your workstation so that the sill is about 3' above the floor and the window head is 6' to 7' above the floor.

• **Heat loss/gain.** Heat loss is always greater overhead than through a wall, so RWs come out worse here. Units with double-glazing, low-E coating and argon gas fill get an R-3.6, which is not too bad. Heat gain is likewise harder to control in overhead glazing. Because the sun is higher in the sky in summer than winter, it pumps more heat through a roof window than

a vertical window surface, while an overhang above a dormer can block almost all unwanted solar heat on a south-facing wall.

BEEFING UP FLOORS

Chances are that your attic was never intended for occupancy, even if it comes with a floor. To support the loads of people, equipment, and furniture for office use, the floor should be able to carry a minimum of 40 lbs. per sq. ft.—more if you have extra-heavy equipment. You can determine whether your floor structure is up to the task by consulting a building professional. The following table can give you a rough idea.

Size of Joists	Spacing	Maximum Span
2" × 6"	16"	8'7"
	24"	7'6"
2" × 8"	16"	11'4"
	24"	9'6"
2" × 10"	16"	14'3"
	24"	11'8"
2" × 12"	16"	16'6"
	24"	13'2"

First measure the joists. Say they measure $1\frac{5}{8}$" × $7\frac{1}{2}$", look under the nearest size in the table: 2" × 8". Next measure the average distance between the joists (spacing). You find it to be around 15". The maximum safe span for the office use is 11'4". Is the floor adequate, as is? You can't tell without determining how far the joists presently span (the length between supports). Say they span to a beam or bearing wall at the center of the house, for a distance of 14'. This is 2'10" over the safe span distance your office floor will safely support. You will need to reinforce or replace the joists for the new use.

If you decide to reinforce, rather than replace, the joists—and I think this is the best choice—you can use the existing joists as part of the new floor and add additional members to gain the needed strength. Here are three ways to reinforce an existing wood-framed floor:

• **Sistering.** If the existing joists are regularly spaced but undersized for the new load, you can strengthen them (and level the tops) by nailing new "sister" joists alongside each. Be sure the sisters extend the full distance between supports.

• **Capping.** It may be difficult to install sister joists over the full span or there may be insulation between the existing joists you want to leave intact (it will help soundproof your attic office). In lieu of sister joists, you can cap the top of each existing joist with a 2" × 4" laid flat to create a composite joist with greater capacity. To ensure that the new built-up joist works as one unit, lay down a continuous bed of construction adhesive over the top of the existing joist with a caulking gun, then nail the cap down with 10-penny nails closely spaced, say no greater than 12" apart.

• **Supplemental joists.** The existing joists may be too wide or uneven to preclude sistering or capping. In many older houses the ceiling joists were not regularly spaced or were spaced too wide to adequately support a floor above. Any spacing wider than 24" is a sure bet for a springy floor. The best approach might be to ignore the existing joists and install new joists, properly sized, at 16" or 24" spacing between the existing ones.

These approaches are illustrated in Figures 11-11 through 11-13 (at right). As with any structural change, to be on the safe side, have a competent building design professional review any system you decide on.

HOW TO KEEP FROM COOKING OR FREEZING

Exposed to the weather overhead, as well as on the sides, attic offices require more care than other spaces to maintain comfortable temperatures. Start with well-insulated walls and roof, as suggested in chapter 8. Opt for vertical windows over roof windows or skylight, if possible, and

Figure 11-11: Sister Joists. *When nailed to each existing joist, these can at least double an attic floor's load carrying capacity. The new joists can be installed from above if you will be adding a new floor, or below if there is no ceiling.*

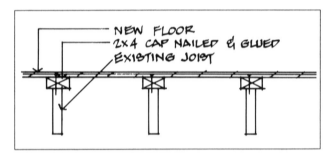

Figure 11-12: Capping Existing Joists. *Adding 2" × 4"s set in adhesive and nailed can also beef up the structure, but the increase is harder to predict.*

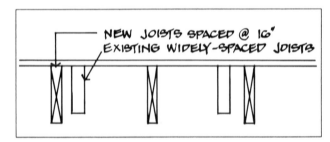

Figure 11-13: Adding New Joists. *Placing these between the existing joists is the best way to get more structural capacity, as well as a regular spacing for a new floor.*

locate them according to the guidelines in chapter 8. If you do select roof windows, equip them with operable controls, such as blinds.

A source of heat might be as easy as a fan installed right in the floor, if the room below is heated, or any of the separate devices discussed in chapter 9. Although some times of the year are uncomfortably hot and humid without mechanical air conditioning, you can get free cooling at other times by opening your well-placed windows. If you are lucky, they might even let you watch geese flying south.

CHAPTER 12

BASEMENT PROBLEMS AND SOLUTIONS

Tangled wires and piping overhead; cold, damp walls; uneven floors and darkness are obstacles you may face in turning a corner of your basement into a home office. Most have solutions. Some, such as inadequate headroom, you may have to make the best of. Let's examine your basement from the top down.

THE MESS OVERHEAD

Unless you live in a recently built house with a basement intended for finishing, the chances are indeed good that your basement ceiling is a jumble of electrical wiring, pipes, and ducts. If you have lived there very long, it might also be home to Junior's first skis, curtain rods, and a lot of other stuff you have long since forgotten but couldn't bring yourself to consign to the yard sale. Though daunting, this miasma can be dealt with. Have that yard sale. Discard. Donate to charity. Don't let the trappings of the past block your plans for the future.

The Headroom Dilemma

A basic lack of headroom is a thornier issue. As we saw earlier, most codes require a minimum clear height of 7'6" in "occupied" spaces. If you don't have the minimum headroom, you can make your office in another part of your house or ignore the requirement. After all, it may be a shame to let this potentially valuable real estate lie fallow. Most people are not 7'6" tall, so a clear height of anything over, say, 6'6" is possible, if not ideal. Of course if you need a building permit for construction, you may not get away with it.

If headroom is tight, make the most of what you have. After you remove the skis and other clutter from between the joists overhead, look for ways to handle the utility lines that may be eating up headroom. Electrical wiring hanging below joists can easily be relocated to a more convenient location. Piping suspended below floor joists can often be raised up to just below the joists with one or two reconnections, unless they are waste (sewer) lines that are pitched to drain.

Even heating ducts that protrude too far down can be altered. In some cases they can be pushed up to run between the joists rather than below them. If not, you can often replace them with a shallower duct of the same cross-sectional area. For example, if you have a 12"×20" duct hanging below the joists at a critical location with the 12" dimension facing down, you can replace it with an 8"×30" duct, to gain 4" of valuable headroom.

Ceiling Finish Options

Rather than installing a new ceiling below one where headroom is tight, consider leaving the ceiling as is, but making all the pipes, wires, and other stuff seem to vanish. You'll be surprised to see how painting everything a single color can unify the plethora of confusion overhead into a single composition. To reinforce the idea, paint the walls a contrasting color. Even if it takes a lot of paint, the cost will still be less than a new ceiling.

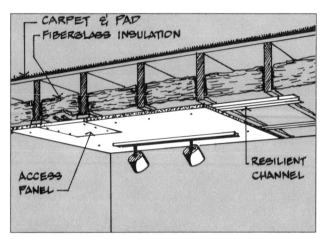

Figure 12-2: Sound-Deadening Ceiling. *Reduce impact noise from footfall on the floor above by adding a carpet, pad and insulation between the joists. Then install a gypsum wallboard ceiling on resilient metal channels (see chapter 10). Provide an access panel at spots where you might need to get to mechanical or electrical devices.*

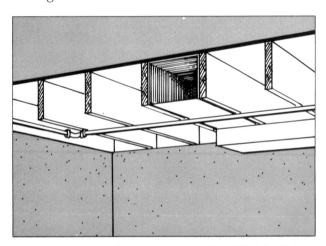

Figure 12-1: Simple Basement Ceiling Finish. *Painting the ceiling structure, pipes, wiring, and ducts all the same color will turn a confusing mess into a unified whole. To make this trick even more effective, paint the walls a contrasting color.*

But you may have other reasons for installing a separate ceiling, space permitting. Basement rooms are highly vulnerable to footsteps on the floor above. This can wreak havoc on your concentration. To reduce this structure-borne noise, you can do one or more of the floor sound-deadening strategies suggested in chapter 10 and shown in Figure 10-2 (page 86).

Enclosing the ceiling with wallboard permanently encases everything above, so before you do this be sure the items you cover won't need to be worked on. Provide a means of access for any others. Anticipate any spots that might require access, such as valves, junction boxes, pipe and duct clean-outs, and install removable access panels at these locations. Sheets of ½" plywood

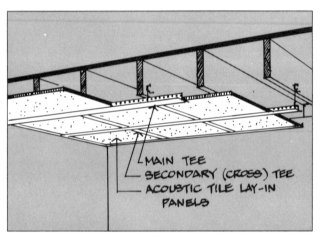

Figure 12-3: Suspended Ceiling. *If you have enough headroom, a suspended ceiling provides universal access and is simple and economical to install. After hanging the main tee members by wire from the joists, install the cross tees to form a grid measuring 24" × 24" or 24" × 48". Acoustic panels that lay into the grid come in various textures and patterns.*

held in place with screws and painted the same color as the ceiling make good, simple, access panels.

If you want to add a ceiling below the joists and sound control isn't an issue, consider a suspended lay-in ceiling composed of metal tee-shape supports with acoustic tile panels loosely laid into the tees. The tees are hung by wires from the joists into a modular pattern of 24″ × 24″ or 24″ × 48″ (the most common size). Infill tiles are available in a wide variety of textures and profiles. You can mount standard light fixtures on the surface of the ceiling or install modular fluorescent fixtures flush, if clearances permit.

Before we leave ceilings, I want to point out another potential source of irritation: noise from waste piping. The cast iron sewer pipes common in older homes were relatively quiet. Newer pipes made of plastic (white PVC or black ABS) can sound like a waterfall each time a toilet is flushed. Concealing them behind a sound-deadening ceiling finish such as the one described above may solve the problem. Otherwise, wrap the pipe with 4″-thick fiberglass insulation and hope for the best.

BASEMENT WALL IMPROVEMENTS

The walls in your basement may serve admirably in their present state, as long as the basement's main purpose is to house the furnace and water heater and provide storage space for seldom-used household trappings. Once the basement becomes the site where you will sit and work for hours at a time, its raw masonry walls and cement floor may well prove too cold, too damp, or too unsightly. In worst cases they may be riddled with cracks that allow entry of cold air, water, radon gas, and rodents. But take heart, there is a remedy for each of these problems.

Water Leaks

Does water run through cracks in the walls after extended rainy periods or seep through at other times? If so you will be wasting your time, effort, or money finishing off the space for an office until you do something to stop the leakage.

Start at the source outside. You can have your walls dug out and properly waterproofed, at the cost of several thousand dollars, or seek cheaper remedies. Most of the water probably originates on the surface, rather than below grade, so your first line of attack should be to redirect the runoff away from the foundation wall.

If the roof drains directly onto the ground by the affected wall, install a gutter at the eave with a downspout that funnels water to a single point on the ground. At this point, create a lined channel to carry the drainage several feet away from the foundation.

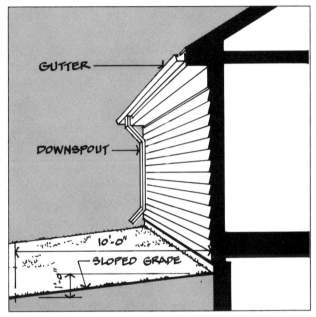

Figure 12-4: Basement Waterproofing. *Do the easiest things first, such as installing a gutter and downspouts at the eaves. Slope the grade away from the foundation wall. As a last resort, a trench can be dug next to the foundation and a waterproofing membrane applied.*

If the ground drains toward the house, see if you can regrade it to slope away at a minimum pitch of ¼″ per foot, for 5′ or so out from the wall.

One system developed in Scandinavia both controls surface runoff near the foundation and stems heat loss from the basement by creating a 4′-wide channel next to the wall, into which is placed a strip of rigid foam insulation that slopes away from the house, as shown in Figure 12-5 (page 102). The insulation board directs surface water out away from the foundation while retarding heat escaping from the mass of earth below it. If you try this method, tape all joints between foam panels and take extra pains not to puncture the foamboard.

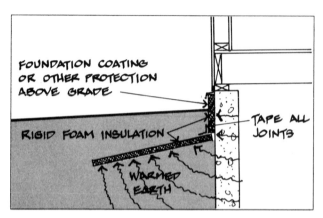

Figure 12-5: Scandinavian Two for One System. *The Swedes developed an approach that both directs surface water from the foundation wall and retards heat loss from the basement. Four-foot-wide rigid foam insulation sheets are laid in the ground and up the outside of the wall. Joints are taped and portions exposed above grade are coated with polymeric foundation coating. The earth below the insulation buffers heat loss from the interior to the outside air.*

Although stopping water leaks from the inside is harder than from the outside, it may be your only choice. If the wall is very old, it may consist of field stones laid up without mortar. You can apply mortar from the inside by using a dry premixed mortar that comes in bags. When I did mine, I started with a trowel, but found it was more effective to pack it in by hand. Be sure to wear heavy-duty rubber gloves to avoid chemical burns from the cement.

Concrete and concrete block foundation walls sometimes have cracks that allow water to seep through. Various materials such as epoxy or cement-based compounds can be injected into the cracks from the inside, but this is tricky work better left to a waterproofing expert. If you go this route, follow the guidelines in chapter 6 for locating a qualified expert.

Dampproofing

Basement walls may also have a problem with dampness. Originating both from moisture-producing sources inside and outside the house, dampness problems are made even worse by the hygroscopic nature of cementitious wall materials. If unprotected by a vapor barrier on the out-

side, the walls absorb moisture from the earth and wick it through to the inside surface where it condenses and runs off or evaporates into the room. The result can be unhealthy for you and unfriendly to anything you want to keep dry.

As with waterproofing, your first line of defense should be a good dampproofing barrier on the outer face of the wall. The best cure from the inside, I believe, is to build a separate interior wall that contains a vapor barrier between the masonry and new wall finish. Before we get down to wall finishes, though, we should consider insulation.

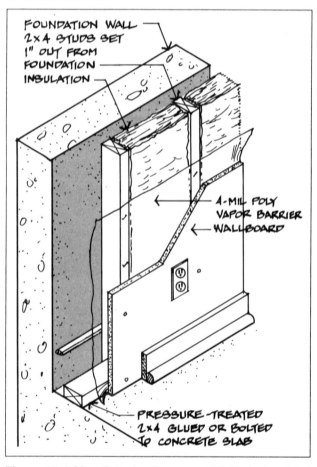

Figure 12-6: New Interior Basement Wall. *An insulated studwall provides a wiring chase, moisture barrier, insulation, and new wall finish in one system. Also, the studs serve as an easy base for securing furniture and shelving.*

To Insulate or Not

If the ground is a natural insulator, why insulate basement walls? Good question. Whereas the ground is warmer than the air above in winter, it remains colder than the comfortable temperature you want inside your office. For example, the average soil temperature 20' deep in Fargo, North Dakota, is around 41°F, much below the comfort level inside (usually 72°F). So in areas with cold winters uninsulated basement walls will continuously leak heat to the adjacent earth.

In summer, the same uninsulated wall might help cool the space. But, because summers are shorter than winters in North Dakota, the main problem is retaining heat in the winter.

In the Gulf region, the soil may be warmer than the desired inside temperature. In Miami, the deep soil temperature stays around 78°F. But because the difference is just 6°F, insulating foundation walls makes little sense.

Because subgrade insulation is not yet a well-defined science, experts don't agree on the optimum level of insulation. In the absence of clear guidelines, I suggest the following levels for the parts of your foundation below grade (above grade foundation walls should be insulated to the same levels as other above-grade walls, as described in chapter 8):

0	Southern Florida and the Florida Keys.
R-8	Western slope of Washington, Oregon, California; Southern half of Texas, Louisiana, Georgia; Northern Florida.
R-11	All other locations.

You can insulate either the outside or inside of the foundation. Insulation on the outside is probably slightly better, because it couples the foundation wall to the inside temperature, while isolating it from the colder outside soil. The wall is kept from freezing and its constant temperature helps stabilize the inside temperature. Good bets for exterior foundation are rigid fiberglass (high-density); rigid sheets of extruded polystyrene (blue or pink board); polyurethane or poly-

isocyanurate (usually cream colored); or phenolic (pinkish).

An inch of extruded polystyrene will get you an R-value of 5, so if you are aiming for R-8, use the 1½" thickness (R-7.5). After you have dug out the dirt 4' down (no minor effort), rigid foam insulation is relatively easy to apply to the outside of the foundation wall with a compatible adhesive. Protect the portion sticking out of the ground with one of several types of cementitious coatings now available.

Wall Finishes

You may want to leave your basement walls exposed inside if they have a special character, such as brick or stone. Even the uneven texture of concrete has a special charm you might want to retain. Leaving it natural or painting it with a good masonry paint will allow the surface character to read through.

More than likely, however, the walls will need some treatment to counter coldness, dampness, or water leaks. A new studwall inside the masonry wall is a good way to solve several problems at once: cure dampness and coldness, provide a chase in which to run wiring, and a base for a smooth, even wall finish.

Use only pressure-treated wood (or redwood, cedar, or cypress) for the studs, because they will constantly be exposed to a damp environment. Fix the sill plate to the floor slab with expansion bolts set into the concrete (the hard way) or a bead of construction adhesive (the easy way). An inch-wide space behind the studs provides an excellent place to run electric wiring.

After wiring, staple kraft-faced fiberglass insulation batts between the studs. On the face of the studs, staple 4-mil polyurethane (poly) sheet. Because this is your barrier between the damp masonry and dry interior, take special care to seal against air leaks. Wrap the poly around the backside of any switch or outlet boxes and seal any holes with silicone caulk (messy, but necessary).

Finally, nail or screw wallboard to the studs

(½" thick for studs spaced 16" apart, ⅝" thick for studs spaced 24" apart).

Wallboard joints should always be taped and filled. This will suffice if you will be applying another finish, such as wood paneling. For a paint finish or application of a wall covering, you'll need to fill all nail holes as well as the joints and sand the entire surface completely smooth. Even the smallest imperfections show through a paint finish.

TURNING YOUR BASEMENT FLOOR INTO AN OFFICE FLOOR

If you are lucky, the basement floor you start with will be a smooth, level concrete slab that stays dry. Finishing it for an office is a simple matter, as we'll see later. But what if your floor falls short of this ideal? An uneven or sloped surface, cracks, dampness, and constant or periodic water seepage all require remedial work before a finish is applied. Some of these are more serious than others, but ignoring water and dampness is a sure bet for future grief.

The Quest for a Dry Floor

As with walls, water and dampness often plague basement floors. Keeping water out can be difficult and expensive, but essential to prevent damage to finishes, equipment, or materials stored in your office. Controlling water coming up through cracks in the floor begins with pinning down the entry points.

Water coming up through the slab may only bedevil you at certain times of the year, such as spring, when the water table rises up higher than the floor level. It might also trace to a subterranean aquifer that dribbles continuously through a porous vein near the floor. Unfortunately, none of the various methods advertised to control this kind of water penetration is foolproof. All are likely to be expensive starting at $3,000 on up. If your problem only affects one or two spots, I'd start with a gallon of hydraulic patching compound you can get from a masonry supplier. If

it stops the leak, you are home free. If not, you haven't lost much in the way of time or money. If this doesn't work, get an evaluation from a qualified waterproofing contractor, along with a firm estimate of the probable cost and type of guarantee you can expect.

Controlling dampness wicking up through an existing concrete floor slab can be done by simply applying a moisture-proof coating or membrane to the slab before applying a floor finish. A moisture-proof coating may limit the type finish you apply, if you are thinking of adhesively bonded resilient flooring or ceramic tiles. A polyethylene membrane will definitely rule out a directly bonded floor finish. But all is not lost, you can apply the dampproofing coating or membrane, then build a wood floor above to serve as a substrate for any floor finish you want.

A Wood Subfloor Over Concrete

This simple addition to your concrete slab can slay several dragons with a single blow: bar dampness, create an even surface, create a chase for wiring, and provide a nailable substrate. But to do it, you should make sure you can lose at least 2¼" from the available headroom.

Sweep the slab, then place a layer of 6-mil polyethylene (poly) sheet down to act as a moisture barrier. Overlap generously and tape the seams with duct tape. Next, lay 2"×4" sleepers flat side down, in rows 24" apart. If the concrete is not level, shim where necessary, as described in the following section.

Finally, place sheets of ¾" plywood over the sleepers with the face grain perpendicular to the direction of the sleepers. If you will be applying an adhesively bonded floor covering, use an underlayment-grade plywood. Nail the plywood to the sleepers with spiral-shank flooring nails.

Leveling an Uneven Floor

Basement floor slabs often slope intentionally toward a drain, or unintentionally because of poor construction or settling. A very minor slope of ⅛"

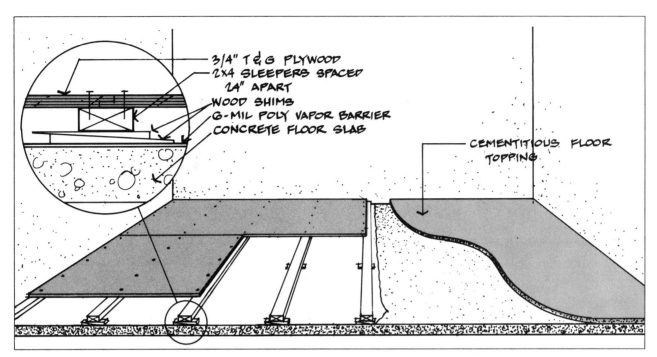

3/4" T & G PLYWOOD
2×4 SLEEPERS SPACED 24" APART
WOOD SHIMS
6-MIL POLY VAPOR BARRIER
CONCRETE FLOOR SLAB

CEMENTITIOUS FLOOR TOPPING

Figure 12-7: Two Ways to Level a Basement Slab. *An uneven concrete slab can be leveled by installing a grid of 2" × 4"s (left) or by a cementitious topping (right). The wood approach is probably more economical and you can run wiring in the cavities. Topping, though more expensive, is quicker and easier if done by specialty contractors (see the appendix for suppliers). If you opt for the wood approach, begin by laying down a plastic vapor barrier sheet. Place 2" × 4"s in position and nail a board across them to temporarily hold them in place. Shim each 2" × 4" with wood (shingle) shims until gridwork is completely level, then nail plywood panels, staggering them as shown above.*

per foot or less probably won't be noticeable, but greater slopes can be unattractive and make it necessary to shim or block each piece of furniture and equipment that sits on the floor. Assuming the water problems have been solved in the area you want to convert to an office, it's a good idea to level a sloping floor before applying a finish. Here are two methods.

Shimming. To fill a low space between the concrete floor slab and wood sleepers, use wedge-shape shingle shims (available from lumberyards in bundles). Place two shims under each low spot. Insert the thin edge of one shim under the sleeper. From the opposite side, insert the other shim, thin edge first. By pushing the shims toward each other their wedge shape makes them fill gaps up to about ¾". For wider gaps, start with a piece of solid blocking below the shims. If you are shimming above a poly membrane, take care not to puncture it.

Topping. Another way to level a concrete slab is to flood the surface with a leveling compound. You can hire applicators licensed to apply portland cement- or gypsum-based toppings, but this isn't cost effective unless you are doing the entire basement floor. At least one product, Ardex™, is designed for nonlicensed applicators. The material comes in bags as a powder. After mixing it with a paddle in a barrel, the slurry is poured over the slab, in thicknesses of up to 3". All of these cementitious toppings (listed in the appendix) yield a smooth, level surface capable of accepting any floor finish. Another plus is that these toppings fill the small cracks that admit radon gas.

BASEMENT WINDOWS

Okay, the lack of windows wasn't enough to turn you off to converting part of your basement into your office. But can you really work for long periods of time without outside light and views? Those people who work in high-rise offices never see the outdoors except at lunch break, if then. Perhaps you're consciously seeking a work environment away from outside distraction.

If you value daylight, you'll want to make the most of any sunlight that penetrates small basement windows, or you might even consider busting holes in the foundation for a new window. Concrete cutting is done all the time by specialized contractors (check the yellow pages for listings under "Concrete sawing"). I could have a contractor travel 50 miles to my town and cut an opening in an 8" concrete wall for $22 per lineal foot, or a minimum job charge of $315—adequate to cut a 48"×36" opening. The diamond-toothed saw cuts a clean slot into which you can insert a window frame.

If you already have windows in the basement, they may be small, three- or four-pane units that swing in from hinges at the top. Until recently, basement windows were single-glazed and not very well sealed. Wood window frames set in a masonry wall are also subject to dry rot. If the frames are shot, your best bet is to replace the entire unit with quality wood or pvc units with double glazing. If the frames are sound, focus your first efforts on weathersealing; cold air streaming in through cracks can cause you real discomfort, as well as waste heat to the outdoors.

Fill any perimeter cracks wider than ½" or so with urethane foam, which is available in pressurized cans. Then caulk smaller cracks with a polyurethane or acrylic latex caulk.

If the sash is poorly weatherstripped (or not at all), install spring bronze (my favorite) or any of the after-the-fact plastic weatherstripping available at your home center.

After stopping air leaks, you can cut the heat loss through the glass itself by adding a storm window to the inside or outside. Check the plastic types available at your local building supply dealer or measure the size of the sash and have a glass shop make up a unit out of glass.

Below-grade basement windows trap water that can enter cracks in the foundation and debris that can block light. You can keep the well clean of water and debris and add another barrier to cold air, by installing a clear acrylic window well cover above the well, as shown in Figure 12-9 (page 107).

Here's how you can increase the amount of light that streams through small basement windows. First, cut back any foliage blocking the path of the sun. Next, increase the size of the window well to prevent the walls from shading the opening. Finally, cut a piece of rigid material (plywood or cardboard) to fit the bottom of the well. Cover the top side with reflective foil. Placed in the bottom of the well, the economical "light shelf" will reflect the sunlight that is otherwise wasted on the ground onto the ceiling, where it will be diffused evenly into the room.

A HABITABLE ENVIRONMENT

Basement offices come with environmental problems found in no other part of the house. Dampness and radon gas can foul the air. Gas- or oil-burning appliances require combustion air. Addressing these concerns is important to your comfort and health. Ways to heat and cool the space were covered in chapter 9, and ways to control dampness from walls and floors were addressed earlier in this chapter. Here's what you can do to control radon and ensure adequate combustion air.

Radon

According to the U.S. Surgeon General, exposing yourself to radon gas at levels exceeding 4 picocuries per liter (pc/l) risks lung cancer. The odorless, colorless, naturally occurring gas is present in varying levels in soils throughout the United States. If you didn't worry much about radon until now, setting yourself up an office in the basement is cause for concern.

Basements are not only the entry point for radon, where it seeps through cracks in the walls

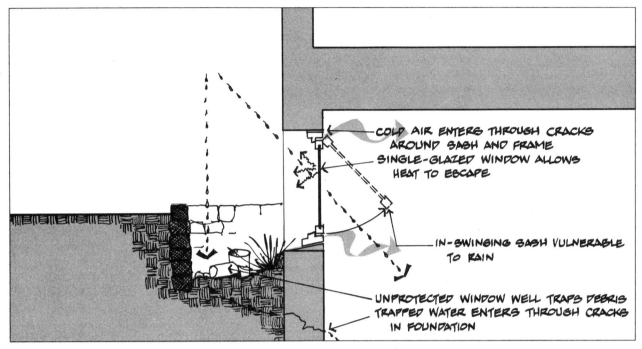

Figure 12-8: Basement Windows. *Many window problems need to be solved before you finish your basement office. Unprotected window wells collect trash and water, which finds its way through the foundation wall. Older types of basement windows leaked cold air, heat, and water when open.*

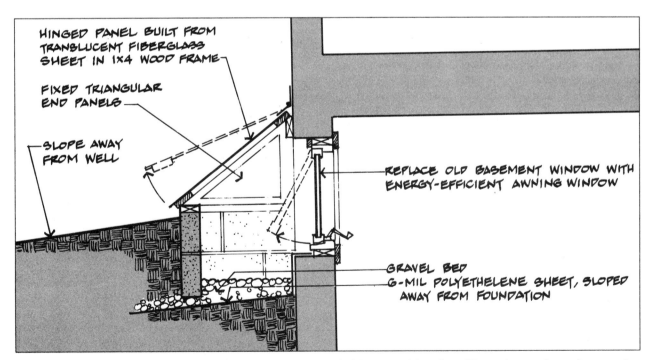

Figure 12-9: Improved Basement Window. *Begin by replacing the old window unit with an energy-efficient, out-swinging unit, caulked around the outside of the frame. Install a sloped membrane in the bottom of the well to direct any collected water away from the foundation. An enclosure will keep most surface water out of the window well, while helping retard heat loss. The enclosure shown here can be custom built for any size window and well. The hinged panel opens for ventilation in the warm months. If your well is small (36" wide by 17" out from the house) you can purchase a prefabricated acrylic area well cover from a lumberyard.*

and floor, but the area of the house where the concentration is likely to be the highest. Unfortunately, sealing up the windows for greater energy efficiency traps even more radon.

You can get an indication of whether you have a radon problem by testing with an activated charcoal test wafer. You can buy these from a building supply dealer or hardware store for around $20. The wafer is exposed to the air in the basement space for five days and is then sent to a lab for analysis (included in the purchase price). You should perform the test in the winter, when openings to the outside are closed. If the first test shows concentrations in excess of 4 pc/l, get a second test within a few weeks.

If you obtain consistently high test results, you should solve the problem before finishing your office space. The Environmental Protection Agency (EPA) recommends hiring a qualified contractor who has been certified by the agency's Radon Contractor Proficiency Program (RCP). Expect to pay anywhere from $500 to $2,500, depending on the house and choice of radon reduction methods used.

If your house has a basement with a slab-on-grade floor, various suction methods can be applied to the underslab, sump hole, or concrete block walls. For houses with a crawl space under the main floor, ventilation from the outside is increased (making insulating the floor and pipes necessary). In either type house, cracks and openings in the walls and floor should be sealed first. This used to be the main means of radon reduction, but it has been found to be ineffective if unaccompanied by more active methods. For detailed advice, request a copy of the pamphlet, *Consumer's Guide to Radon Reduction*, from the EPA listed in the appendix.

After completing your radon upgrades, retest to see how effective your efforts have been before finishing the office.

Combustion Air

Oil- or gas-burning furnaces need oxygen (combustion air) during their burn cycle. In poorly sealed houses, enough combustion air infiltrates through cracks to ensure an adequate supply. In sealing up some of these cracks to conserve heat, you may have reduced the supply of outside air to your combustion appliances to a level that threatens the quality of the indoor air as well as the efficient burning of the appliance. If, in remodeling the basement for an office, you seal off the space around the appliance with partitions, you also stand to choke off an adequate supply of combustion air.

Do not backslide on your energy-saving measures or chuck your proposed layout. But do provide make-up air to the furnace and/or water heater in another way. You may be able to do this with vents in the walls around the appliance or by bringing a duct from the outside to the area near the burner. For details and advice ask a heating contractor or consult informative pamphlets such as *Introducing Supplemental Combustion Air to Gas-Fired Appliances*, which is available from your state energy office or the U.S. Department of Energy (see appendix).

CHAPTER 13

PORCHES

My introduction to porches as home office sites came when a client asked me to look into the feasibility of the idea. The upstairs spare bedroom he had been using served his one-person accounting firm most of the time, but the lack of privacy from the rest of the house became a problem as his two young kids grew older and got more active. His 1920s-vintage home came equipped with a long but narrow porch on the side next to the driveway. Some previous occupant had installed windows above the railing to enclose the porch, but though pleasant and sunlit, the porch was seldom used by the present young family.

When I visited the site, I felt this porch cried out to be converted to an office. Besides the windows, a separate entry off the driveway meant excellent separation from the main house.

But one drawback loomed: The porch seemed awfully narrow. My solution was to bump out the side walls over the foundation by two feet, extending the main portion from 8' to 10' wide—a workable width.

Was narrowness the plague of all porches, I wondered. I drove around the older part of the city to find out (porches were common on houses built before the 1940s, but fell out of fashion after that). I found a remarkable variety of porches:

long, narrow porches; deep porches set into a corner of a house; porches that wrapped around two sides of the house; porches that contained wonderful round or octagonal spaces; and porches that rose two stories.

Some of these could easily be turned into offices. Others were too narrow, too small, or poorly situated with respect to the house. Some could be converted, but not without losing the charm they added to the house as porches.

The opportunity for abundant windows, an outside entry, and good separation from the rest of the home make any porch worth considering for an office, but you should weigh the assets carefully against the liabilities and the cost of conversion.

First, make sure closing your porch in won't degrade the appearance of your home. The generous porches that graced many older homes made pleasing transitions between inside and outside. Even if you no longer sit out on the porch on summer evenings to sip lemonade with neighbors, your porch may still be an integral part of your home's character that can be lost with insensitive remodeling.

Next, check into the legal aspects. Some zoning ordinances measure required setbacks to the main house wall, allowing porches to encroach into the setback. Once you close the porch in,

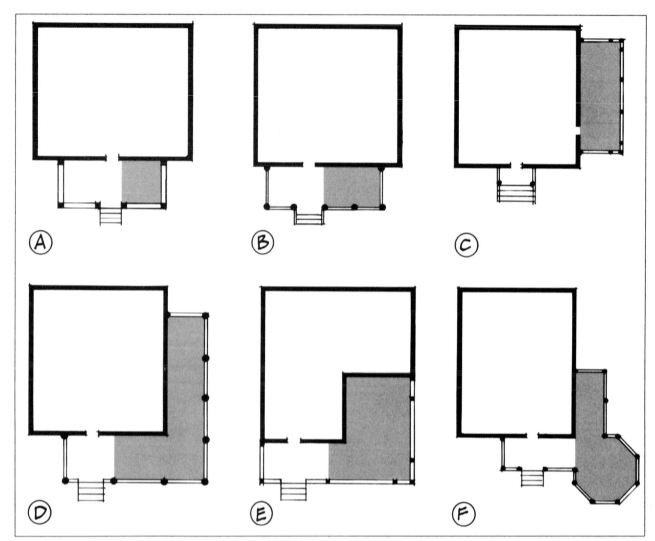

Figure 13-1: Porches Come in Many Varieties. *Not all porches will make a good office. The house entrance that bisects the porch in example* **(A)** *leaves little free space to either side. The offset entry in* **(B)** *offers more usable space. Houses with a separate side porch* **(C)** *and side-wrapped porches* **(D)** *offer plentiful space for office use. Porches deep-set into a corner of the house* **(E)**, *often wide as well as deep, are naturals for conversion. Round or octagonal porches such as* **(F)** *may make small, but interesting office candidates.*

you effectively move the house wall out.

Naturally your porch has to be big enough for an office. In chapter 5 I suggested that the minimum width is 5'4", with a minimum length of around 8', after deducting for space needed for passage into the house.

When considering minimum clearances, don't short the distance needed to get into the house. If you make the mistake of closing off the porch for an office with no separation between the office and the passage corridor, you have no

protection against the distraction of traffic of people into and out of the house, your office won't be secure, and the blast of cold air in winter will devastate your comfort. What's more, forced passage through an office isn't the way most homeowners would choose to welcome their nonbusiness visitors. A friend of mine spotted an opportunity for a stained glass studio in the wide porch of her Salt Lake City bungalow. She didn't plan a separation between the studio and door to the house. But stained glass can be messy, and

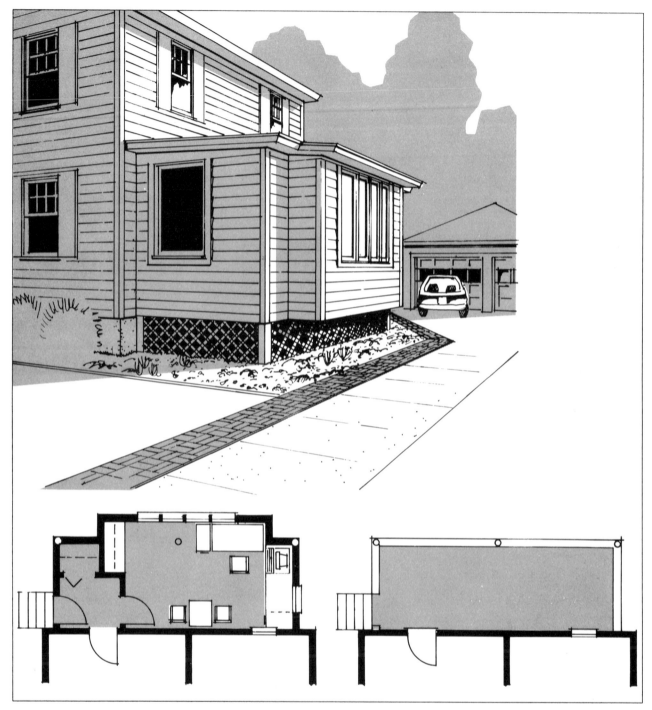

Figure 13-3: Porch Bump Out. *This porch was well situated for a home office, thanks to its location at the side of the house near the driveway and its separate entrance to the rear. To gain additional width, a portion of the long wall was bumped out 2′ over the foundation. A separate vestibule partition at the rear directed traffic between the back door of the house and the office.*

outer beam 2′ to support the wall at the bump-out.

You could also level the floor by tearing out the old floor completely and rebuilding it. This is the right approach if sistering isn't possible or if the old joists have insect damage.

To raise the porch floor to the height of the house floor, you might add sister joists set at the

same level as the house floor, rebuild the floor completely, or frame a new floor above the existing one. If the difference in floor levels is no less than 5″, you can use 2″ × 4″ joists, spaced 16″ set on flat 2″ × 4″ sleepers, as described in the section, "Leveling an Uneven Floor," in the previous chapter. This method works for both wood and concrete porch floors. You can also raise and level an existing concrete porch slab by pouring a new concrete slab above it, but not without sacrifice. It will cost more and you'll lose the space between joists; this is invaluable for containing wiring, insulation, and heating piping or ducts.

Warm Floors

Porches start out exposed to the weather from above, at the sides, and often from below. You can insulate the floor either directly, leaving the space below cold (Figure 8-4, shown on page 63), or insulate the foundation down to the ground (Figure 8-5, shown on page 64). Both methods work if properly done, though my choice is to insulate the wall. You can even maintain the appearance of an open lattice by constructing a solid foundation wall, painting it dark, and placing the lattice in front of it a couple of inches. If you go this route, however, make sure to provide a hinged or removable access panel at one side and cover the earth below to prevent moisture migrating up into the enclosed crawl space.

If you build a wood floor above an existing concrete porch floor, you'll gain an opportunity to insulate the floor. Take it. You'll be glad you did, if you are in an area with cold winters (refer to chapter 8 for tips on procedure and how much to insulate a floor).

PORCH WALLS

Originally built as the weather barrier for the house, the tightly sealed and insulated wall between the house and the porch offers an excellent barrier against household sights and sounds, except for one thing: windows. If the office were the only thing that mattered, you could solve the problem by simply replacing intervening windows with solid infill panels, gaining useful wall space on the office side for storage or display in the process. But the room inside the house would lose its daylight and view to the outside. Leaving the windows intact preserves much of the light, and view, but sacrifices your office's privacy. Can the needs of both spaces be met?

Yes. If you want to preserve the natural lighting—and the opportunity to reconvert the office to a porch at some future time—consider installing a translucent panel on the office side of window openings. Several patterns of obscure glass (glass that lets light but not vision through) are available, or choose a white-colored textured plastic sheet similar to the lenses in fluorescent lighting fixtures. Have the panel material cut to fit over the outer window frame, leaving a gap of an inch or so, then screw wood stops (moldings) over the panel edges into the window frame.

The new outer wall can be built as described in chapter 8, as modified to blend with the design of the porch. If your porch has an ornate wood railing or posts with period details, you can preserve this charm by letting your new infill walls play second fiddle to these features. If space allows, build the new wall behind the railing and select windows of a module and size that blends with the house. If space is tight, consider removing the railing and reinstalling it to the outside of the new wall as a decorative feature. Figure 13-4 shows examples of how offices can be built to blend into various kinds of porches without compromising the house's architectural character.

CAPPING IT OFF

Unless your porch roof leaks or you bump the wall out, you won't have to do much about the roof. But you will probably need to tear out the porch ceiling to run wiring and install insulation. Follow the guidelines for insulation described in chapter 8. Insulate between the rafters if you

want a sloped (cathedral) ceiling; otherwise, fit the insulation between the ceiling joists.

If you bump the outer wall out a few feet, try to maintain the same pitch in order to blend with the porch's appearance. You should be able to do this simply by removing the fascia board and

Figure 13-4: Enclosing a Porch Without Destroying Its Character. *A series of windows above the ornamental railing helps preserve the charm of this two-story porch (top right). Bungalows often come with generous porches and solid railings. Enclosing them can be as simple as adding windows that blend with the house (middle). To preserve the highly articulated details of this octagonal porch, narrow windows were placed on each side of the support posts. Between and above the windows is siding that matches the house (bottom right).*

adding short-length sister joists to the porch roof joists. Doing so might mean a short length of sloped ceiling at the outer wall, but this can add to the design in much the same way as do the sloped walls of attic ceilings.

HEATING AND COOLING YOUR PORCH OFFICE

Count on your porch office gaining more unwanted heat in the summer and needing more heat in the winter than the rest of your house because of its long exposure to the exterior and the likelihood that much of the outside wall is taken up by windows. You can reduce the amount of additional cooling or heating by insulating the roof, solid walls, and floor to the greatest practical level. High-performance windows of the types discussed in chapter 8 will cost a bit more but will pay for themselves in energy savings and greater comfort.

Heating a wood-framed porch can be as simple as tapping off a hot air duct or hydronic pipe in the basement and running an extension duct or pipe through the house foundation wall and under the porch floor. Your heating contractor should be able to tell you if this is feasible. If not, or if the porch floor is a concrete slab, consider installing electric radiant heat around the outer wall or any of the wall-mounted unit heaters described in chapter 9.

If you have enough windows that open, in many parts of the United States you can cool the office with natural ventilation for much of the year. If your office windows are exposed to direct sunlight, particularly if they face south or west, you can control the unwanted solar heat gain and glare with the proper natural or artificial controls, as described in chapter 8.

High-performance windows, well-insulated walls, and proper shading devices can cut your summer heat gain to the bone. A window air conditioner or all-purpose wall-mounted package unit can keep you cool during the hottest and most humid periods. They'll have to, because you won't have a porch to go out and sip a cool drink on anymore.

CHAPTER 14

GARAGES AND OUTBUILDINGS

The back two-thirds of my 16' × 22' single garage made a fine site for my first architectural office when I started my practice in 1976. Having used the garage as a workshop from the beginning, I squeezed the workshop down into the remaining third of the front portion containing the garage door. My garage office served nicely except in summers, when the kids played in the backyard and I often ended up going outside to play with them.

To house his structural engineering practice, Wayne King created a beautiful office with dramatic sloping cathedral ceilings in the top floor of an unused barn on his Ipswich, Massachusetts, property. Few changes were needed by Salt Lake City structural engineer, Ron Weber, to convert a mobile home on his farm in Ibapah, Utah, into an office he uses when at the farm.

Detached buildings such as garages, barns, sheds, and mobile homes make excellent offices, if you do it right. At first glance, conversion may seem like an easy task. After all, the most difficult part, the structure, is already there.

But don't be deceived. The structure only represents a third or so of the total construction. Organizing and finishing the interior, insulating, wiring, and installing heating and cooling equipment can account for much of your time and effort or cost a bundle if you hire someone to do it. Ron Weber had to tear out an interior wall of his mobile home to create a central room big enough for his office. You need only consider your office requirements when you replan a mobile home, barn, or shed. When converting all or part of an actively used garage, you must also decide on what to do with the car.

GARAGE SPACE PLANNING

Here are some possible solutions to the car/office dilemma, whether your garage is part of your house or detached:

- Divide the space between car and office.
- Move the car out and convert the entire garage to office space.
- Convert the entire garage to office and provide alternative protection for the car.

Sharing Space With the Car

Each bay of a multicar garage contains between 200 sq. ft. and 300 sq. ft. of floor space. About the size of a large bedroom, this should be enough area for many one-person offices.

Figure 14-1 (page 119) shows a typical two-car garage (A) and the most obvious way to divide the space (B): a partition right down the middle. There's probably a support post or two there anyway, making this an even more natural dividing line. The main entrance can be in the front, with a secondary door to the office carved out of an existing window or through the connecting wall to the garage. Any door to the garage, as well as the connecting wall, will need to adhere to fire safety standards, which is discussed further on.

If you install a flat ceiling above the office side (Figure 14-1, C), you can use the loft above for storage. But if you can sacrifice this storage, extending the dividing wall all the way to the roof creates the opportunity for a cathedral ceiling (Figure 14-1, E), which yields a more interesting interior. If this idea grabs you, get some professional advice for how best to remodel the roof framing if necessary.

One of the most attractive features of garages, when converting them to offices, is the wide door opening at the front. Complete with header beams, you need simply to remove the overhead garage door to gain a ready-to-use rough opening 8' or 9' wide, if a single-car opening, or 16' or 18' wide for a double-size opening. With garage door removed, the clear opening height will be 6'8" or 7'0"—either size just right for a standard swinging door.

Figures 14-1 and 14-2 (shown on pages 119 and 120) suggest some window and door configurations you might consider for the garage door opening. The clerestory window in the roof dormer of Figure 14-1, F, floods the high open space of this office with daylight.

Using the Entire Garage

If you need more space than a single car bay, consider taking over the entire garage. Our typical two-car garage reappears in Figure 14-2, this time entirely converted into two different kinds of offices. Example A shows how the space might serve the needs of a design professional, such as interior designer, architect, or engineer. The entrance door leads directly into the public area, equipped with a reception/administration desk, couch, and conference table. A bookshelf/work

table divides the public area from the production room, which contains three drawing board workstations. In this case, there is also a nearby bathroom.

The second example is a wedding consultant's office. Here, the public area contains an L-shaped couch where clients can sit comfortably while looking over selections in catalogs. Toward the rear there is a small washroom and an adjacent refreshment center. A desk at the front serves the consultant's administrative needs. In the large showroom in the upper right corner, fixed displays enable clients to view actual samples of wedding dishes, dresses, and decorations.

YOU STILL CAN'T FORGET THE CAR

Whether you use all or just part of your garage, you'll still have to park cars somewhere. Your planning board may even require a site plan showing parking facilities as a condition of issuing you a permit for your project.

Cars need, at the very least, a clear space of 8' × 18' with a space of equal size behind each parking space to enable access. Your local zoning ordinance may call for larger spaces. If you don't already have a driveway large enough to accommodate both resident and visitor traffic, see if you can extend it to the side or front. Zoning ordinances that require setbacks of 10' or more for buildings often allow parking to extend right up to the property line.

If you intend to convert the entire garage to office space and you live in a climate with a lot of snow, you might want to consider building a roof over one or two parking spaces to form a protected carport, as shown in Figure 14-2, A and C.

Plantings, in raised planters or dug into the driveway, can soften the appearance of the driveway and provide a welcoming entrance for visitors.

LOFTY OPPORTUNITIES

If your garage or outbuilding is a single-story with a roof pitch less than, say, 9 in 12, the attic

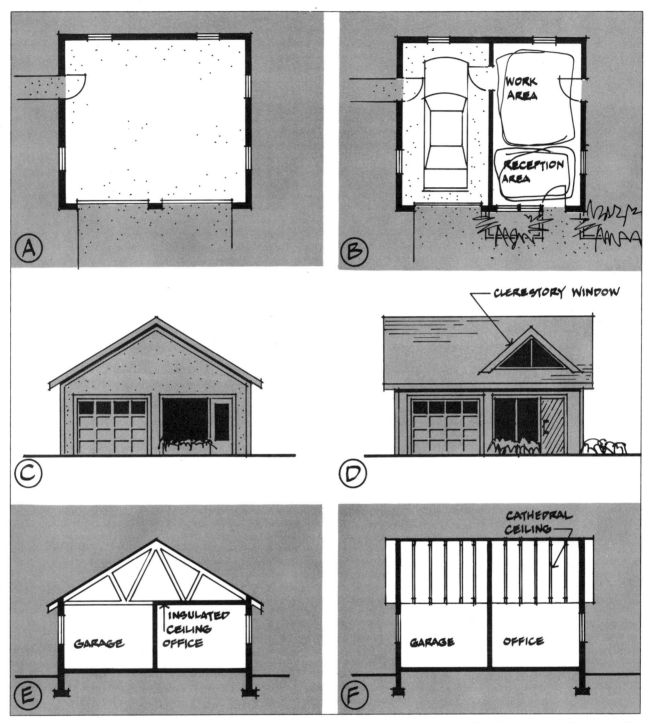

Figure 14-1: Sharing Part of a Garage. *The typical double garage* **(A)** *becomes a single garage/office with the addition of a partition down the center* **(B)**. *Drawing* **(C)** *suggests how the office entry might appear if a flat ceiling is constructed above the office side, as shown in section* **(E)**. *Extending the dividing partition full height to the roof, as shown in cross-section* **(F)**, *creates the opportunity for a cathedral ceiling and clerestory window* **(D)**.

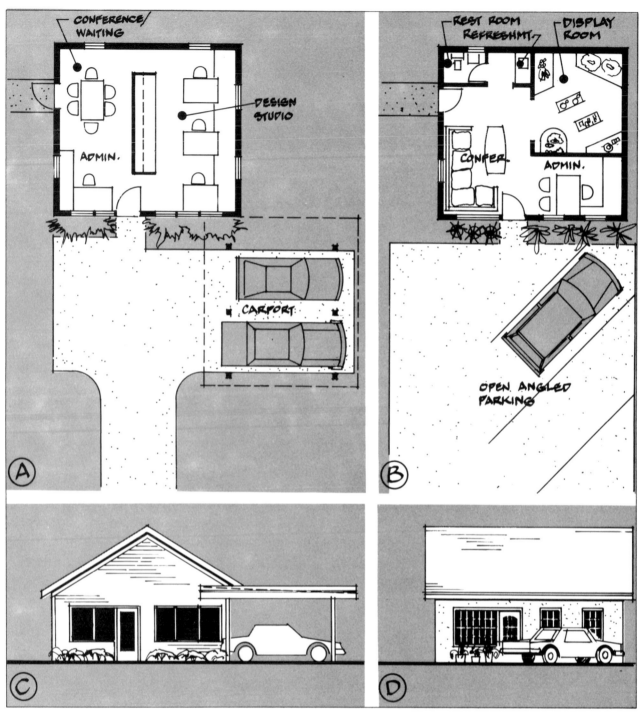

Figure 14-2: Using the Entire Garage. *The designer's office shown in* **(A)** *contains an administrative/reception area with a conference table to the rear that doubles as a client waiting area. A dividing partition contains display space on the public side and shelves above a work surface on the studio side. Three drawing stations fit nicely to the right. The garage houses a wedding consultant's office in example* **(B)**. *Clients can look through catalogs while seated in the conference area or wander through the exhibits of wedding accessories in the display room. A small rest room and refreshment area in the upper left provides amenities so that clients won't have to go into the main house. A covered carport provides client parking in example* **(C)**, *and open angle parking is used in example* **(D)**.

space probably contains insufficient headroom to develop into usable office space. You can still use it for storage (Figure 14-1, C) or develop a high cathedral ceiling (Figure 14-1, E). You may be lucky enough to have a garage in a former "carriage house" with more space above. If so, the roof doesn't rise from the garage ceiling—as in modern garages—but from a kneewall 3' or 4' above that level. Converting this space to an office may require beefing up the floor structure and adding a stairway if guest traffic is expected. Because these changes affect all attics, they are discussed in chapter 11.

OUTBUILDING FLOORS, WALLS, AND ROOFS

Finishing the interiors of outbuildings is the same as finishing off any unfinished space, as described in chapter 8. If you start out with 2"×4" studs exposed to the inside, seize the opportunity to add any wiring or plumbing lines and insulation before applying the interior finish material.

Your floor surface may already be carpeted (as in mobile homes) or it may be a sloping or uneven garage slab, or it may be a dirt floor in a shed or barn.

Civilizing an Outbuilding Floor

Count yourself lucky if the floor is a smooth, level concrete slab. Put down a sheet of 6-mil polyethylene sheeting to keep moisture at bay, a foam pad and carpet, and you have an office floor that can give any rented office a run for its money. Chances are, though, your floor will need one or more of the following alterations:

- A level surface
- A way to reduce heat loss to the cold earth
- Some way in which to run electrical wiring, piping, or heating supply ducts

Expect head-height problems where garage floors meet the remodeled overhead door openings. When you replace garage doors with some combination of windows and a swinging door,

you won't want to replace the header beam as well. If you start out with less than 6'10" overall clearance, you'll need it all for a standard 6'8" door with threshold and frame (you can get by with an inch or so less if you install the door in the opening without a frame or with a custom frame). With little height to spare, your only floor finish option may be a carpet and pad laid directly over the concrete (see Figure 14-3, Example A, page 122).

Your options increase if the door clearance height exceeds 7'0". You can build some kind of wood floor above the slab or earth, thereby gaining a warm, level surface under which you can run wiring or pipes. Three approaches are suggested in Figure 14-3.

Example B assumes a level slab, 7' or more below the header beam. Lay pressure-treated 2"×4" sleepers down directly over the slab (or lay down a layer of 6-mil poly and nontreated 2"×4"s). Fill the voids between the 2"×4"s with 1½"-thick rigid insulation. You can also run wiring in these voids if you keep it snug to the concrete, or run it in a metal conduit to prevent accidental puncture by nails. Finally, nail the plywood subfloor to the sleepers. You can get by with ½" plywood if the sleepers are spaced 16" apart, but use ¾" plywood if you space the sleepers at 24".

Example C shows how to deal with a sloping floor and generous rough opening (7'1", minimum). A gridwork of 2"×4"s floats above the sloping slab, supported by combinations of wood shims and blocking.

Don't despair if you are starting with a dirt floor. You'll have to build a concrete or wood floor from scratch, but be able to do so in a way that accommodates insulation, ducts, and wiring needed in your office. Figure 14-3, D shows how you might do this with a wood floor system.

Garage Fire Walls

Because building codes treat garages as hazardous areas that contain flammable materials, most

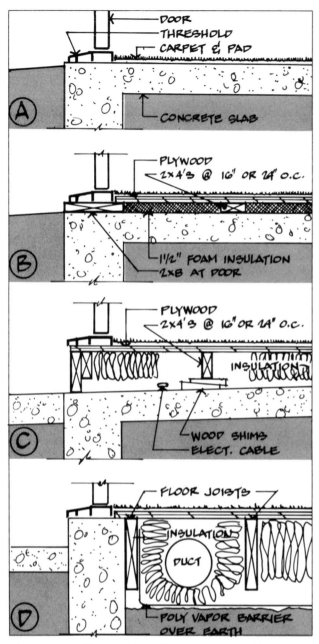

Figure 14-3: Garage Floor Improvements. *If you start with a smooth, level concrete slab, the simplest floor treatment is a carpet and pad (A). Installing plywood subfloor over 2×4 sleepers (B) allows you to insulate the floor, bridge imperfections in the concrete, and run wiring. If there is to be a door between office and garage, the office floor should be raised for fire safety. Drawing (C) shows how to do this with a network of 2"×4"s on end. Use shims to level the 2"×4"s. In example (D), a new wood floor is built over an existing earth garage floor, with space below for ducts, wiring, and insulation.*

now require some degree of protection between garages and abutting living spaces, which include offices. The requirements are most stringent for garages built into the ground floors of houses, with abutting basements and rooms above. Any walls and ceilings between garage and living space have to be rated to a "1-hour" level, which simply means it takes one hour for a fire to burn through the floor or wall assembly.

For garages attached alongside living spaces, the requirements are somewhat less: a single layer of ½" gypsum drywall board on the garage side of the separating partition.

If you convert one half of your garage into an office, you can get a 1-hour rating in the wall or ceiling separating the office from the garage simply by facing both sides of the wall or ceiling with a type "X" gypsum wallboard such as Sheetrock Firecode C™.

Doors between ground-story garages and living spaces have to be fire-rated, as well. Because doors are not rated separately from frames, it's best to buy a prehung unit—either a solid-core wood door or steel-faced one, such as those manufactured by Stanley Works, Inc. To make sure you get a fire-rated unit, look for a "B-Label" on the inside of the door frame. Doors between main-level garages and living spaces need only to be 1¾" solid-core construction.

Codes also require the thresholds abutting living spaces to be a minimum of 4" above garage floors to prevent gas vapors from leaving the garage and crawling along the floor of an adjacent room until they meet a pilot flame of a combustion appliance and go "poof!" You can satisfy this requirment by building your office floor 4" higher than the garage, as shown in Figure 14-4, A (page 123), or—if you are stuck with a floor at the same height—by installing the connecting door 4" higher than the floor, as shown in Figure 14-4, B. In the latter case, the 4" step will pose an obstacle to trip over if the door is left open, so you might want to install a closer to automatically close the door.

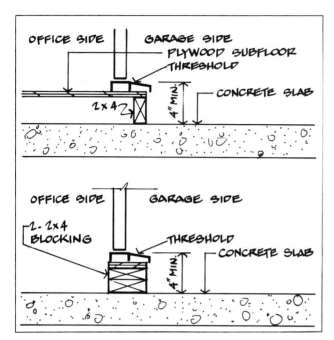

Figure 14-4: Garage/Office Doorways. *These require raised door sills at a minimum of 4" to prevent ground-hugging gas fumes from entering the office side. You can do this by elevating the entire office floor, as shown at top, or by raising the door sill only (bottom). Raising the entire floor provides the extra advantage of a chase for insulation, ducts, piping, and wiring.*

HEATING AND COOLING

Chances are your outbuilding office will need a heating/cooling system separate from the main house. Chapter 9 described the ways you can heat a space remote from the central system. A small heat source without ducts, such as a package window or wall unit, can heat an office in a converted single-car garage bay. If you're converting a double garage, you probably need a small furnace with ducts to distribute the heat to remote corners, particularly if the space is carved up into separate rooms.

One final thought: Outbuildings either come with windows or outside walls that can contain windows. Make the most of these openings to the outside for natural lighting, heating, and cooling, as pointed out in chapter 8. The cooling breezes that waft through them in early summer and fall can reduce your dependence on air-conditioning while keeping your office comfortable inside. Natural daylight and views are also assets.

ADEQUATE WIRING

Before you apply new wall finish to your converted outbuilding, make sure you have adequate electrical wiring for lighting and power outlets. A garage may have, at most, one power circuit. A barn or shed may have no wiring at all or antiquated knob-and-tube wiring with birds nesting above. You will need a minimum of two separate 110-V power circuits for your office — one for lighting and one for outlets. An additional line dedicated to computers would be better still. If you share space with a garage, figure on a few circuits for garage power and lighting.

The Connecting Cable

To get more than one circuit from your house, you'll need a branch panel box in the outbuilding, connected to the house's main panel by the proper size and type of cable. Electrical engineer Wayne Whippie suggests hiring a qualified electrician to do the work or at least to advise you about what to use and how to install it. You'll need a tap off the main house panel, probably off of two 30- to 50-amp circuit breakers connected to a disconnect switch. If your connecting cable is to be buried, you can use "direct burial" type cable buried at least 12" in the ground, or single conductors encased in a 2" plastic (PVC) conduit. Conduit has the additional plus of accommodating phone lines. If you want to run the connecting cable overhead, you'll need a special type of cable designed for this purpose.

Wayne Whippie strongly recommends that the connecting cable carry, in addition to the two power conductors, a full-size neutral wire and ground. Although a separate ground rod can be driven at the outbuilding, don't depend on this alone.

The Branch Panel

Branch panels come in six-, eight-, and twelve-circuit sizes. An eight- or twelve-circuit panel box costs only slightly more than the smaller size and allows you the flexibility to add circuits.

What About Lightning?

Lightning is always a concern where vulnerable electronic equipment is present. Wayne Whippie suggests installing a surge protector device at the branch panel as basic protection. If your out-building is on a hill or you live in a lightning-prone area, look into lightning rods on the roof as an additional protection. When you leave your office for more than a few days, shut off the power at the branch or main house panel.

CHAPTER 15

ADDITIONS

No question about it, an addition is the most expensive home office space. But if you have a site and can swing the financing, it is the surest way to get exactly what you need in terms of space, privacy from the main house, and a separate outside entrance.

WHERE TO ADD?

Unless you have only one place to add on, deciding on a location comes down to two questions: Where can I add? Where should I add? Let's look at each in turn.

Limitations Imposed by the Site

Your lot limits your options in two ways:

- Legal setbacks from the property line
- Physical obstacles (landscape features, utilities)

Start with a copy of the zoning ordinance for your municipality. From the maps in the front part you should be able to determine the zone you live in. If you live in a detached dwelling, your house is probably located in a "residential" zone of one sort or another. Next, turn to the chapter that sets requirements for your zone. Here, you'll find the minimum lot sizes and minimum setbacks, that is, the distances required between buildings and property lines. Front and rear setbacks are generally larger than side yards. If you live on a corner lot, you may be required to maintain frontyard setbacks at both streets.

The detailed zoning requirements may also limit the percentage of lot you can cover with buildings.

To find out where you can legally add, you'll need a scale plan of the site (plot plan) showing how the house fits on the site, the street, drive, and property lines. If you don't have a plot plan as part of your purchase records, you can draw one from the legal description of your property. That is, if you know how to translate statements such as "thence north thirty six degrees forty minutes fifty-two seconds east to a point" into a line on paper that has the proper length, bearing and position. Otherwise ask an architect, surveyor, or drafting service to make you a plot plan to a scale of 1" = 10'0" or larger.

Next draw in the location of utility lines (such as buried piping for water, sewer, and gas) and overhead power and telephone lines. If you have a septic system, you should have the location of the tank, drain field, and all piping. You may have to find this information from other records or track it down personally. Overhead cables are easy enough to spot. Buried lines are harder, but not impossible. To find your water line, for example, find the point where the water supply main enters the basement. Look for a meter in the frontyard. The main should run in a straight line between these two points into the street. Sewer and gas lines can be similarly located. Figure 15-1 shows a typical urban/suburban lot with this data drawn.

Next draw (or have drawn) lines parallel to the property lines to indicate all required zoning setbacks. If your lot is small, you probably can't build anywhere except to the rear. Many homes on suburban and innercity lots already snug as close to the front and side property lines as legally allowed.

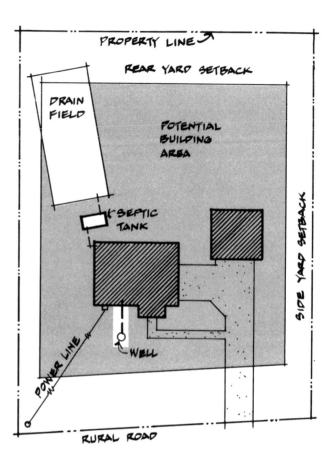

Figure 15-2: Rural Plot Plan. *A rural plot plan shows the same information as one for a city or suburban location, except that water and sewer lines running to the street may be replaced by a water well and septic system, which cannot be built over.*

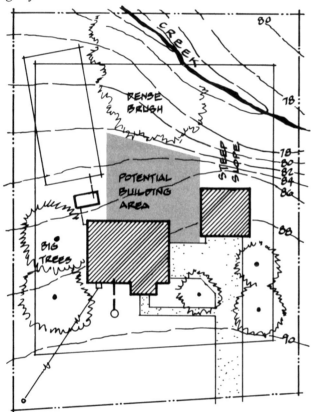

Figure 15-1: Urban/Suburban Plot Plan. *A drawing made to scale showing your property, the adjacent street or streets, buildings, paving, utility lines, and required zoning setbacks. The area within the setbacks (shaded) shows where you can add on.*

Things might not be so easy for rural dwellers. For example, I recently modified the plan for a proposed addition to a lakeside home when I discovered that a well head lurked 6″ below the ground at the new location. To find the hidden

well head, we first found where the well pipe came through the foundation wall. We then used a rented metal detector to locate the well head outside.

Locating septic systems may also be daunting. You're lucky if you start with record drawings of the system. The tank may be apparent from the clean-out port. If you don't have drawings showing the location of the drain field, you will have a hard time finding it without digging. In this case, I would completely avoid building anywhere downslope from the tank. Figure 15-2 (above) shows a rural lot with its well and septic system pinned down, along with the building setbacks.

Physical features within the area where you

can legally build may further narrow your choices. What if the site slopes steeply up or down from the house? What about that old oak tree that provides shade in the summer? You should be able to approximate the locations of trees, rocks, and standing water sufficiently to draw them on the site plan. If not, you may want to have a site survey done by a licensed surveyor.

If your lot slopes seriously in the area where you think you can build, I would suggest hiring a surveyor to do a topographic survey and draw gradient lines at 2' intervals, such as shown in Figure 15-3.

And Don't Forget the House

As if site constraints weren't enough, a successful marriage between house and office addition calls for attention to the house's internal circulation, the locations of existing windows and doors, and roof shapes.

Say the only place you can add on is to the rear of your house. A kitchen, bath, and two bedrooms occupy the length of that wall. Butting the addition up to this wall at any point incurs penalties. Blocking off a bedroom window wipes out that room's cross ventilation and reduces its light and view. (You can't block two bedroom windows, even if you want to, without providing another way out of the room to satisfy fire codes.) Backing the addition up to the bath is possible, but you must be willing to sacrifice the light and view of the window and provide an exhaust fan for ventilation. And placing the addition next to the kitchen may mean losing the window above the sink.

How you get to the office from the house bears equal consideration. A ground floor addition offers an excellent opportunity for a separate entry. But whereas this may be great for visitor traffic, do you really want to have to go outside the house to get to your office? And what about the future? How will having only an outside entry affect your home's resale potential? A buyer might want to use the office addition as another

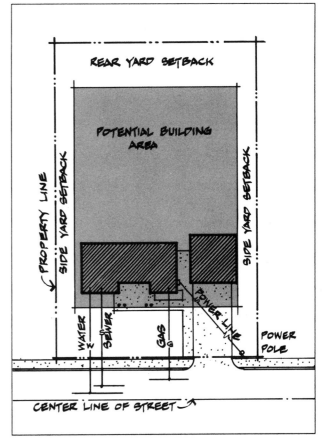

Figure 15-3: Physical Limitations. *Before finally establishing where your addition will go, make sure the location won't conflict with physical features. If your site is not level, you may need a survey to establish grade lines, as shown here at 2' intervals. The shaded area represents the only feasible area for building in order to stay within setback lines, clear the septic system, avoid the steep slope behind the garage, and dodge the dense brush.*

bedroom that connects directly to the house.

The best solution is to provide both an internal connection as well as an outside entry. For the interior link, try to get a passage through the most public part of your house, such as off a main entry hallway. Failing that, seek access through a living, dining, or other "front" room, or through a closet.

Rating Your Options

If, after considering the site constraints, you end up with more than one possible place to add on, it might help to create a list of pros and cons for each possibility. Figure 15-4 (page 128) shows a

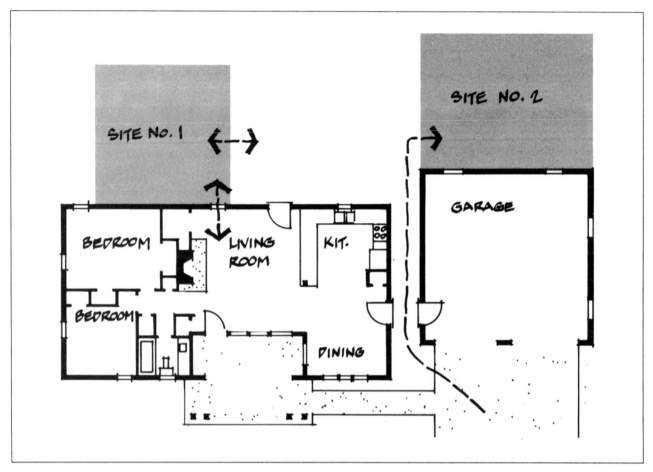

Figure 15-4: Two Candidate Sites. *Two choices emerge for the house shown in Figure 15-1. The first site is behind the bedroom, and the second site is behind the garage. The pros and cons of building an addition in each location are listed below. Which choice would you make?*

COMPARING POTENTIAL BUILDING SITES

Site No. 1: Adjacent to Bedroom No. 1

Advantages
1. Close to house (share common wall, may extend heating system)

Disadvantages
1. Have to go through living room to get to office
2. Have to convert living room window to doorway and create new window
3. Office will reduce size of backyard near house

Site No. 2: Behind Garage

Advantages
1. Well separated from household activity and noise
2. Easy to get to office from driveway (through breezeway)
3. Doesn't infringe on backyard near living room

Disadvantages
1. Have to go outside house to get to office (liability in winter)
2. Can't extend house heating to serve office

comparison of two possible locations for our typical single-family urban/suburban house.

ADDING OUTWARD

The opportunity for a separate outside entry makes an addition to the ground floor a compelling choice if you have a feasible spot next to the house. Because you will be starting from scratch, you can plan the addition to fit your business needs. Despite the office function inside, the addition's outer face should look residential rather than commercial if you want to enhance your home.

Blending New to Old

Because you'll be investing thousands of dollars in your office addition even if you build it yourself, the addition should increase the value of your home. Adding space alone won't necessarily add resale value. The addition has to also enhance the visual or "curb appeal" of the house, to put it in real estate jargon.

Designing an addition that will enhance an existing structure is always a challenge, even for professionals who devote years to learning the art. Unless you are skilled at design, get some guidance from an architect or home designer.

Buying a few days of their time to come up with a sketch or two will pay off over the long haul. Even if you ultimately hire a professional, you might want to try some sketches of your own. There is no harm in doing so, and here are some tips that can help you blend new to old:

1. Maintain horizontal lines expressed on the house. Match tops of windows and doors, floor lines, and roof eaves.

2. Try to maintain the same roof pitch. If your addition abuts the side of the house at the roof eave, consider intersecting the main roof with a double-pitch gable roof, rather than a single shed roof of lesser pitch.

3. Repeat geometries. To be consistent with the vertical look of double-hung windows, you can use double-hung or casement windows. If you want a wider window than the single units on the house, group windows together in multiples.

4. Repeat materials, but not without thought. Say your house is brick veneer trimmed with painted wood. You may not want to pay for brick construction on the addition, or even be able to match the existing brick. Instead, use wood siding on the addition, painted to match the house's wood trim.

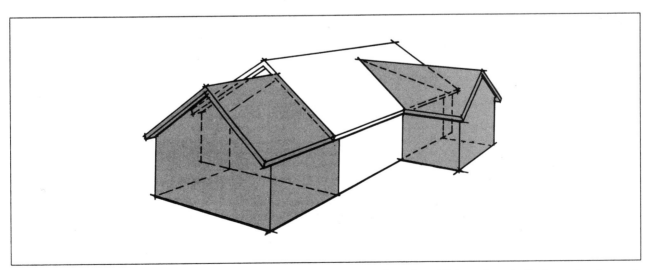

Figure 15-5: Wing or Tee? *Adding onto the gable end of a roof (area shaded at left) is simpler than adding an intersecting tee (right). But, the decision should be made by considering how the addition relates to the house in plan and how the new form affects the existing house.*

5. Repeat the colors of the house's roof, trim, and wall surfaces.

In short, copy the house.

Basement or Crawl Space?

An addition to the ground floor requires a substructure that can be as minimal and economical as a shallow foundation around the edges of a concrete slab floor or as elaborate as a full basement. The right type depends on your plans for the space below, the type of heating system, and your budget. Let's look at each substructure contender.

Shallow foundation/slab floor. The most economical way to underpin your addition is a foundation/footing wall extending only to the frost line (3' to 4' in most of the United States) and a concrete slab floor sitting on the ground within. With no cavity below for heating ducts, the cost of rigid ducts encased in concrete can eat up any

advantage gained from the system. But there are other ways to heat and cool the space, as described in chapter 9. Ducts can be run through the ceiling/roof cavity. If interior partitions won't block the air flow, a wall-mounted heater can heat the space without any ducts. A slab also offers opportunity for a radiant heating system imbedded in the slab, though you should get the opinion of a local engineer or heating contractor to determine if this approach is cost effective for a small space.

Shallow foundation/wood floor over crawl space. The same shallow foundation wall can support a wood-framed floor, leaving 2' or 3' of crawl space below to contain pipes, ducts, and wiring. You'll pay around 60% more for a wood-framed floor over a slab on grade, but get much more in the way of flexibility.

Full basement foundation/wood floor. Extending the foundation down another 3' or 4'

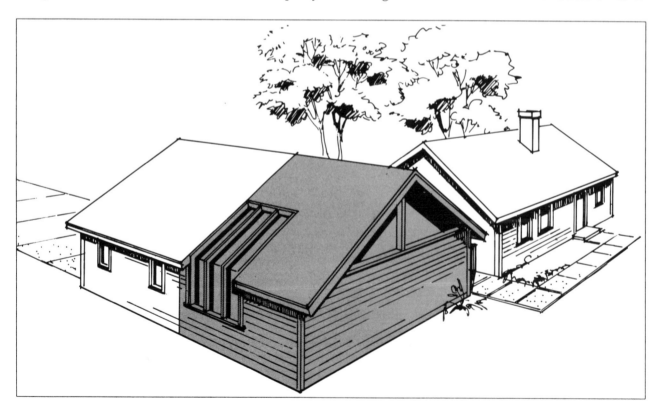

Figure 15-6: Adding Onto the Back of a Garage. *If we added to the back of the garage of the example shown in Figure 15-4, the result might look something like this. The materials and form follow the garage, but windows and doors are designed to make the office a light-filled, pleasant work space.*

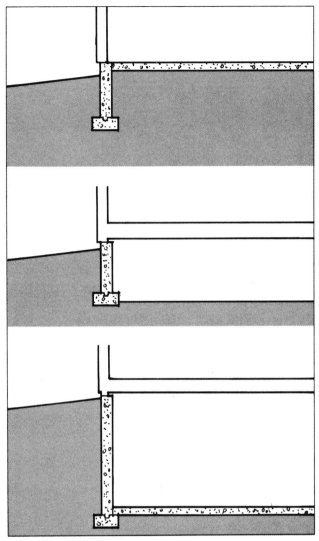

Figure 15-7: Three Floor Choices for an Addition. *Each choice has pros and cons. In all but one case your choice won't limit your options for floor finishes; if you choose a concrete slab with an imbedded radiant heating system, you should not lay down carpet.*

Slab on Grade

Pros
1. Least expensive floor system
2. Potential for running radiant heating tubes through slab

Cons
1. Cold underfoot, unless insulated
2. No spaces in which to run piping, wiring, and ducts

Wood Floor over Crawl Space

Pros
1. Space underneath can be used for piping, wiring, and ducts

Cons
1. No space available for heating equipment

Full Basement

Pros
1. Basement ceiling space accommodates piping, wiring, and ducts
2. Additional floor space for storage, heating equipment, or finished room

Cons
1. Most expensive system
2. Most vulnerable to water penetration
3. Requires stairway or opening from house basement

and pouring a concrete floor slab yields a full basement that can double your added space. Because unfinished basement space is cheap compared to the aboveground space, this choice is appealing.

The Common Wall
Adding on at ground level offers the opportunity to save by sharing a common wall between house and addition. Think twice though. Even if the

new roof can be tied into the old without additional supports, doing so will lose other benefits of a separate wall, such as a place to run wiring and opportunity for acoustic privacy. A separate wall on the office side offers these perks at little extra cost, because you would probably have to

Figure 15-8: Three Ways to Add an Office Above a Garage. *You can add space above a ground-floor garage by abutting part of the existing second floor or popping up a separate structure. To make sure the addition blends well with the house, repeat roof forms, window types, and exterior finish materials and colors. By extruding one end of this house's second story (top left), the vacant space above the shallow-sloped garage roof becomes an office space that can be converted at a future time into a den or guest bedroom. The office addition perched above the garage (middle) recalls the geometry of the second floor portion. This garage was big enough to allow for a new stairway at the rear to serve the office upstairs. In the bottom right example, space was too tight inside the garage for a stairway, so one was built outside on the end of the garage.*

add a drywall or other finish to the house wall anyway.

ADDING UPWARD

If you can't add on at ground level, maybe you can go upward. Do you have unused vertical space above a first-floor garage or other room? To exploit this space successfully you'll need to solve all of the usual problems of shared walls and floors, as well as provide a way in.

Shared Floors and Walls

As with ground floor additions, you can save one wall by using the existing house wall, but should do so only after considering the advantages gained by building a separate wall. A separate wall will provide an easier support for a roof and afford cavities for soundproofing and wiring (you may need one for roof support, in any case).

The floor may be capable of supporting the new loads (40 lbs. per sq. ft.) if it served pre-viously as a flat roof over a first-story garage. To be sure, get professional advice or check the framing against the guidelines under "Beefing up Floors" in chapter 11. If an unheated garage underlies your office addition, then you'll need to insulate the floor or insulate the garage walls (but some cold air will still leak in through sectional overhead garage doors).

Getting Up There

Your early planning should figure in a practical way into your second-floor office addition. If you need to receive visitors, will their path take them through the most private part of the house? If so, you may want to consider building a separate stairway from the ground, assuming, of course, there is a place to build one and you can afford to. If you do plan one, follow the guidelines for stairs in chapter 11. A roof above the stairway is a good idea everywhere and enclosing it with walls and roof is a must in areas with cold, wet winters.

PART FOUR

FINISHING AND EQUIPPING

CHAPTER 16

FINISHING TOUCHES

You probably don't want your home office to echo the last office you worked in. Now that you are calling the shots, you can create a more humane environment that suits your personality and style of working. But there are a few things to keep in mind.

If clients come to your office, they should guide your decor. The mood you create affects the message you send to them. Patterned drapes and wall coverings and oriental rugs on the floor may say "homey" to an interior designer's clients but read as "unprofessional" to clients of a management consultant.

And don't forget the future of your office space. How much change will be necessary and how easy will it be to make the changes if you need to convert to another use when you move your office or sell the house?

These constraints, though limiting, leave you plenty of elbowroom. If you know your options and plan thoughtfully, you can create a comfortable workspace that echoes your personality while creating just the right ambience.

AMBIENCE

So what kind of ambience *do* you want in your office? Something that stirs you to action? Relaxes? Recalls nature? Evokes high-tech? Rustic?

Maybe you just want a friendly kind of place that doesn't call attention to itself but lets you go about your business without distractions.

The colors, forms, and textures of every surface contribute to the total mood. How you light the space can spell the difference between success and failure. Manipulating this palette of variables isn't easy; designers spend years learning how to do it well. You may want to buy some professional consulting time to ensure that yours is successful. If you make your own decisions, the guidelines in this chapter may be of help.

USING COLORS AND TEXTURES TO ADVANTAGE

Psychologists say color affects mood, but they disagree as to how and to what extent. I read somewhere that mauve is the most calming color. This explains the popularity of the mauve-plum-gray scheme. But if you're looking for something different, here's the most generally agreed upon list of color associations:

Yellow	Happiness
Red	Energy, excitement, anger
Green	Refreshment, nature
Blue	Restfulness, peace

There are other associations, as well. Reds and yellows suggest physical warmth, whereas blues imply cool. Orange, green and purple are, supposedly, heat neutral.

Of course you can achieve an infinite number of variations by mixing the three primary colors (red, yellow and blue) with each other, and with black and white. You shouldn't use any primary color full strength on the floors, walls, or ceilings in your new office because it would be overpowering. Instead, use subdued tints over the major surfaces to create the mood. Save full-strength color for accent trim and accessories, or avoid it altogether. The approach I like is to reserve the main color interest for the floor covering and keep wall and ceiling surfaces less interesting. When your eyes are focused at the work surfaces or walls beyond, you will avoid distraction.

Textures also call forth associations, though they are not as well defined as colors. I can't look at a ceiling covered by acoustic tiles perforated with tiny holes without thinking back to the schooldays when I counted the holes in one tile, then estimated the number in the whole ceiling. Or, think about who, in the stereotypical office, most likely rates a deep plush carpet? Who gets stuck with the commercial-grade, low-pile, type? Well, you get the idea.

Be aware of any common associations the colors and textures of your finish materials call forth. If you are unsure, try them out on your family and friends. Some books advise selecting home office colors and textures to blend with the rest of your house. I recommend the opposite. Treat the office as distinct from the house. For example, whereas my home is done in off-whites with earth-tone accent colors, my office is a muted scheme of blue-greens.

How Color Can Alter the Space

Color can't actually change the space, but it can affect one's perception of it. Light surfaces tend to recede; dark ones foreshorten. If your attic ceiling presses down, a lighter color will push it up. But, if the same attic is long and narrow,

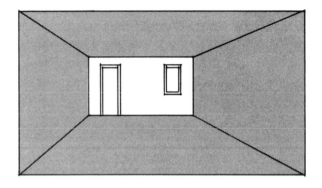

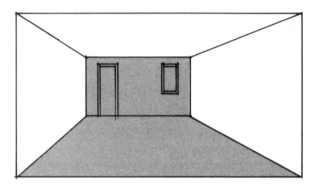

Figure 16-1: Color Value Affects Apparent Depth.
Light-colored surfaces seem to recede (top), whereas darker ones appear to be closer (bottom). One way to use this effect to advantage is to paint a low attic ceiling white or off-white to make it seem higher.

painting the end wall a dark color can bring it forward visually.

The shade of walls and ceiling also affects how light diffuses in your office. Light colors reflect light; dark colors absorb it. Light-colored surfaces will throw daylight coming in from windows or skylights farther into the space and spread it more evenly.

The lighting sources make matters still more interesting by affecting how you perceive surface colors. Incandescent lamps bring out the warmth of colors, particularly noticeable on reds, oranges, and yellows. The cool-white light of fluorescent lighting, until recently, muted these colors, while boosting blues and greens. Because human flesh is warm colored, it too looked sickly under cool-white fluorescent lighting.

Modern fluorescent lamps are kinder to surface colors, but the choices can be daunting, as you may conclude from Figure 16-2 (shown below). Though these "full spectrum" lamps yield better color balance than their predecessors, they still favor daylight or warm light. As a result, if you have both incandescent and fluorescent lamps on simultaneously, things tend to look a bit weird. The best compromise, in my view, is deluxe cool white or deluxe warm white fluorescent, or incandescent only.

Selecting Colors and Textures

The choices in colors and textures are so numerous as to bewilder you the first time you investigate paint chips or wallcovering sample books. It might help to make a list of goals for the color scheme. You might ask yourself:

- What emotions should the colors stir?
- What mood do I want my office colors to communicate to my clients?
- What colors do I work best amid?
- What items (equipment, predetermined surfaces such as wood or stone) do the colors have to blend with?

- Does my office space need to be visually enlarged, or reduced?

And don't forget your own personality. In a commercial workplace you don't have the opportunity to express yourself. Use it now. All things considered, I suggest the following guidelines:

- Keep ceilings as close to white as possible for good light distribution.
- Choose light colors for most walls (except walls at the end of long rooms that you want to foreshorten).
- Choose colors based on large samples if possible (small paint chips can fool you).

WALL AND CEILING FINISHES

Here's a rundown of the most apt finishes for home offices.

Paint

Paint still reigns as the most economical and easiest wall finish to apply over most substrates. Unlike other finishes, once on, it is easy to change.

LAMP TYPE	COOL WHITE	DELUXE COOL WHITE	WARM WHITE	DELUXE WARM WHITE	DAYLIGHT
EFFICIENCY (LUMENS PER WATT)	HIGH	MEDIUM	HIGH	MEDIUM	MEDIUM-HIGH
EFFECT ON NEUTRAL SURFACES	WHITE	WHITE	YELLOWISH-WHITE	YELLOWISH-WHITE	BLUISH-WHITE
COLORS STRENGTHENED	ORANGE, BLUE, YELLOW	ALL NEARLY EQUAL	ORANGE, YELLOW	RED, ORANGE, YELLOW, GREEN	GREEN, BLUE
COLORS MUTED	RED	NONE APPRECIABLY	RED, GREEN, BLUE	BLUE	RED, ORANGE
EFFECT ON SKIN COLOR	PALE PINK	MOST NATURAL	SALLOW	RUDDY	GREYED
REMARKS	BLENDS WITH SUNLIGHT, GOOD COLOR ACCEPTANCE	BEST OVERALL COLOR RENDITION. SIMULATES SUNLIGHT	BLENDS WITH INCANDESCENT LIGHT, POOR COLOR	GOOD COLOR. SIMULATES INCANDESCENT LIGHT	SIMILAR TO COOL WHITE

Figure 16-2: Fluorescent Lamp Choices. *Because the five fluorescent lamp types in the chart emit different wavelengths of light, they strengthen some solid colors and muddy others. Deluxe cool white probably has the best capacity to render most colors true. If your office gets a lot of sunlight, cool white will blend best. If you intend to use incandescent lamps (such as desk lamps) and fluorescent simultaneously, deluxe warm white will mix best.*

If your wall paint must double as a vapor barrier in lieu of a plastic membrane (as was discussed in chapter 8), start with a moisture-resistant primer. Shellac-based white primers such as BIN™ work well, if you can stand the fumes of the alcohol solvent. Apply at least two coats of topcoat for an even finish.

Latex wall paints now come in four sheens: satin (dull, flat), eggshell (slightly shinier), semi-gloss (shiny but not as much as gloss) and gloss. The flatter the sheen, the better it hides surface imperfections, but the harder it is to clean. Semi-gloss is washable, which makes it the choice for kitchens and baths, but too shiny for office walls. Eggshell, a nice compromise, can also coat woodwork, but because wood surfaces are more likely to need cleaning than walls I suggest semi-gloss or gloss here.

Wall Coverings

"Wallpaper" no longer describes the product that you buy in rolls and apply with an adhesive. Though many wall coverings are still backed with paper, their facings are now washable vinyl. You can cover all walls, only some walls, or the lower half (wainscot) of your office walls with any of the hundreds of patterns available. And, for every field pattern, there is a complementary border.

You can install roll-stock wall coverings yourself to almost any smooth, dry substrate that has been sized (coated with a solution that controls the bond). If your walls already have wallpaper, you'll have to strip it off. Glossy walls have to be dulled by sanding for a good bond.

It's no longer necessary to brush the backside of the paper with a flour paste. Now you dip the roll in water to activate the coating on the back, then stick it on the wall.

Paneling

Do you long for the mood of a traditional English drawing room? You can create this feel with real oak, cherry, or walnut paneling over all or part of the walls, if you can spare the expense. Or, if rustic is your flavor and you are on a beer budget, consider barnboards or knotty pine. In either case, I suggest real rather than fake wood. Wood veneer paneling has the look of a cheap motel.

The classical wood paneling that graced the drawing rooms of eighteenth-century English manors consists of solid boards, square or nearly square, whose tenon edges fit into the mortises (grooves) of a grid of muntins. Installing a system like this competently is the province of the skilled finish carpenter or cabinetmaker.

Installing board paneling is much more forgiving. You can probably do it yourself with a few hand tools (though a portable electric saw makes it a lot easier).

Don't choose dark woods like walnut, red oak, and mahogany, or light woods stained dark, unless you want a dark office. Choose a light wood like ash, white oak, birch, or pine, or limit your paneling to the lower portion of the walls and apply a light-colored finish above.

Other Wall Treatments

After positioning your equipment and installing shelves, your free wall space will probably shrink considerably. The right finish can help absorb sound, or provide a tack surface or something you can write on. Here are some options.

Carpeting. Putting carpet on some walls or the lower (wainscot) portion of all walls can add interest and soften their appearance. It also provides an excellent surface to tack things onto. Carpeted walls also soak up noise produced in the office, but won't staunch sounds from outside the office.

To work well as a tack surface without looking like a floor covering, choose a uniformly colored carpet with a level-loop and low pile height ($\frac{3}{16}$" or $\frac{1}{4}$"). Bond the carpet to the wall with carpet adhesive. A piece of wood trim (chair rail) makes a good transition where the carpet meets plain wall.

Cork and fiberboard. These also make good

The Frame-and-Panel System. *These horizontal and vertical rails are first attached to wood nailers. The panels (beveled edge shown here) sit into the rail frame and are held in place by moldings around the edges.*

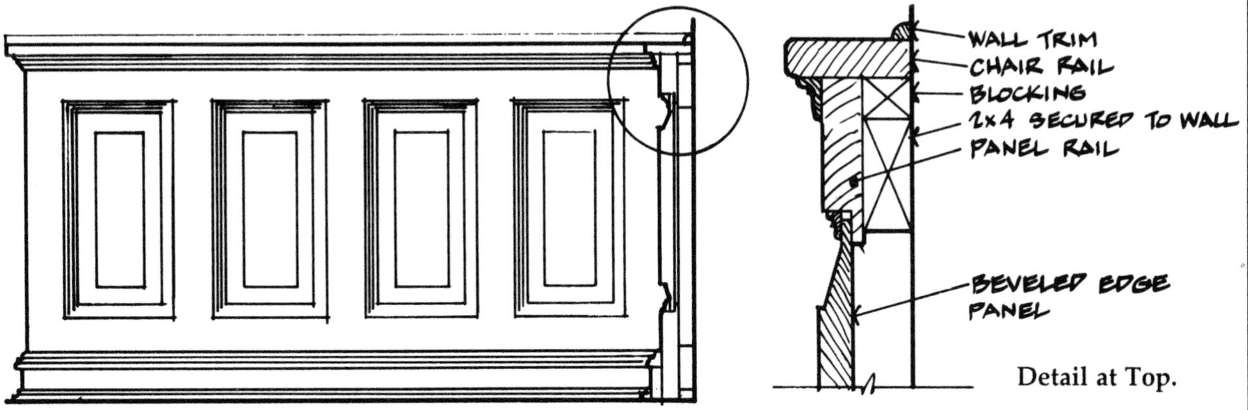

WALL TRIM
CHAIR RAIL
BLOCKING
2x4 SECURED TO WALL
PANEL RAIL

BEVELED EDGE PANEL

Detail at Top.

Tongue-and-Groove Board Paneling. *This type is more economical and easier to install than the classic type. Boards come in various widths and nominal 1" thickness. Install boards horizontally by blind-nailing through the tongue at each stud, or vertically by securing horizontal nailers to the wall at 16" or 24" spacing.*

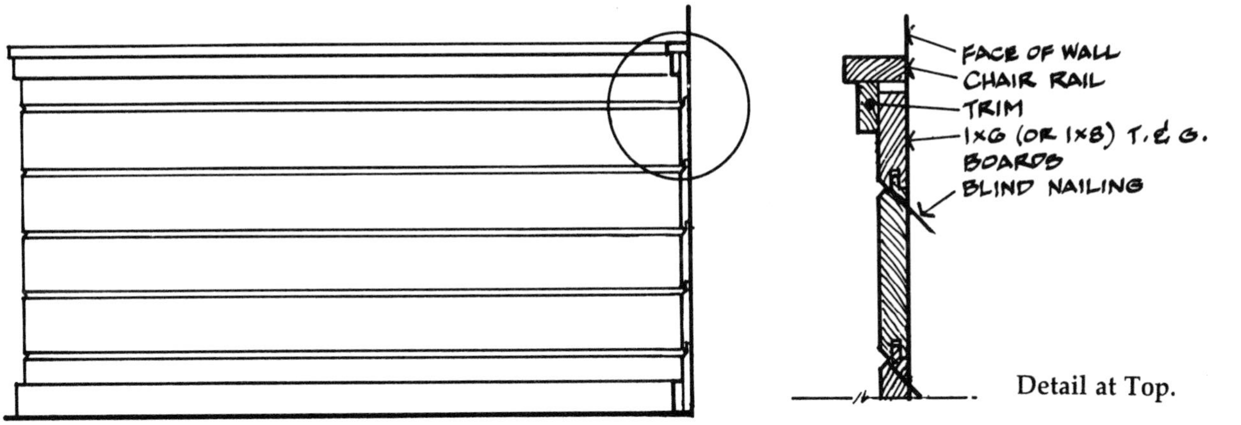

FACE OF WALL
CHAIR RAIL
TRIM
1x6 (OR 1x8) T.&G. BOARDS
BLIND NAILING

Detail at Top.

Board and Batten Paneling. *This creates a deep texture for an informal mood. Choose smooth boards such as pine, cedar, or redwood, or use rough-sawn or barnboards for a really rustic look. For vertical installation (as shown) first attach horizontal nailers to the wall 24" apart.*

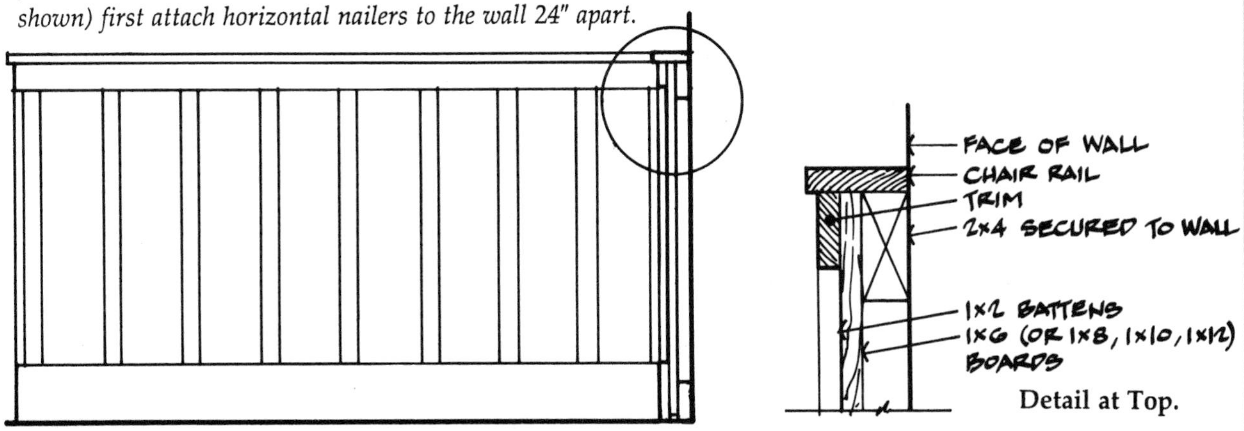

FACE OF WALL
CHAIR RAIL
TRIM
2x4 SECURED TO WALL

1x2 BATTENS
1x6 (OR 1x8, 1x10, 1x12) BOARDS

Detail at Top.

Figure 16-3: Three Types of Wood Paneling. *You can create many different looks with wood paneling, through choice of wood specie, panel design, and finish. Three possibilities are shown above on a 3' wainscot.*

tack surfaces. Cork comes in roll stock or square tiles backed with adhesive, or nail or screw bulletin boards framed in wood or aluminum to the wall. Prefabricated boards range in sizes from 24" × 18" to 48" × 72". More economical fiberboard is available from lumberyards in 4' × 8' sheets, ½" thick. Most types have a white facing on one side that can be left as is, painted, or covered with a fabric.

Dry erase boards. If you like writing on dry erase boards, installing them on your office walls will consume less floor space than mounting them on easels. They come framed in 24" × 18" to 48" × 72" sizes.

Wallboard. Good old gypsum drywall makes a good tack board, but not a writing surface. After the pinholes get too many, simply fill them in with a spackling compound and repaint.

FLOOR FINISHES

Many factors enter into choosing the right floor finish: the substrate, acoustic qualities, durability, color and texture, whether you can install it yourself, and cost. Let's start with the most economical and work upward.

Paint

If you are pinching pennies, you can transform a raw concrete or other hard-surface floor into a warm looking and practical office floor with nothing more than a good paint job and an area rug. Paint only slabs that are dry and stay dry. Begin by patching holes or cracks with a masonry patching compound, then prime the surface with a primer designed for concrete. Finish with two coats of gloss enamel. Alkyd (oil-based) enamel yields the best finish, but is being phased out by water-based acrylic enamels.

Resilient Flooring

Thin floor coverings composed of vinyl, rubber, or cork make the most durable floor surfaces and the most suitable if liquids are likely to be spilled. Resilient flooring comes in a wide range of colors

and patterns in both tile and sheet form. Tiles, the easier choice if you are doing it yourself, can be applied in a bed of troweled-on adhesive or, in some cases, you just peel off the backing paper and stick. I have installed self-stick tiles in two houses with good results. If you use this type, you'll get a better job by first filling in any dents, cracks, and imperfections in the substrate. Depending on the adhesive, concrete slabs may require sealant as a first coat.

Carpeting

Carpeting is the most common office floor covering because of its soft texture, warm feeling, and ability to cushion footfalls. It will absorb sounds generated inside the office, which is important if you have more than one person working or noisy equipment.

If you have ever chosen carpet, you know the variety of choices in material, color, texture, pattern, and underlayment. Any of the currently available natural or synthetic fibers will suit your office use. Prices vary widely, with nylon or polypropylene at the bottom end and wool at the top. A low, even-textured carpet (level-loop or tufted) will prove more practical than a texture with uneven height, both for keeping clean and moving around on. Protect any carpet subject to repeated traffic from chair casters with vinyl chair mats.

Although pads under carpets increase their softness and give them a feel of luxury, you should resist the temptation. They prove harder to walk on and moving equipment around on a padded carpet takes a greater toll on its fibers.

Your carpet color and texture is a wise place to begin your overall color scheme because you're less likely to change it. For flexibility, pick a color and pattern that can go with more than one wall color. Neutral solid colors or multicolor carpets make versatile choices.

There are two legitimate ways to install a carpet. But there is also one not-so-legitimate way that is simpler and workable. Your first option involves nailing down thin plywood, tack-

Figure 16–4

COMPARING WALL FINISHES

CRITERIA	Paint (primer plus two coats rolled on plaster or wallboard)	Wall Coverings (paper or vinyl)	Wood Paneling Classical Frame and Panel	Wood Paneling Vertical or Horizontal Boards	Carpeting	Cork (12x12 tiles)	Dry Erase Board
	WALL FINISH MATERIAL						
Acceptable Substrates							
Plaster or Wallboard	◆	◆			◆	◆	◆
Existing Wallpaper (if sound)	◆	◆			◆	◆	◆
Masonry	◆				◆	◆	◆
2x4 Vertical or Horizontal Nailers			◆	◆			
Mood and Effect							
Formal	◆		◆		◆		
Informal but Efficient	◆	◆		◆	◆		
Informal and Homey	◆	◆		◆			
Acoustic Properties							
Deadens Internally-Generated Noise					◆	◆	
Durability							
Washable	◆	◆	◆	◆			
Cleanable by Vacuuming					◆		
Relative Cost							
High			◆				◆
Medium				◆	◆	◆	
Low	◆	◆					
Ease of Installation							
Easy, even for beginners	◆					◆	◆
Difficult, requires practical skills		◆		◆	◆		
Difficult, hire a professional			◆				

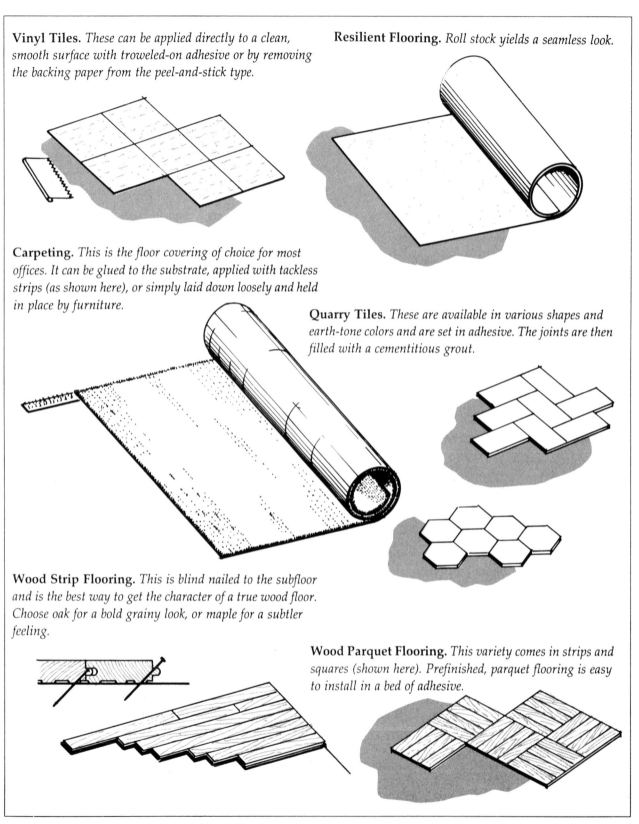

Vinyl Tiles. *These can be applied directly to a clean, smooth surface with troweled-on adhesive or by removing the backing paper from the peel-and-stick type.*

Resilient Flooring. *Roll stock yields a seamless look.*

Carpeting. *This is the floor covering of choice for most offices. It can be glued to the substrate, applied with tackless strips (as shown here), or simply laid down loosely and held in place by furniture.*

Quarry Tiles. *These are available in various shapes and earth-tone colors and are set in adhesive. The joints are then filled with a cementitious grout.*

Wood Strip Flooring. *This is blind nailed to the subfloor and is the best way to get the character of a true wood floor. Choose oak for a bold grainy look, or maple for a subtler feeling.*

Wood Parquet Flooring. *This variety comes in strips and squares (shown here). Prefinished, parquet flooring is easy to install in a bed of adhesive.*

Figure 16-5: Office Flooring Choices. *Carpeting may seem the natural choice for your office floor, but not the only one. Resilient flooring, quarry tiles, and various types of wood offer different expressions with easy-to-clean durability.*

imbedded strips around the edges of the room (glue them, in the case of a concrete slab). With edge strips in place, lay the carpet over the floor and use a carpet stretcher (borrowed from the supplier) to stretch the carpet over the tacks.

The second legitimate method is to glue the carpet to the substrate with a troweled-on adhesive. This is a common method for commercial applications, but I don't recommend it for your home office. If you ever want to remove the carpet you will curse the day you glued it down.

The third method is simply to lay the carpet down without the aid of a chemical or mechanical binder. In time it will lose the curl at the edges and lie flat. It won't go anywhere under normal office use, and the weight of furniture and equipment eliminates lateral movement.

Quarry Tiles

Quarry tiles, though not the cheapest choice, make a handsome home office floor. Like resilient flooring, their surface is durable and easy to clean. These are available in rectangular sizes from around 4″ up to 12″ on a side, as well as hexagons, octagons, and other shapes. Their unglazed surface makes walking on quarry tiles safe, if not soft. Colors range from earth tones (buff, browns, and reds) to various grays.

You can probably install quarry tiles yourself over a plywood subfloor or concrete slab by first troweling on an adhesive (depending on the type, you may have to prime a concrete slab first), then forcing a grout into the joints with a squeegee. The few simple tools required can be bought or borrowed from the tile supplier.

Wood Flooring

Another hard-surface floor finish is natural wood. Though expensive, its beauty and warmth add unmistakable class underfoot, while providing a surface tolerant of spills.

There are two basic choices: unfinished and prefinished. Then you've got to decide on the type of wood and shape.

Unfinished wood flooring comes as random length planks or strips with tongue-and-groove (T&G) edges. Strip flooring measures 2¼″ and ²⁵⁄₃₂″ thick, whereas planks will vary from 1″ × 4″ to 1″ × 10″ nominal size. Oak and maple are available almost everywhere; walnut, fir, and southern yellow pine are somewhat less common. You might look for plank flooring in pine, mahogany, and fir.

Installing strip or plank flooring is hard, back-straining work, but not beyond the ability of most do-it-yourselfers. After coaxing the grooved side of each strip into the tongue of the previous one, you drive a nail at an angle through the tongue into the subfloor (blind nailing). The nails are concealed by the grooved side of the next piece.

When all strips are installed, fill any cracks or holes with a filler of matching color and smooth the surface with a rented floor sander. Two or three coats of penetrating oil finish such as Watco™ may be the easiest and most durable finish you can apply. The excess oil is wiped off the surface to allow the oil that has penetrated to enhance the natural grain and character of the wood. If you want something other than a deep, satin finish, choose a clear polymeric formulation that you brush on. My favorite is three coats of high-gloss polyurethane.

Prefinished wood flooring, the lazy person's choice, comes in planks that can be glued down to concrete slabs or nailed to wood subfloors, and as 12″ × 12″ parquets to be glued down. Installing parquets, like laying down floor tiles, is easier than cutting, placing, nailing, and finishing raw wood flooring. The result, though, can't hold a candle to raw wood strips or planks installed and finished with care.

Composite Floor Finishes

If wet spills are likely in some areas of your office, but you don't want hard-surface utilitarian floors throughout, why not consider more than one floor finish? One way to do this is to apply a hard

Figure 16–6

COMPARING FLOOR FINISHES

CRITERIA	FINISH FLOORING MATERIAL							
	Paint	Carpeting	Resilient Flooring Tiles (peel and strip)	Resilient Flooring tiles (adhesively applied)	Resilient Sheet Flooring	Quarry Tiles	Wood Strip Flooring	Wood Parquet Flooring
Acceptable Substrates								
Concrete Slab	●	●	●	●	●	●		●
Plywood	●	●	●	●	●	●	●	●
Particle Board	●	●					●	
Existing Resilient Flooring		●	●	●	●			
Mood and Effect								
Formal		●						
Informal but Efficient	●		●		●	●	●	●
Informal and Homey	●					●	●	●
Acoustic Properties								
Deadens Internally-Generated Noise		●						
Durability								
Needs No Protection at High Wear Areas			●	●	●	●	●	●
Suitable for Wet Spills	●		●	●	●	●	●	●
Relative Cost								
High					●	●	●	
Medium		●	●					●
Low	●							
Ease of Installation								
Easy, even for beginners	●		●					
Difficult, requires practical skills		●			●		●	●
Difficult, hire a professional						●		

floor to the entire floor, then place throw rugs or area rugs over areas not subject to heavy wear. Another less flexible approach is to permanently fix carpeting where you want it and apply hard flooring elsewhere.

FINISHES FOR CABINETRY AND FURNITURE

Because you will also have to finish any cabinets, furniture, shelving, and work surfaces you build yourself, you should think about their finish before beginning construction. Wood to receive a natural finish has to be selected for specie, grain character, and type of stain, if any. Items to be painted need only a smooth, paintable surface. I always use particle board rather than plywood where possible. It takes paint better and costs far less. Where you have to use solid wood, such as trim and edging, use #2 pine rather than select or "D" pine. When filled, sanded, and sealed, the knots disappear and the extra effort will save you plenty. Even with flaw-free lumber, you still have to fill and sand nail holes and joints.

Paint

You can paint wood and wood-composition furniture as you would walls, but, because most furniture is subject to abrasion, a more durable finish makes better sense. Gloss or semi-gloss enamels applied over a coat of wood primer work well. A second coat of primer, lightly sanded, yields an even better look to the topcoat.

One carryover from wall painting that does make sense is a paint roller. Using one to coat wide expanses of furniture yields a smoother finish in far less time than a brush. Use a low-nappe (¼" or less) mohair roller for enamel-type paints.

Natural Finishes

You can coax almost any expression you desire out of natural wood by combining the right specie of wood with the appropriate finish and a lot of work:

Grain: strong (oak) or weak (birch, maple)

Sheen: glossy, semi-gloss, dull (satin)

Color: white, blond, reddish, browns, and dark

Because of the expense, it might make more sense to save natural wood finishes for places where they really count, that is, surfaces that show the most. Why apply natural finishes to the tops of shelves and insides of cabinets when you never see these surfaces? Paint them instead.

Penetrating finishes such as tung and linseed oil and proprietary oil finishes (Watco™, Minwax™) sink down into the wood to bring out its true character with the least effort. Stain the wood first if you want to alter the color. Then use a brush or sponge to flood the surface with oil and then give it a few minutes to penetrate. Finally, wipe off the excess for a rich, satin look. Waxing adds luster and depth.

Superficial coatings build a film that rides the surface without penetrating. Clear varnish, polyurethane, and shellac are usually brushed on in three successive coats to achieve a choice of sheens from satin to high gloss. As with penetrating finishes, you can stain the wood first. Single-step coatings that contain colorants offer another avenue, but the color isn't as deep as with a stain-plus-coating finish.

Laminated Plastic

Surfaces of prefabricated office furniture are likely to be finished with a matte-sheen laminated plastic (Formica™, Wilson Art™). The work surfaces of furniture you build yourself may be durable enough by simply painting or varnishing them, but if subjected to continual abrasion or wet spillage, consider topping them with laminated plastic. Installing the material requires precision cutting, trimming, and bonding with contact cement (which allows no second chance), so you may be wise to call on a carpenter who has done a few kitchen cabinets.

WINDOW TREATMENTS

Today's energy-efficient windows can do much to control light and solar heat, but even the best of them can't do everything you may want for your office environment: maintaining a view while preserving privacy, controlling glare, reducing winter heat loss while blocking summertime heat gain, enhancing the interior and promoting physical security, and so on. These demands call for additional controls in the form of window treatments, which can respond to the time of day, season, and outside weather conditions.

Window treatments take many forms. They can be layers of glass or plastic that you add to the inside or outside of the window, opaque barriers, or fabric-based covers that permit various amounts of light and heat to enter or escape. Most of them share one important feature: adjustability.

Choose a window treatment that will enhance your work efficiency and comfort, and one that supports the mood you are seeking. Your climate, the location of your office with respect to your house, and the proximity of neighbors and the street can serve as starting points. Your final selection will have to accommodate the type and size of windows, your work habits, the appearance you want, and your budget. Here are a few of your choices.

Storm Windows

If you have ever been chilled working next to single-glazed windows on a cold winter day, you know your first priority is physical comfort. Replacing leaky windows with energy-efficient windows will do the trick, but if this overwhelms your budget, consider storm windows. They can mount to the inside or outside, but make sure the storm window can be opened and closed without removing the entire unit.

Plastic Window Films

Plastic films bought in rolls and stuck to the inside of windows with water can cut various amounts of solar heat gain and glare, depending on their tint (shades of gray or brown) and whether they are coated with reflective metals. Because these materials block solar gain year-round, they are best suited for windows in hot climates exposed to the south or west.

Blinds

You can't beat blinds for variable solar control. Two types of slatted blinds enable you to direct the sunlight where you want while maintaining view to the outdoors. Horizontal mini-blinds (Venetian blinds) made of aluminum or vinyl slats are best adapted to south-facing windows. By adjusting the angle of the slats you can direct the noontime sunlight up onto the office ceiling, which then returns it to any work surfaces as a soft, filtered light.

For windows on the east and west, vertical blinds work best. These are available in various tints, fabrics, and widths, and can be rotated to direct sunlight where you want it, closed completely, or drawn open to the side of the window.

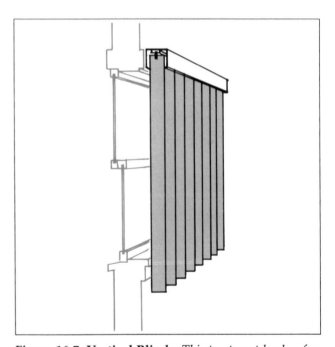

Figure 16-7: Vertical Blinds. *This treatment lends a formal air to a window and offers one of the best ways to control the sun's direct rays through east- and west-facing windows. Blinds swivel from completely open to completely shut, or can be drawn to stack at the side.*

Shades

Whereas blinds render the window almost "blind" when fully closed, shades allow some light to filter through the fabric. The simplest and most economical are rolling shades. At the bottom of the heap are the simple vinyl roller shades you can buy at any department store. Used alone, they look austere and sometimes tacky. You can hang drapes to dress them up, or check into the classier versions that use different fabrics and ride in side tracks (available at window accessory stores).

Pleated shades stack, rather than roll up, and are contained within tracks at the sides. Single-layer pleated blinds fold up like an accordion. Another type weds two layers of fabric to form honeycombs when the shade is pulled down. The air entrapped within each honeycomb cell helps cut heat loss. Hunter Douglas claims R-values ranging between 1.2 and 4.2 for their Duette™ models. Pleated blinds are elegant without other window treatments, but, as with roll blinds, you can't see through them when closed.

Drapes

Drapes can add softness and elegance to your office interior, but don't control sunlight with the same agility as blinds. When closed, they can beef up the R-value of double-glazed windows by from 0.3 (conventional drapes) to 2.0 (quilted with a filling). But when closed, heavy drapes block all sunlight, along with its light and warmth. This feature might be an advantage if you need darkness for occasional video presentations or projected media.

Window Quilts

Window quilts are a heavier type of drape consisting of a fabric bonded to an insulating filler and mounted in a fully surrounding frame. When closed, they block all outside light and view and increase the R-value of a double-glazed window by 3.3. I can't see much advantage for installing them in an office used primarily in the

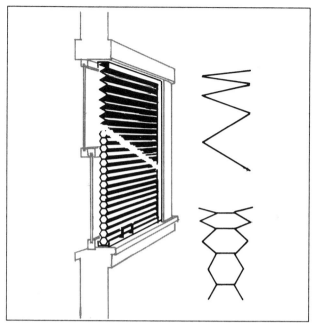

Figure 16-8: Pleated Shades and Honeycomb Shades.
Both pleated shades (top half) and honeycomb shades (lower half) control glare from a window facing any direction while diffusing sunlight to control glare. Because these units ride in tracks at the side, the airspace between window and shade helps insulate the window for greater comfort. An airspace in each slat of the honeycomb shade adds another insulating barrier.

day, but they will benefit a cold-climate office used at night. If you sew, you can make your own on a basic machine from patterns and materials generally available.

Exterior Shutters

If hurricanes or tornadoes threaten the safety of your office or if burglary looms as a concern, look into the various devices that mount to the outside of windows.

Exterior roll-down shutters, in use for years in Europe, are still not popular in the United States. The devastation wreaked by Hurricane Andrew in 1992 might spur their acceptance, along with other forms of exterior window protection. One type consists of foam-filled hollow vinyl or aluminum slats (Enviroblind™). When closed, the units block most light, noise, and storm damage (winds of up to 105 mph), and dis-

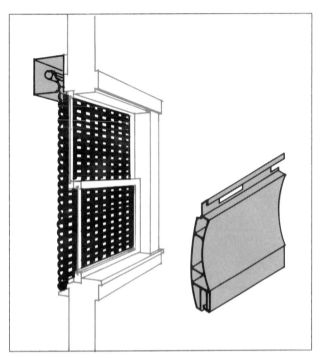

Figure 16-9: Exterior Rolling Shutters. *In use in Europe for years, these are now gaining more interest in the United States, thanks to the barrier they offer against break-in and their ability to protect from high winds. The slats, made of extruded vinyl (as shown) or aluminum, ride in tracks at the side and roll up into a drum above the window. When fully closed, some daylight filters in through slots in the slat linkages.*

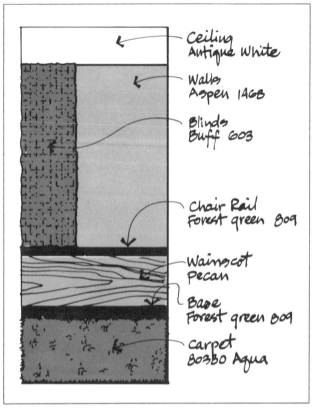

Figure 16-11: Make a Color Scheme Board. *Glue swatches of proposed fabrics and paint chips to a piece of letter-size cardboard. To get the best idea of how the colors will relate in your office, size each item according to its importance (that's why the wall chip is the largest above, and the chair rail trim the smallest). Then arrange each item on the board next to the item it will be seen against.*

courage intruders. Slots in the joints between slats admit small amounts of ventilation and light. The R-value of the window is increased by around 2. Units can be controlled by straps or cranks from the inside, or by an electric motor.

Exterior shutters also come as flat, louvered, panels that fold shut (Colonial), hinge at the top (Bahama) or roll sideways in tracks. Most products are aluminum, available in various colors. Shutters provide the same kind of protection as roll-down shades, with two differences: the open louvers allow continuous ventilation and more light, but they provide no thermal insulation.

Shading Screens

Another exterior-mounted device for offices continually exposed to direct sunlight is shading screens. Not to be confused with screens that keep flies and mosquitoes out, this type is specifically designed to control sunlight. One brand made from woven fiberglass and available in eight colors claims to block up to 70% of solar heat and glare (Phifer SunScreeen™). Phifer also makes a metal version stamped from flat black aluminum that contains hundreds of tiny louvers that work like venetian blinds to cut solar gain by 85%.

Awnings

Awnings can also effectively block direct sunlight from entering the window. They work best on south-facing windows, though. To keep late-afternoon sunlight out of west-facing windows,

Figure 16–10

WINDOW TREATMENT SELECTOR

CRITERIA	Pleated Shades	Storm Windows	Window Films	Shading Screens	Drapes	Rolling Shades	Venetian Blinds	Vertical Blinds	Window Quilts	Exterior Shutters	Awnings
Light Control											
Controls Glare on East & West Windows	●		●	●	●	●		●		●	
Controls Glare on South Windows	●		●	●	●	●	●			●	●
Adjustable	●				●	●	●	●	●	●	
Mood and Effect											
Formal	●		●		●		●	●		'	
Informal						●			●		
Acoustic Properties (when closed)											
Reduces Internally-Generated Noise					●				●		
Reduces Externally-Generated Noise		●							●	●	
Energy Factors (when closed)											
Cuts Daytime Heat Loss/Gain	●		●	●	●		●	●	●	●	●
Cuts Nighttime Heat Loss/Gain	●	●			●				●	●	
Relative Cost											
High										●	
Medium								●			
Low			●			●	●				
Ease of Installation											
Easy, even for beginners		●		●		●	●				
Difficult, requires practical skills	●				●			●	●		●
Difficult, hire a professional										●	

you'll need awnings that lower to cover almost the full depth of the window.

MAKE A COLOR SCHEME BOARD

After you've selected a window treatment you'll need to pick a fabric and color, whether you end up with interior blinds, drapes, or shades. To help you coordinate your choices into an entire scheme and explore alternatives, mount them on a color board.

You should be able to get samples of carpets or floor tiles from a supplier. Next collect samples of any wallcoverings and paint chips. If possible, get a full set of paint chips so that you can use them to approximate colors of items for which small samples may be unavailable (such as furniture).

Begin your board by gluing down a carpet or floor tile sample near the bottom of the board. If you use rubber cement, you can easily change items that don't work. Add, successively, samples of each contiguous material, ending with the ceiling at the top. When your board is complete, you'll be able to get a feel for the entire scheme. If things don't work together, you can quickly pluck out the offending sample and try others. When you have a scheme that reflects the needs of your office and your personal tastes, you will really start to appreciate the advantages of being your own boss. And remember, you can always change the scheme without asking anyone else.

CHAPTER 17

FURNITURE AND EQUIPMENT

*Contradictions abound in the business communications world today. Why do we grip
a hand-held calculator to perform a series of sums, when the computer on our desk has the power
of thousands of calculators? Why do we type a document on our computer, print it
to convert it into paper, then shove it into a fax machine to convert it into phone signals,
then print it out again at the receiving fax machine? Chances are very good the document will
be typed in again and put right back into digital format.*
Paul Schofield[1]

Many of these contradictions no doubt trace to the fact that progress in technology outpaces our ability to integrate its fruits rationally into our work. A glance at a computer catalog can leave you scratching your head. Much of the stuff is a mystery, and I wonder if the revolution has a momentum that rolls on regardless of its real value.

For most of the new equipment, I find myself thinking:

1. Gee, what a great idea!
2. But do I actually need it?
3. Would the cost really save me time and effort over the long haul?
4. I can probably do just as well without it, at least for the time being.

I usually don't make my final decision on the basis of monetary cost because stuff gets cheaper after the first generation. What's important is the time and effort required to learn how to use it. The qualifier, "for the time being" leaves the option of reconsidering at some time in the future.

It used to be much easier. When I started writing professionally in 1983, most writers got by splendidly with an electric typewriter (except for the few purists who scratched out their first draft on a yellow legal pad). Then came word processors, which added speed and utility. But where you could switch from a manual to electric typewriter with little difficulty, word processors required learning a whole new way of working. Modems, faxes, video cassettes, and interactive computer online networks all followed, in turn, and a spate of software that does everything but read your mind.

FINDING AND GETTING EQUIPMENT
Sources

Gone, too, are the days when your only source for office supplies and equipment was Ajax Office Supplies on Main Street. With the growth of home offices, a new generation of office stores has come on the scene that take on many of the trappings of large discount stores. Add to that the specialty computer stores and mail-order sources (see the listings in the appendix), and you have many sources for equipping and supplying your office.

If you are the least bit handy with tools, consider building much of your fixed office furniture. You can get just what you want at a cost many times less than buying it prefabricated, and you can alter it easily, as needs change, without worrying about decreasing its value.

Buy, Finance, or Lease?

Of course, you can't build everything. After deciding what equipment you need, you have to figure out how to acquire it. Should you buy it outright, over time, or lease it?

According to Nancy A. Nichols, senior editor of the *Harvard Business Review*,[2] paying cash for a piece of equipment is generally the least expensive option, and it enables you to depreciate the total cost of the item. But doing so depletes operating capital you may need for other expenses. And, you may get stuck with something bound for obsolescence in a short time.

Borrowing to pay for equipment also allows you to depreciate the equipment and deduct the interest from your tax liability. But ownership also risks obsolescence and reduces your line of credit.

Leasing protects you best from obsolescence, doesn't show up as a liability on your balance sheet, and permits you to get full financing. You'll be able to deduct the lease payments from your tax liability. Keeping the ownership with the supplier means they will be responsible for maintenance and repairs. On the downside, leasing incurs the highest total cost, and the equipment reverts to the lessor at the end of the term, unless you pay a buyback sum. Another problem is that you may get penalized for cancelling mid-term.

Nichols suggests scrutinizing your cash position, the ease and cost of borrowing, and the potential obsolescence of the equipment, before deciding among options.

HIGH-TECH EQUIPMENT

To advise you in a book like this about which computers or other rapidly evolving electronic equipment to get is to risk the advice becoming obsolete even before the book comes off the press. So my advice is to use other sources to stay current (such as trade magazines, professional peers, newsletters, and periodicals such as *Home Office Computing, Inc.*, and *Money*).

But whereas equipment and tools change, the human body doesn't. Whatever computer, fax, phone, or copy machine you select, you still need a way to fit it into your total scheme so that you can work with it efficiently. The rest of this chapter focuses on your office infrastructure, that is, all of the stuff that houses or supports those ever-changing tools.

FURNITURE

Chronic backaches have plagued office workers since clerks first sat for long periods bent over desks or tables. Along with backache, we now face eyestrain and headaches from staring at computer monitor screens, carpal tunnel syndrome from entering data, and possibly unknown perils from the electrical waves emanating from the electronic equipment.

All of these health hazards have spawned a new science, *ergonomics*, which aims to design tools and furniture to fit the human body without causing it discomfort or harm. The height, width, and depth of your desk and the angle of your keyboard can not only affect your comfort and health, but your working efficiency, as well.

Desks and Work Surfaces

With the advent of portable phones and notebook computers, many of us will be free to spend more of our working time in the car or our favorite living room chair. But even traveling salespeople spend some time at a desk. And some things—drafting, for example—simply can't be done in a car.

The example of drafting brings up an important point when selecting a desk or working surface: Can you get by with only one? For my writing studio/architect's office, I use four different workstations, each tailored to a specific activity. Rather than spend several hundred dollars for a hardwood drawing table with an adjustable top, (I don't think most people ever change the angle of an adjustable top anyway) I found the angle I liked to work at and spanned a simple piece of plywood between two side tables consisting of hollow-core wood doors on particle-board sup-

Figure 17-1: Workstation Ergonomics. *To lessen the strain on your body, take a few pains to create a more ergonomically correct arrangement at your workstation.* **(1)** *Start with a good chair with a seat that adjusts up and down.* **(2)** *The backrest should both adjust vertically and allow you to change the horizontal tension.* **(3)** *Maintain a vertical posture.* **(4)** *Your eyes should be between 16" and 28" in front of the document or screen.* **(5)** *The monitor screen should adjust in vertical angle and swivel from side to side.* **(6)** *Situate your screen or document so that you view it at an angle between 10 and 40 degrees from a horizontal line at eye level.* **(7)** *Use a wrist rest to take strain off your wrists.* **(8)** *Most people find a keyboard height of 24" to 27" the most comfortable.* **(9)** *Try using a wedge-shaped foot rest for better foot and leg comfort.*

ports, along the lines of the system shown in Figure 17-2 (page 154).

If you buy a desk or workstation for your computer, adjustability may well be the most important single thing to look for. Fortunately, you have much to choose from:

• **Pedestal desks.** The least sexy option is the common pedestal desk, open at the center and a drawer pedestal on one or both ends. I think they are better suited to impressing visitors (at least the more upscale versions) than they are practical. A home office worker likely has to do many

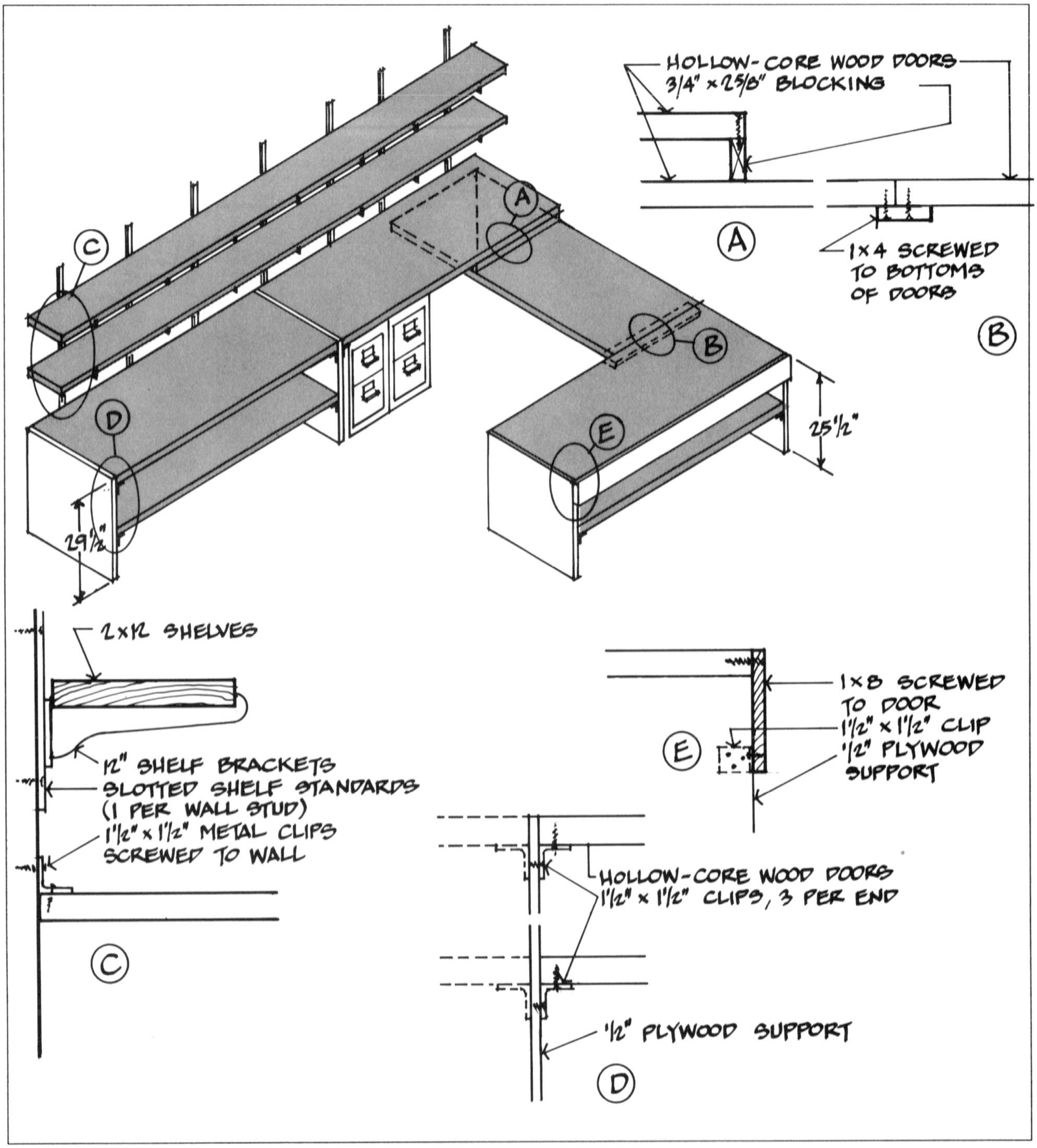

Figure 17-2: Simple Office Furniture You Can Build.
Using a small range of widely available materials, you can build a variety of work surfaces and storage facilities. Besides being economical, you'll be able to disassemble and reconfigure these components as your needs change. Hollow core doors (2'6" × 6'8" × 1⅜") make excellent work surfaces and wide, low shelves for equipment or supplies. Rip supports out of ½" plywood or particle board. Join horizontal surfaces to vertical supports with steel corner brace clips and wood screws. For above-desk shelving, cut lengths of 2 × 12's to the length you want, then mount them on steel shelf standards screwed to the wall.

kinds of work, some involving computers. If you do intend to use a standard desk with a computer, get one with a lower support for the keyboard.

• **Bilevel workstations.** Bilevel workstations come with a low front section for keyboard and CPU; a raised rear surface houses the screen. One version mounts on castors for mobility.

• **Modular workstations.** Many combinations of open-bottom desks, drawer bases, and above-desk shelves are possible in a modular workstation. Though the standard work surface height is 29″, some have keyboard drawers that fit below the top, putting the keyboard lower, and therefore better ergonomically. You can arrange modular systems into *L*s, *U*s, or corners with an angled center. They are available in plastic laminate finish or more expensive natural wood.

Computer Workstations

Personal computer equipment in its present physical form is akin to today's hi-fi sound equipment. If you are old enough, you may remember when home sound systems packaged a radio, record player, amplifier, and speakers in one cabinet. Though you can still buy sound equipment this way (think of boom boxes) serious audiophiles prefer to buy separate modules—pickup, radio, amplifier, and speakers—because they enable greater choice between components and the ability to change one component without replacing the works.

People also want this flexibility to mix and match computer components. It has become an imperative, with technology changing so rapidly. Why should you have to replace your CPU if you move from a dot matrix up to a laser printer, for example? And people like the freedom to configure their components into a spatial arrangement that suits their working style. Notebook (or laptop) computers allow you to work anywhere you can sit (except maybe in the bath), but at the sacrifice of comfort. Their tiny keyboards are nowhere as easy to navigate as a stan-dard separate keyboard and the display screens are harder to read than a cathode-ray monitor. Portable units are a great adjunct for getting some work done inflight, but if you need to spend hours at a time working with a computer, you will more comfortably work with equipment sized to fit your body.

You can, with some additions, stuff the many possible computer peripherals into a standard pedestal desk, but it's a force fit. Bilevel desks are somewhat better, modular workstations still more flexible, as is building your own modular system out of wood doors on supports. If you go this route, the most important advantage is the capacity to store individual components in many possible configurations vertically as well as horizontally. Several off-the-shelf computer workstations achieve this goal, though some sacrifice comfort in the interest of saving space.

• **Portable workstations.** Portable workstations achieve great economy of floor space by stacking components vertically in either a closed or open-rack cabinet. Most mount on castors that make them portable (interestingly, none of the catalog pictures show any wiring coming out the backside).

• **Desk-integrated workstations.** Expect more office furniture companies to offer modular components designed to house electronic equipment for the home office market. Nova Office Furniture builds the major components into an imaginative ergonomically conceived desk that puts the monitor below a glass pane in the desk top, behind a keyboard rack that pulls in and out. The arrangement allows users to look down constantly, instead of horizontally or shifting from a horizontal screen to a lower keyboard. The desk top, unencumbered by computer equipment, is free for other uses. The desk unit comes with racks for mounting printers under the left side and storage for the CPU on end in the other. Shelves can be added to the rear of the desk top for other equipment or storage.

The Pedestal Desk. *Clerks and executives have used this type of desk in years past, but it lacks the flexibility to adapt to modern office equipment.*

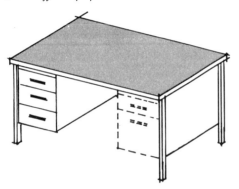

Bilevel Work Surfaces. *The advantage here is a flexible arrangement. The lower front surface adjusts on many models to provide an ergonomically correct keyboard height.*

Modular Workstations. *Kits are available in U- or L-shaped arrangements. Though work surface height is at the standard 29", pull-out shelves below the task level allow for proper keyboard height.*

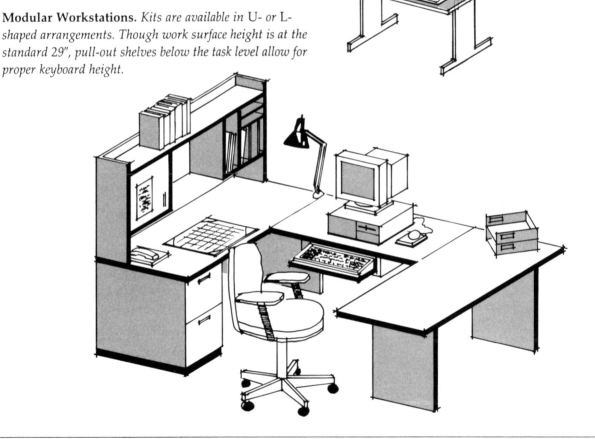

Figure 17-3: Desks and Workstations.

Tables

Tables are likely the single most useful of all your office furniture. They can replace (or supple-

ment) desks as a primary work surface, serve conference needs, and support other furniture and equipment. Laying a wood door over one

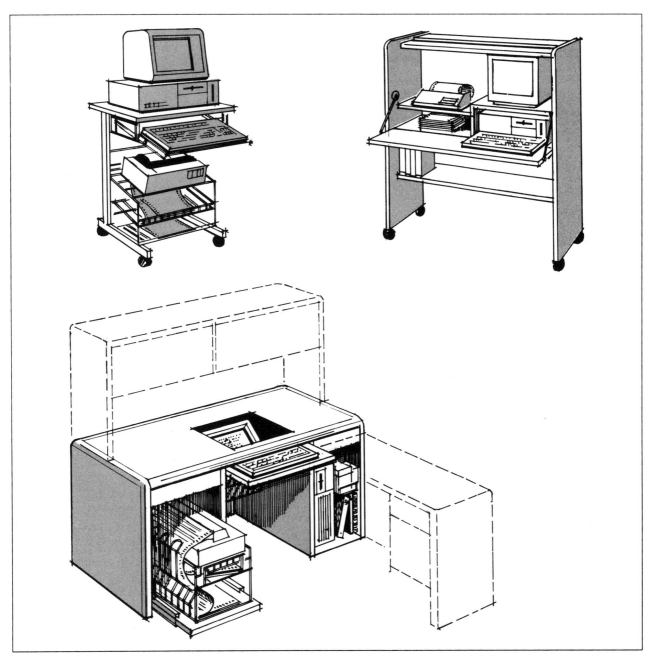

Figure 17-4: Computer Workstations. *A wide variety is available to suit even the most modest floor space. Racks on casters (top left) hold computer, keyboard, and printer in one open cabinet. If security is an issue, consider a cabinet as shown at top right. To close the equipment compartment, the cover pulls down from the top to meet the hinged work surface folded upward. The system at bottom left embodies a new, different approach to computer ergonomics. Placing the monitor below a tinted-glass panel on the desk provides a more comfortable viewing angle (according to the manufacturer), while enabling the top of the desk to remain uncluttered for writing tasks. A printer fits into one side of the main console and a computer on end fits in the other. Accessories are available to extend the workstation upward or outward.*

end of two tables creates a "U", for example, yielding an extra work surface with no additional legs below to encumber space for knees, files, or shelving.

Most prefab tables come 29" high, but have little else in common. Wood and metal conference tables are available in sizes starting at 3' × 6'. You can select from many finishes, including hardwoods, laminated plastic, and glass.

Folding tables, usually laminated plastic tops on folding metal legs, come in sizes from 30"x60" to 36"x96". These tables will provide you the most flexibility at the least cost.

You can make your own demountable tables inexpensively by using wood doors, as shown in Figure 17-2 (page 154). Check your local building supply outlet for doors damaged on one side. You might pick them up at a good discount and never notice the dent or scratch on the side turned to face down.

Chairs

If you spend many hours each day sitting at a desk or computer, do it in an ergonomically designed chair. Your back will appreciate it. A good chair with arms and adjustable back and seat will cost a couple of hundred bucks and is one piece of furniture you probably can't build as well yourself. Here are the two main contenders:

• **Adjustable task chairs.** These sit on a single post over a "star" of horizontal legs on casters. All come with a padded seat and back. Some have permanent arms; others have removable ones. On a quality chair, the back adjusts up or down, with the back-and-forth movement controlled by an adjustable-tension spring. Up-and-down movement of the seat is controlled by a pneumatic cylinder, by a side-mounted lever. A taller version of this chair adapts to drawing boards.

• **Backless task chairs.** Developed in Norway as a way to help prevent lower back pain, these chairs look incomplete at first glance. They have an adjustable padded seat, slightly bent forward, and a knee rest, but no back support. The manufacturer claims the chair distributes your body weight more naturally than conventional chairs, and reduces pressure on the lumbar and seat bones by up to 50%. Because these chairs require an entirely different sitting posture, try one out for several hours before buying.

STORAGE EQUIPMENT

Remember when futurists were predicting that the electronic revolution would translate to less storage space for hard copy? Home office workers I talk to say that if anything, they need more space, because they have to store computer disks and paraphernalia as well as hard copy files. To make your storage work for you, scrutinize your work style and rank everything according to how frequently you use it. Then organize your office so that hot items are close at hand and older accounts are most remote. Periodically purge the "dead" stuff completely.

Desktop Storage

I like to keep files for projects I am working on right now on top of my desk. Plastic file tubs work for this, but I prefer a combination of vertical divided units and open racks of the type used as inserts in metal filing cabinets. Consider also shelves or foot-wide desktop storage additions that come with a combination of shelves, drawers, and slots to get the most out of the rear part of your work surface.

Hard Copy Storage

For less active materials, don't default to standard vertical metal file cabinets until you have considered the options in light of the type of material you store.

• **Vertical filing cabinets.** These prevail as the workhorse of filing storage. Their big advantage is that they fit nicely under a horizontal work surface, leaving space for knees. On the downside, the stuff at the front of the drawers is much more accessible than that at the rear.

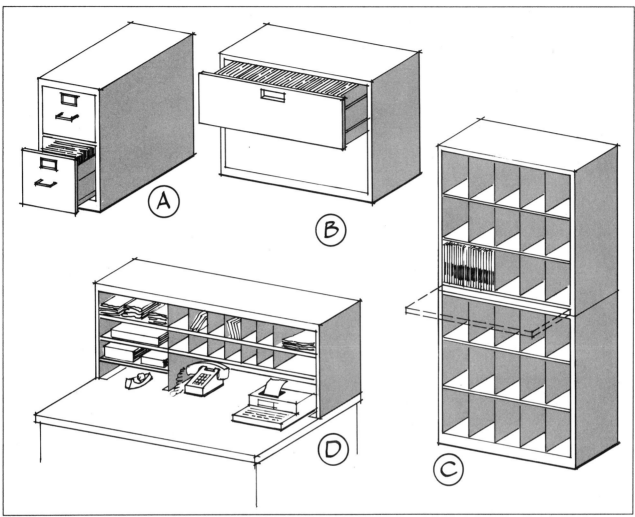

Figure 17-5: Storage Options. *Storage equipment comes in an endless variety to suit your needs.* **(A)** *Standard vertical filing cabinets accomodate letter- or legal-size files. Two-drawer units fit neatly under a work surface, whereas four-drawer units require separate floor space.* **(B)** *Horizontal filing cabinets allow easier file retrieval, but you'll have to leave their front uncluttered for access.* **(C)** *Medical file cabinets store files tabbed on the end for fast and simple re-trieval. Three-unit-high modular units fit atop one another or over a work surface. An optional pull-out shelf below each module provides a handy sorting surface. Magazine file cabinets, like medical file cabinets turned on their side, provide useful storage for pamphlets, journals, and brochures.* **(D)** *Desktop organizers can be fitted with shelves and slots to house a variety of diverse items you need ready access to.*

• **Lateral filing cabinets.** More expensive than vertical units for the same quality and size, lateral filing cabinets make all files equally accessible, at the sacrifice of space, because their largest face has to remain unobstructed for access.

• **Medical filing systems.** If you have many files that you need to retrieve immediately, this might be the system for you. Files tabbed on the ends stack vertically into an array of slots. The all-steel cabinets accommodate letter- or legal-size files and are modular for stacking above one another. An optional pull-out shelf allows you to set down files while placing or retrieving.

• **Literature organizers.** Turn the medical filing system on its side and you have an array of horizontal slots to store papers, pamphlets, brochures, or documents. These steel cabinets also come in modular sizes for stacking two or three high.

Soft Copy Storage

Storage for computer media won't eat up much space, but needs care. A wide variety of plastic and metal storage cabinets are available for 5¼", 3½", and ROM disks. You can store them on top of your work surface, or on shelves below or above. But remember to keep them away from anything with a magnet, including refrigerator magnets, speakers, or headphones. Also, it's wise to store permanent and irreplaceable disks in a secure location, such as a safe-deposit box.

Selecting each piece of furniture and equipment with attention to how it works within your total office system will help you minimize redundancies and contradictions. And you will gain the quiet satisfaction of having designed a system tuned to your own specific needs.

PART FIVE

FROM PLAN TO ACTION

CHAPTER 18

WHAT WILL IT ALL COST?

When my writer friend, Dennis, left his position as a magazine editor to become a full-time freelancer, he had already been banging out occasional freelance stories nights and weekends, working out of a small storage room in his basement. He reasoned that this space would work just as well for full-time service.

The arrangement worked at first, but it wasn't long before the walls started to close in. And it lacked storage space. Dennis's eyes glowed with envy when he first saw my office. I planned and executed it from the beginning, with a space for everything and space to grow.

Like Dennis, many professionals simply turn a weekend workspace into a full-time base of operations, assuming there won't be additional costs or that they can meet the costs as they arise.

ESTIMATING BASICS

Well, things always have a way of costing more than you expect. Why be victim to the unknown when a little cost planning at the outset can give you a handle on the costs? You can use the handle to establish an overhead budget and assign priorities, create a business plan, and go after financing.

You aren't the government. An overrun in your expected startup costs might well put you in Chapter 11. Reliable unit cost data can enable you to peg your costs to within 5% or 10% of the actual costs. This chapter contains worksheets to enable you to list and estimate the expense of converting a spare room, attic, basement, porch, or outbuilding into an office, or building an addition onto your home. Another worksheet combines these construction costs with costs common to all home offices—furnishings, equipment, site work, supplies—to arrive at a total figure you can use for the "things" portion of your startup expenses.

Whether you are estimating the cost of your weekly groceries or the cost of building a home office addition, the process really comes down to five steps:

1. Identify each item that costs.
2. Assign a quantifiable unit to each item, such as "each," "square feet," "pounds," etc.
3. Quantify the units of each item.
4. Multiply each quantity by an assumed unit cost.
5. Add up the line-item totals for a grand total.

The process is simple and straightforward for some things, more complicated for others. You can quickly estimate the cost of items you can buy through mail-order catalogs, even with an additional amount thrown in for shipping and handling.

Getting an accurate fix on the construction costs will be harder on several counts. In addition to the variations in costs you can expect from different suppliers, there may be rapid price fluctuations with time. But the real stumbling block is accurately forecasting quantities, especially with remodeling. Can you really predict how many $2'' \times 4''$s you'll need?

For this reason, you may want to turn this task over to a consultant. If you have plans drawn in sufficient detail to describe your project, builders, architects, or home designers could estimate the costs for the price of their time. Or, you can request the estimate from a builder in the form of a bid; in this case you will get it without cost, but don't do this unless you intend to enter into an agreement with this contractor (or the lowest qualified bidder, if you are soliciting quotes from more than one).

The construction cost worksheets that follow are for those of you who would like to spend the time and effort to estimate your own project (and those who want to get a preliminary idea of construction costs before dealing with a contractor).

THE CONSTRUCTION COST WORKSHEETS

A new stairway probably won't figure into a porch conversion. But you may have to beef up the porch's foundation, which you wouldn't have to do if you are converting an attic space. To account for these and other differences, a separate worksheet follows for spare rooms, attics, porches, outbuildings, and additions. At first glance the worksheets might seem overwhelming. You may have neither the time nor interest to estimate every $2'' \times 4''$ or square foot of wallcovering that may make up the construction portion of your total costs. In that case, get a contractor's bid or buy some consulting time from a building professional.

The Construction Cost Estimate (Worksheets

18-1 through 18-7, starting on page 167) is similar to forms architects and contractors use to estimate all jobs, except that the line items listed have been preselected to suit the kind of area you will be remodeling. Additional spaces allow you to fill in items particular to your project. Use this method only if you have a fair understanding of exactly what your project will require and some experience with remodeling.

The estimate is organized by building components (line items) in the approximate sequence in which they occur in the construction process. Five columns at the right combine data into a total cost for each line item.

In the first column, DIY/C, indicate whether the unit cost is based on you doing the work (DIY = do it yourself) or hiring a contractor (C). List the quantity in the second column. In the third column, "unit," indicate what unit the quantity refers to, such as square feet (SF), lineal feet (LF), single units (E = each), or other units.

Enter the cost for each unit in the third column (more about where to get unit costs in the next section). Then multiply the quantity times the unit cost to get the total construction cost for each line item. Though tedious, the line-item method enables you to see where your heavy costs lie and make substitutions to bring them into line with your budget. If you have a computer with a spreadsheet program and are adept at using it, you can import the form onto a spreadsheet with the appropriate line-item formulas and a formula to sum the totals. When set up, you can make numerous revisions and iterations and get an instant bottom line total each time.

TRACKING DOWN UNIT COSTS

When reliable unit costs are at hand, the rest of the process is fairly mechanical. But tracking down reliable unit costs takes time. Here are some ways to get them.

Construction Costs

Construction costs change constantly. Building professionals depend on computerized data bases and annually published figures (such as those by the R. S. Means Co. and others listed in the appendix). These are not cheap, but you may be able to borrow one through a library. The *Means Repair & Remodeling Cost Data* book should be the most useful volume published by R. S. Means. It contains thousands of line-item costs organized in the same sequence as the Construction Cost Estimate worksheets at the end of this chapter. If you will be doing the work yourself, use only the line-item costs under the heading "materials." For work you will hire out, use the last cost figure (at right), "Total incl. O&P" (total including contractor's overhead and profit).

For anything not listed in the Means or other data base, call local specialty subcontractors listed in the yellow pages. Never ask for a quote for your project unless there's a chance you will hire them for the work. Instead, describe your project and ask for approximate square-foot costs you can use for a preliminary estimate.

Equipment and Supplies

Your quickest source is mail-order catalogs for office and electronic equipment supplies (several are listed in the appendix). Be sure to allow for shipping and handling charges. Can you live without new stuff? If so, visit a used office equipment outlet. You may be pleasantly surprised to find that you can save bundles on certain items of furniture and equipment.

Other Startup Costs

Fees, licenses, insurance, and other costs of starting a business vary with location and the type of business. Unless you are starting a new business as well as establishing a home office, you probably already have a handle on these costs. If not, your best source of information might be your professional network—your professional or trade society and acquaintances you can call on for advice.

THE SUMMARY SHEET

Worksheet 18-7, Summary of Costs, breaks down your setup costs into six categories: construction, furnishings, equipment, supplies, and other startup costs. In the subtotal box for Category 1, Construction, enter the total construction cost you got from one of the previous worksheets or from a contractor or consultant. Fill in the line-items for the other five categories in much the same method suggested for the construction cost worksheets. The sum of the subtotals should give you a reasonable approximation of your home office startup costs.

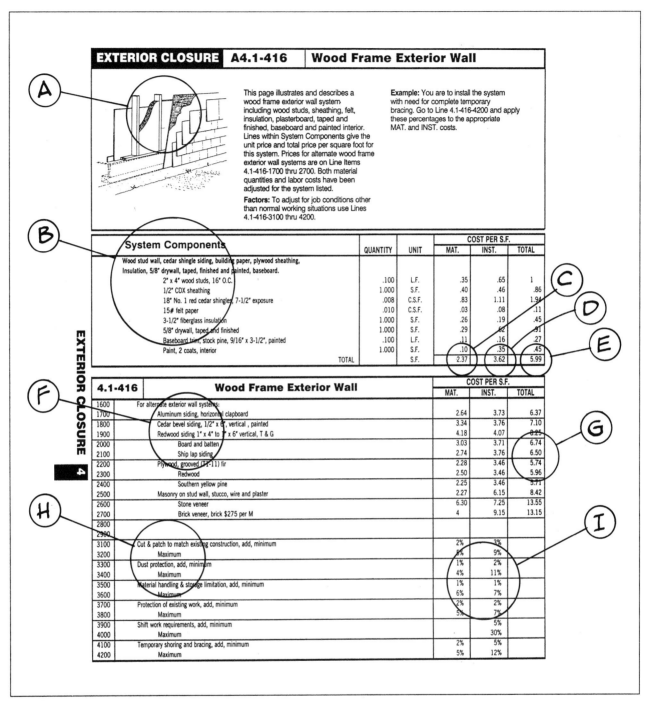

EXTERIOR CLOSURE	A4.1-416	Wood Frame Exterior Wall

This page illustrates and describes a wood frame exterior wall system including wood studs, sheathing, felt, insulation, plasterboard, taped and finished, baseboard and painted interior. Lines within System Components give the unit price and total price per square foot for this system. Prices for alternate wood frame exterior wall systems are on Line Items 4.1-416-1700 thru 2700. Both material quantities and labor costs have been adjusted for the system listed.

Factors: To adjust for job conditions other than normal working situations use Lines 4.1-416-3100 thru 4200.

Example: You are to install the system with need for complete temporary bracing. Go to Line 4.1-416-4200 and apply these percentages to the appropriate MAT. and INST. costs.

System Components	QUANTITY	UNIT	MAT.	INST.	TOTAL
Wood stud wall, cedar shingle siding, building paper, plywood sheathing, Insulation, 5/8" drywall, taped, finished and painted, baseboard.					
2" x 4" wood studs, 16" O.C.	.100	L.F.	.35	.65	1
1/2" CDX sheathing	1.000	S.F.	.40	.46	.86
18" No. 1 red cedar shingles, 7-1/2" exposure	.008	C.S.F.	.83	1.11	1.94
15# felt paper	.010	C.S.F.	.03	.08	.11
3-1/2" fiberglass insulation	1.000	S.F.	.26	.19	.45
5/8" drywall, taped and finished	1.000	S.F.	.29	.62	.91
Baseboard trim, stock pine, 9/16" x 3-1/2", painted	.100	L.F.	.11	.16	.27
Paint, 2 coats, interior	1.000	S.F.	.10	.35	.45
TOTAL		S.F.	2.37	3.62	5.99

COST PER S.F.

4.1-416	Wood Frame Exterior Wall	MAT.	INST.	TOTAL
1600	For alternate exterior wall systems:			
1700	Aluminum siding, horizontal clapboard	2.64	3.73	6.37
1800	Cedar bevel siding, 1/2" x 6", vertical , painted	3.34	3.76	7.10
1900	Redwood siding 1" x 4" to 1" x 6" vertical, T & G	4.18	4.07	8.25
2000	Board and batten	3.03	3.71	6.74
2100	Ship lap siding	2.74	3.76	6.50
2200	Plywood, grooved (T1-11) fir	2.28	3.46	5.74
2300	Redwood	2.50	3.46	5.96
2400	Southern yellow pine	2.25	3.46	5.71
2500	Masonry on stud wall, stucco, wire and plaster	2.27	6.15	8.42
2600	Stone veneer	6.30	7.25	13.55
2700	Brick veneer, brick $275 per M	4	9.15	13.15
2800				
2900				
3100	Cut & patch to match existing construction, add, minimum	2%	3%	
3200	Maximum	6%	9%	
3300	Dust protection, add, minimum	1%	2%	
3400	Maximum	4%	11%	
3500	Material handling & storage limitation, add, minimum	1%	1%	
3600	Maximum	6%	7%	
3700	Protection of existing work, add, minimum	2%	2%	
3800	Maximum	5%	7%	
3900	Shift work requirements, add, minimum		5%	
4000	Maximum		30%	
4100	Temporary shoring and bracing, add, minimum	2%	5%	
4200	Maximum	5%	12%	

Figure 18-1: Estimating Data Base—Whole Systems.
Annually updated data bases such as the Means Repair & Remodeling Cost Data *enable you to estimate construction costs by whole systems or individual components. In the wood-framed wall system pictured (**A**), the components are described (**B**), followed by their material cost (**C**) and cost of installation (**D**). If you are doing the work yourself, subtract the installation cost. The total (**E**) is the cost of each square foot of wall. You can adjust the system using the options in (**F**) for new total unit costs (**G**). Additional fine tuning factors are listed (**H**) with the percentages to be added to the unit cost (**I**). Used by permission.*

061 | Rough Carpentry

061 100 | Wood Framing

		CREW	DAILY OUTPUT	MAN-HOURS	UNIT	MAT.	LABOR	EQUIP.	TOTAL	TOTAL INCL O&P	
138	1002	16" O.C.	F-2	90	.178	L.F.	4.62	4.15	.18	8.95	12.25	138
	1102	24" O.C.		115	.139		3.52	3.25	.14	6.91	9.50	
	1182	12' high, studs 12" O.C.		55	.291		6.60	6.80	.30	13.70	18.95	
	1202	16" O.C.		70	.229		5.30	5.35	.24	10.89	14.95	
	1302	24" O.C.		90	.178		3.96	4.15	.18	8.29	11.50	
	1402	For horizontal blocking, 2" x 4", add		600	.027		.30	.62	.03	.95	1.40	
	1502	2" x 6", add		600	.027		.44	.62	.03	1.09	1.55	
	1600	For openings, add		250	.064			1.49	.07	1.56	2.57	
	1702	Headers for above openings, material only, add				B.F.	.60			.60	.66	
	9000	Minimum labor/equipment charge	1 Carp	4	2	Job		46.50		46.50	78	
140	0010	ROUGH HARDWARE Average % of carpentry material, minimum					.50%					140
	0200	Maximum					1.50%					

061 150 | Sheathing

		CREW	DAILY OUTPUT	MAN-HOURS	UNIT	MAT.	LABOR	EQUIP.	TOTAL	TOTAL INCL O&P	
154	0010	SHEATHING Plywood on roof, CDX										154
	0032	5/16" thick [R061-020]	F-2	1,600	.010	S.F.	.28	.23	.01	.52	.71	
	0052	3/8" thick [R061-030]		1,525	.010		.30	.24	.01	.55	.75	
	0102	1/2" thick		1,400	.011		.36	.27	.01	.64	.86	
	0202	5/8" thick		1,300	.012		.42	.29	.01	.72	.95	
	0302	3/4" thick		1,200	.013		.55	.31	.01	.87	1.15	
	0502	Plywood on walls with exterior CDX, 3/8" thick		1,200	.013		.30	.31	.01	.62	.87	
	0602	1/2" thick		1,125	.014		.36	.33	.01	.70	.97	
	0702	5/8" thick		1,050	.015		.42	.36	.02	.80	1.07	
	0802	3/4" thick		975	.016		.55	.38	.02	.95	1.27	
	1000	For shear wall construction, add						20%				
	1200	For structural 1 exterior plywood, add					10%					
	1402	With boards, on roof 1" x 6" boards, laid horizontal	F-2	725	.022		.70	.52	.02	1.24	1.65	
	1502	Laid diagonal		650	.025		.70	.57	.03	1.30	1.76	
	1702	1" x 8" boards, laid horizontal		875	.018		.70	.43	.02	1.15	1.66	
	1802	Laid diagonal		725	.022		.70	.52	.02	1.24	1.65	
	2000	For steep roofs, add						40%				
	2200	For dormers, hips and valleys, add					5%	50%				
	2402	Boards on walls, 1" x 6" boards, laid regular	F-2	650	.025		.70	.57	.03	1.30	1.76	
	2502	Laid diagonal		585	.027		.70	.64	.03	1.37	1.87	
	2702	1" x 8" boards, laid regular		765	.021		.70	.49	.02	1.21	1.61	
	2802	Laid diagonal		650	.025		.70	.57	.03	1.30	1.76	
	2852	Gypsum, weatherproof, 1/2" thick		1,050	.015		.33	.36	.02	.71	.97	
	2902	Sealed, 4/10" thick		1,100	.015		.31	.34	.01	.66	.93	
	3000	Wood fiber, regular, no vapor barrier, 1/2" thick		1,200	.013		.36	.31	.01	.68	.94	
	3100	5/8" thick		1,200	.013		.47	.31	.01	.79	1.06	
	3300	No vapor barrier, in colors, 1/2" thick		1,200	.013		.51	.31	.01	.83	1.10	
	3400	5/8" thick		1,200	.013		.62	.31	.01	.94	1.22	
	3600	With vapor barrier one side, white, 1/2" thick		1,200	.013		.50	.31	.01	.82	1.08	
	3700	Vapor barrier 2 sides		1,200	.013		.78	.31	.01	1.10	1.39	
	3800	Asphalt impregnated, 25/32" thick		1,200	.013		.31	.31	.01	.63	.88	
	3850	Intermediate, 1/2" thick		1,200	.013		.27	.31	.01	.59	.84	
	9000	Minimum labor/equipment charge	1 Carp	2	4	Job		93.50		93.50	156	

061 160 | Subfloor

		CREW	DAILY OUTPUT	MAN-HOURS	UNIT	MAT.	LABOR	EQUIP.	TOTAL	TOTAL INCL O&P	
161	0010	FLOORING, WOOD See division 095-604										161
164	0012	SUBFLOOR Plywood, CDX, 1/2" thick [R061-020]	F-2	1,500	.011	SF Flr.	.36	.25	.01	.62	.83	164
	0102	5/8" thick		1,350	.012		.42	.28	.01	.71	.93	
	0202	3/4" thick		1,250	.013		.55	.30	.01	.86	1.12	
	0302	1-1/8" thick, 2-4-1 including underlayment		1,050	.015		.99	.36	.02	1.37	1.70	

WOOD AND PLASTICS 6

Figure 18-2: Estimating Data Base — Components. *You could also use the* Means *guide to estimate the wall system of Figure 18-1, item by item. Beginning by finding the section dealing with the outer skin, the sheathing* **(A)**, *locate the type you want to use* **(B)**. *Column* **(C)** *tells the unit, in this case S.F., or square feet. The material cost* **(D)** *and labor (installation) cost* **(E)** *combine for a total unit cost* **(F)**. *Use this total minus the labor cost if you are doing the work yourself. The total in column* **(G)** *represents the total with the contractor's overhead and profit figured in. Used by permission.*

Worksheet 18-1

CONSTRUCTION COSTS: SPARE ROOM OFFICES

	DIY/ Contr.	Quantity	Unit	Unit Cost	Total
Doors and Windows					
New outside entrance	——	——	——	——	——
New or replacement windows	——	——	——	——	——
_____	——	——	——	——	——
_____	——	——	——	——	——
New Interior Partitions	——	——	——	——	——
Floor, Wall & Ceiling Finishes					
Painted walls and ceilings	——	——	——	——	——
Tackboard surfaces	——	——	——	——	——
Vertical writing surfaces	——	——	——	——	——
Carpeting	——	——	——	——	——
Resilient floor covering	——	——	——	——	——
_____	——	——	——	——	——
_____	——	——	——	——	——
Heating/Cooling/Air-conditioning					
Extending ducts/heating lines	——	——	——	——	——
Unit heater/air conditioner	——	——	——	——	——
_____	——	——	——	——	——
_____	——	——	——	——	——
Plumbing					
New sink	——	——	——	——	——
_____	——	——	——	——	——
Electrical					
Surface wiring	——	——	——	——	——
Wiring/rewiring	——	——	——	——	——
Light fixtures	——	——	——	——	——
_____	——	——	——	——	——
_____	——	——	——	——	——
Misc. Other					
_____	——	——	——	——	——
_____	——	——	——	——	——
_____	——	——	——	——	——
_____	——	——	——	——	——
_____	——	——	——	——	——

Total _____

Worksheet 18-2

CONSTRUCTION COSTS: ATTICS AND LOFTS

	DIY/ Contr.	Quantity	Unit	Unit Cost	Total

Floor Structure Upgrades
New framing & subfloor
Insulation

_____

_____

_____

_____

Exterior Walls
Framing & drywall
Insulation

_____

_____

_____

_____

Interior Partitions

_____

_____

_____

_____

Roof/Ceiling Improvements
Additional framing
Ceiling enclosure
Roofing/reroofing
Dormer window units
Skylights

_____

_____

_____

_____

Ladders or Stairways

_____

_____

_____

Windows

_____

_____

_____

Doors

_____

‗‗‗‗‗‗‗‗‗‗

Floor, Wall & Ceiling Finishes
Painted walls and ceilings

‗‗‗‗‗‗‗‗‗‗
‗‗‗‗‗‗‗‗‗‗
‗‗‗‗‗‗‗‗‗‗

Tackboard surfaces
Vertical writing surfaces
Wood flooring
Other floor covering

‗‗‗‗‗‗‗‗‗‗
‗‗‗‗‗‗‗‗‗‗

Heating/Cooling/Air-conditioning
Extending ducts or heating lines
Unit heater/air conditioner

‗‗‗‗‗‗‗‗‗‗
‗‗‗‗‗‗‗‗‗‗
‗‗‗‗‗‗‗‗‗‗

Plumbing
New sink
New toilet

‗‗‗‗‗‗‗‗‗‗
‗‗‗‗‗‗‗‗‗‗

Electrical
Surface wiring
Wiring/rewiring
Light fixtures

‗‗‗‗‗‗‗‗‗‗
‗‗‗‗‗‗‗‗‗‗

Misc. Other

‗‗‗‗‗‗‗‗‗‗
‗‗‗‗‗‗‗‗‗‗
‗‗‗‗‗‗‗‗‗‗
‗‗‗‗‗‗‗‗‗‗
‗‗‗‗‗‗‗‗‗‗
‗‗‗‗‗‗‗‗‗‗
‗‗‗‗‗‗‗‗‗‗
‗‗‗‗‗‗‗‗‗‗
‗‗‗‗‗‗‗‗‗‗
‗‗‗‗‗‗‗‗‗‗

| **Total** | ‗‗‗‗ |

Worksheet 18-3

CONSTRUCTION COSTS: BASEMENT OFFICES

	DIY/ Contr.	Quantity	Unit	Unit Cost	Total
Floor Improvements					
Wood sleepers/plywood	___	___	___	___	___
Cementitious floor leveling	___	___	___	___	___
_____	___	___	___	___	___
_____	___	___	___	___	___
_____	___	___	___	___	___
Foundation Wall Improvements					
New insulated inner studwall	___	___	___	___	___
_____	___	___	___	___	___
_____	___	___	___	___	___
_____	___	___	___	___	___
_____	___	___	___	___	___
Interior Partitions					
_____	___	___	___	___	___
_____	___	___	___	___	___
_____	___	___	___	___	___
_____	___	___	___	___	___
Ceiling Improvements					
Ceiling enclosure	___	___	___	___	___
_____	___	___	___	___	___
_____	___	___	___	___	___
_____	___	___	___	___	___
Stairways					
_____	___	___	___	___	___
_____	___	___	___	___	___
_____	___	___	___	___	___
Basement Window Improvements					
Replacement windows	___	___	___	___	___
_____	___	___	___	___	___
_____	___	___	___	___	___
_____	___	___	___	___	___
Floor, Wall & Ceiling Finishes					
Painted walls and ceilings	___	___	___	___	___
Tackboard surfaces	___	___	___	___	___
Vertical writing surfaces	___	___	___	___	___
Painted concrete slab	___	___	___	___	___
Other floor covering	___	___	___	___	___
_____	___	___	___	___	___
_____	___	___	___	___	___
_____	___	___	___	___	___

Heating/Cooling/Air-conditioning
Extending ducts or heating lines
Unit heater/air conditioner

_____

_____

_____

Plumbing
New sink
New toilet

_____

_____

_____

Electrical
Surface wiring
Wiring/rewiring
Light fixtures

_____

_____

_____

Misc. Other

_____

_____

_____

_____

_____

_____

_____

_____

_____

_____

_____

_____

_____

_____

_____

_____

| **Total** | _____ |

Worksheet 18-4

CONSTRUCTION COSTS: PORCH OFFICES

	DIY/ Contr.	Quantity	Unit	Unit Cost	Total
Foundation Work					
Concrete piers/footings	___	___	___	___	___
_____	___	___	___	___	___
_____	___	___	___	___	___
_____	___	___	___	___	___
Floor Structure Upgrades					
New framing & subfloor	___	___	___	___	___
Insulation	___	___	___	___	___
_____	___	___	___	___	___
_____	___	___	___	___	___
_____	___	___	___	___	___
_____	___	___	___	___	___
Exterior Walls					
New exterior studwalls, complete	___	___	___	___	___
_____	___	___	___	___	___
_____	___	___	___	___	___
_____	___	___	___	___	___
_____	___	___	___	___	___
Insulation	___	___	___	___	___
Drywall	___	___	___	___	___
_____	___	___	___	___	___
_____	___	___	___	___	___
_____	___	___	___	___	___
_____	___	___	___	___	___
Roof/Ceiling Improvements					
Additional framing	___	___	___	___	___
Ceiling enclosure	___	___	___	___	___
Roofing/reroofing	___	___	___	___	___
Insulation	___	___	___	___	___
_____	___	___	___	___	___
_____	___	___	___	___	___
_____	___	___	___	___	___
_____	___	___	___	___	___
Interior Partitions					
_____	___	___	___	___	___
_____	___	___	___	___	___
_____	___	___	___	___	___
Doors and Windows					
New outside entrance	___	___	___	___	___
Windows	___	___	___	___	___

——————————————

Floor, Wall & Ceiling Finishes
Painted walls and ceilings
Tackboard surfaces
Vertical writing surfaces
Wood flooring
Other floor covering

——————————————

Heating/Cooling/Air-conditioning
Extending ducts/heating lines
Unit heater/air conditioner

——————————————

Electrical
Surface wiring
Wiring/rewiring
Light fixtures

——————————————

Misc. Other

——————————————

| Total | _____ |

Worksheet 18-5

CONSTRUCTION COSTS: OFFICES IN OUTBUILDINGS

	DIY/ Contr.	Quantity	Unit	Unit Cost	Total

Floor Improvements
Wood sleepers/plywood
Cementitious floor leveling
New wood floor
New concrete floor

Exterior Wall Improvements
Framing & drywall
Insulation

Interior Partitions

Roof/Ceiling Improvements
Additional framing
Ceiling enclosure
Roofing/reroofing
Dormer window units
Skylights

Ladders or Stairways

Windows

Doors

_____

_____

Floor, Wall & Ceiling Finishes
Painted walls and ceilings
Tackboard surfaces
Vertical writing surfaces
Wood flooring
Other floor covering

_____

_____

_____

_____

Heating/Cooling/Air-conditioning
Extending ducts or heating lines
Unit heater/air conditioner

_____

_____

Plumbing
New sink
New toilet

_____

_____

_____

Electrical
Extend wiring from house
New panel boxes
Surface wiring
Wiring/rewiring
Light fixtures

_____

_____

_____

Misc. Other

_____

_____

_____

_____

_____

| Total | _____ |

Worksheet 18-6

CONSTRUCTION COSTS: ADDITIONS

	DIY/ Contr.	Quantity	Unit	Unit Cost	Total
Foundation					
Excavation	_____	_____	_____	_____	_____
Full basement foundation	_____	_____	_____	_____	_____
Crawl space foundation	_____	_____	_____	_____	_____
Slab-on-grade foundation	_____	_____	_____	_____	_____
_____	_____	_____	_____	_____	_____
_____	_____	_____	_____	_____	_____
_____	_____	_____	_____	_____	_____
_____	_____	_____	_____	_____	_____
Floor					
Framed wood floor	_____	_____	_____	_____	_____
Slab on grade	_____	_____	_____	_____	_____
_____	_____	_____	_____	_____	_____
_____	_____	_____	_____	_____	_____
_____	_____	_____	_____	_____	_____
_____	_____	_____	_____	_____	_____
_____	_____	_____	_____	_____	_____
New Exterior Walls					
Wood-frame walls	_____	_____	_____	_____	_____
Brick veneer walls	_____	_____	_____	_____	_____
_____	_____	_____	_____	_____	_____
_____	_____	_____	_____	_____	_____
_____	_____	_____	_____	_____	_____
Roof/Ceiling					
Roof/ceiling system	_____	_____	_____	_____	_____
Dormer window units	_____	_____	_____	_____	_____
Skylights	_____	_____	_____	_____	_____
_____	_____	_____	_____	_____	_____
_____	_____	_____	_____	_____	_____
_____	_____	_____	_____	_____	_____
Interior Partitions	_____	_____	_____	_____	_____
_____	_____	_____	_____	_____	_____
_____	_____	_____	_____	_____	_____
_____	_____	_____	_____	_____	_____
_____	_____	_____	_____	_____	_____
Windows	_____	_____	_____	_____	_____
_____	_____	_____	_____	_____	_____
_____	_____	_____	_____	_____	_____
_____	_____	_____	_____	_____	_____

Doors
Exterior doors
Interior doors

_____

_____

Floor, Wall & Ceiling Finishes
Painted walls and ceilings
Tackboard surfaces
Vertical writing surfaces
Wood flooring
Other floor covering

_____

_____

_____

Heating/Cooling/Air-conditioning
Extending ducts or heating lines
Unit heater/air conditioner

_____

_____

Plumbing
Sink
Lavatory
Toilet

_____

_____

Electrical
Wiring
Light fixtures

_____

_____

Misc. Other

_____

_____

_____

_____

_____

_____

_____

| **Total** | _____ |

Worksheet 18-7

SUMMARY OF COSTS

	Quantity	Unit	Cost per Unit	Total Cost

1. Construction

(Total from Construction Cost
Worksheets or from outside source)

Subtotal #1, Construction:	_____

2. Furnishings

	Quantity	Unit	Cost per Unit	Total Cost
Desks	_____	E	_____	_____
Drafting tables	_____	E	_____	_____
Other tables	_____	E	_____	_____
Chairs, desk	_____	E	_____	_____
Chairs, conference/waiting	_____	E	_____	_____
Bookshelves	_____		_____	_____
Blinds/drapes/shutters	_____	E	_____	_____
_____	_____	_____	_____	_____
_____	_____	_____	_____	_____
_____	_____	_____	_____	_____
_____	_____	_____	_____	_____
_____	_____	_____	_____	_____

Subtotal #2, Furnishings:	_____

3. Equipment

	Quantity	Unit	Cost per Unit	Total Cost
Computers	_____	E	_____	_____
Printers	_____	E	_____	_____
Modems	_____	E	_____	_____
Other computer equipment	_____	_____	_____	_____
Telephones	_____	_____	_____	_____
Answering machines	_____	_____	_____	_____
Software	_____	_____	_____	_____
Copy machines	_____	_____	_____	_____
_____	_____	_____	_____	_____
_____	_____	_____	_____	_____
_____	_____	_____	_____	_____
_____	_____	_____	_____	_____
_____	_____	_____	_____	_____
_____	_____	_____	_____	_____
_____	_____	_____	_____	_____
_____	_____	_____	_____	_____
_____	_____	_____	_____	_____
_____	_____	_____	_____	_____

Subtotal #3, Equipment:	_____

4. Supplies
Paper
Pencils/pens
Computer disks

———	———	———	———	———

Subtotal #4, Supplies ———

5. Misc. Other Startup Costs
Fees & licenses
Insurance

Subtotal #5, Misc.: ———

Total Startup Costs ———

CHAPTER 19

GETTING BUILT

Now that you've planned your office, gotten a building permit, and arranged financing, you are ready to begin remodeling. You even know which parts of your project you will do yourself and which ones you'll hire out (if not, go back and read chapter 6). What's next?

If you intend to do it yourself, you can get out your tools and start buying materials. But even ardent do-it-yourselfers hire outside contractors for some things. To get quality work from contractors without getting stung, you should know your way around bids, estimates, contracts, and guarantees. All of these have legal implications. The advice I offer is from the vantage point of an architect. I strongly suggest that all bids, estimates, and contracts be in writing and that you have them reviewed by an attorney.

WORKING ARRANGEMENTS

Managing the Construction Work Yourself

For projects more complex than, say, putting up some wallboard and extra wiring, your first question might be how to coordinate the various trades to keep the work moving smoothly along. You wouldn't want to have to pay the framers to stand around waiting for the foundation to be poured, or for the electricians to twiddle their pliers while the framers put up the studs.

If you have the expertise, time, interest, and patience, you can manage your own project. Acting as your own general contractor is a feasible approach if you have only one or two other trades to coordinate, but daunting if there will be many different trades. Before assuming this mantle, ask yourself if you feel qualified to:

- Find qualified subcontractors.
- Prepare contracts.
- Schedule the work of each subcontractor in the proper sequence and with minimal conflicts.
- Inspect the work of subcontractors and know what to look for.
- Process any changes in the work.
- Pay subcontractors for work completed, but not for work still to be done.

If you don't feel up to taking on any of these responsibilities, the next approach may be better.

Hiring a Contractor to Manage the Work

The easiest way to coordinate the various trades on your project is to hire a general contractor to manage the entire project. There are two ways to do this:

- Hire subcontractors independently, but entrust their coordination and management to a general contractor who acts as project manager. This person will do the scheduling, coordinating, and paying of subcontractors. The project manager may charge a fee amounting to 15% to 30% of the total construction cost.

• Contract with the general contractor to take complete responsibility for all aspects of the project under one of the contractual arrangements described next. You will deal only with the general contractor, who will oversee and administer the subcontractors.

CONTRACTS

However you choose to get the work done on your project, I can't overemphasize the importance of a written contract. For one specialty contractor to do a simple, straightforward job—such as putting in a unit heater—a contract may be as simple as a single-page proposal describing the materials, labor, and guarantee. You can add language to amend or flesh out the contract, if necessary. If you hire a general contractor to take on the whole project (method 2 above), you need something more elaborate. Lump-sum and cost-plus-fee contracts are the most common for this type of project.

Lump-Sum Contracts

Lump-sum (or fixed-fee) contracts guarantee that the contractor will do the work agreed to for one price. This is the best arrangement for you, if you can define the project adequately at the outset. You should have a good set of drawings and specifications that leave few unanswered questions.

But even with a lump-sum contract, the inevitable happens. Unforeseen conditions lurk in all remodeling work, so be prepared to accommodate changes, which usually means additional work that increases the cost of the contract. It's a rare occasion when change orders result in reductions to the original contract amount (more about changes later on).

Cost-Plus-Fee Contracts

All remodeling is a flight into the unknown. Even with good plans and specifications, it may not be possible to accurately pin down the exact extent of the work. Cost-plus-fee contracts suit projects with many unknowns. You agree to pay the contractor on the basis of the costs of material and labor, as documented by receipts, plus a fee to cover overhead and profit. The 15% to 30% fee is the same fee that you pay in a lump-sum contract, but with a lump-sum you don't see it as a separate item. This form of agreement is always to the contractor's advantage, so don't use it if you don't have to.

What to Include in Your Contract

A good contract for construction should name each party to the agreement, the date of signing, and spell out the following items:

• A description of all work to be included (may say "as described in the plans and specifications" or list in detail the products and materials to be used)
• The date of commencement and completion, if time is of the essence
• The total sum (if lump-sum contract) or fee (if cost-plus-fee contract)
• How progress payments are to be scheduled and the conditions for final payment
• A list of other documents that are part of the contract (plans and specifications)
• Statement on guarantees
• Insurance provisions
• Provisions for changes in the work

My favorite contract form for small projects is the *Abbreviated Form of Agreement Between Owner and Contractor* published by the American Institute of Architects (AIA) and available through AIA chapter offices in each major city. Request form number A107 for lump-sum contracts and form A117 for cost-plus-fee contracts. In addition to the clauses listed previously, these contract forms contain several pages of "general conditions" that clarify your responsibilities, and those of the contractor, as well as clauses describing subcontracts, changes in the work, time, payments, insurance, correction of unsatisfactory work, and contract termination provisions. Each contract form comes wrapped in a sheet of instructions, but you may need an attorney to help you tailor the contract to your project.

FINDING GOOD CONTRACTORS

Nothing beats word of mouth for finding an expert. When I'm looking around for qualified contractors for my clients I first cull through my file of "builders." If I come up short, I rely on the advice of other architects. You, too, can use your network. Do you know anyone who has recently had an addition built? Do you know someone who regularly deals with contractors, such as architects, designers, engineers, real estate agents, or bankers? Just be sure your advice is objective.

Most professionals who deal with builders will probably be happy to suggest a few competent ones, as long as you understand that they are in no position to make guarantees. Or, you might get some decent leads from lumberyards; they at least can tell you which contractors are busy. Some home-improvement books suggest calling trade associations, but doing so will likely get you a list of their members, and not much else.

One home improvement writer, Tom Philben, thinks contractors who advertise on radio, TV, or print media are tainted. "The yellow pages always struck me as a crazy place from which to hire a contractor.... One would hardly get a heart surgeon, or even an endodontist, from the yellow pages."[1] Maybe so, but this strikes me as a bit too harsh if you're trying to track down leads. Use the yellow pages only as a starting point, then make your final decision on the basis of a personal interview.

After you have found at least three contractors, phone them to briefly describe your project and schedule and ask if they would be interested in bidding on it. If so, invite them to come to your home for an interview. Serious, competent builders will happily agree to this, although you might have to bend a bit to their schedule, partic-

ularly if they are busy (a good sign).

The initial interview has two goals:

1. Informing the contractor about your project and expectations
2. Acquainting you with the contractor's personality and qualifications

The first goal is the reason you should have the meeting on your turf. The contractor can look over the actual site of the project to get a feel for the real scope of work.

Begin the meeting by going through your plans. Here's where you'll be miles ahead if you have professionally prepared plans rather than something scratched out on the back of an envelope. Good drawings and specifications define the work so that very few decisions are left to the builder. Answer any questions the contractor may have, explain your schedule, when work can begin, and what hours of the day the contractor will have full access to the site. The more completely you can describe the project, the more accurate the bid will be and there will be fewer surprises during construction.

Next comes your turn to find out about the bidder. Ask if the company is licensed, how long it has been in business, and request a list of recent customers you can contact for references. Ask about complaints. Every contractor receives them, so what you need to know is their nature and how the contractor handles them. Here are some questions to ask the contractor:

- Has your firm ever failed to complete any project? If so, why?
- Do you have any judgments, claims, arbitrations, or suits outstanding against you or your firm?
- Have you sued or requested arbitration with any client within the last 5 years?

You can also check complaints outstanding against contractors by contacting your Better Business Bureau, but I wouldn't expect much help here.

If you will be doing much of the work yourself, you will naturally want to discuss how your work will mesh with the contractor's. If your personal chemistry doesn't blend, your work probably won't either.

Finally, ask about the bidder's financial footing, that is, whether that person can obtain insurance to cover personal injury, property damage, worker's compensation. Say you will require written confirmation of these later, if you enter into agreement.

GETTING BIDS

After interviewing several contractors, prepare a short list of bidders. For home remodeling and additions, I think three is the minimum and anything more than six counterproductive. Give each bidder a set of plans and specifications (or an equivalent detailed description of the work to be included) and a list of items you expect to be included with the bid. A bid form provides a systematic way to do this and ensures that you will be comparing apples to apples. Include the following items:

- Your name and address and the name and address of your project
- How long the bid will remain valid
- Reference to the plans and specifications, including their date
- Record of any addenda (changes issued to the bidders before their bid is due)
- A general description of the work (if there are plans and specifications to describe the work in detail) or detailed description, if not
- The lump sum price, or fee (if cost-plus-fee arrangement)
- Description of any alternates, along with a space for the cost of each
- A space for the bidder to indicate how long the project will take to complete
- Who to contact for clarifications about the project (you or your architect)

Give your bidders at least two weeks to figure their bids; they will be under the crunch of time pulling together bids from their subcontractors.

When you have all bids in hand, open them privately (or with your designer). If you are confident the lowest bidder can do the work, pass on the news over the phone. Tell that person he or she is the lowest bidder and you intend to sign on, pending verification of financial qualifications and making any adjustments to the contract that may have come along in the bidding period. Along with bank references, request a financial statement that lists the firm's current assets, liabilities, and name of agent who prepared the statement.

Call the other bidders to thank them for their efforts. It's up to you as to whether or not you tell them the amounts of any other bids. I usually do. The information may help them with future bids and will be the only thing they get out of their time and effort.

CONSTRUCTION

When you are satisfied that your low bidder is financially able to complete your project, complete and sign the contract for construction. Make sure copies of any insurance required by the contractor are appended to the contract. After obtaining a building permit, which is usually the contractor's responsibility, you are off and running.

The contractor should submit a payment schedule early on to show how the total amount is divided up for the various trades. Each invoice should detail the actual work completed under each category and the percentage of the total, providing a constant check of the job's progress against money paid out. Though an up-front payment of 10% to 20% of the total isn't amiss to pay for the contractor's initial materials, you don't want the cash paid out to get ahead of the work completed. It is common to withhold up to 10% of the total value of completed work (called retainage) until the end of the project to cover you in this regard. If you are working with an architect or designer, their responsibility can include reviewing the contractor's payment requests.

Who's Watching?

Besides checking the progress of the project against the contractor's payment requests, someone other than the general contractor should keep an eye on the progress of the work to answer questions about the intent of the drawings or specs and ensure that the quality is consistent with the contract. If you don't feel confident of this, arrange to extend your designer's services to include "construction observation." Your designer should visit the site periodically to observe the progress of construction and act as your agent in resolving issues that come up with the contractor. If this service is not included in the designer's basic fee, it can be arranged on an agreed-on hourly rate.

Handling Changes

The first rule of remodeling is: Always expect changes. You can never accurately predict what you will find when you tear into the existing structure. I call this the "law of the missing substrate." It works like this: You're pulling up the planks in your attic to install carpet and you notice a suspicious deposit on the sides of some of the joists. A few pokes with a screwdriver reveals termites. You end up replacing the floor boards as well as several joists.

Which leads to the second rule of remodeling: The changes caused by the first rule always end up adding to the construction cost. If the change comes within the contractor's purview, ask for a written estimate of the change before giving the go-ahead, even if it slows the progress of the job. When you get the estimate, you have to evaluate whether it is fair; this is another reason to keep your designer on board through the construction phase. If you are flying solo, you might ask another builder for an opinion, though this can get sticky.

All changes, of course, don't necessarily arise from construction contingencies. You should allow some kind of cushion, say 5% to 10% above the amount of the contract, for changes you may want to make for your own reasons.

THE END GAME

As your project nears completion, the contractor will want to close out the books and ask for a final inspection. Schedule an inspection with the contractor and your designer (if you have retained one for this phase). Record any incomplete or defective work on a "punch list."

The contractor will notify you again when the punch list has been completed, and another inspection will ensue. Hopefully, you'll clear everything this time, but you may have to play another round or more. No new deficiencies should be discovered on the second inspection. Because contractors have by this time collected most of the contract amount, they may not feel the urgency to square final details. All you can do is hang onto the retainage, cajole, and coerce until you are satisfied that the work is complete as agreed to. Then you can sign off and pay out the retainage.

Finally, the day comes when you move in and set up your equipment. This is an exciting milestone. When the newness wears off, you'll realize the point of all your time and efforts was to create a space for your work. Then you'll be able to get down to business.

My space has changed several times since I moved in, constantly evolving with my changing needs and equipment. Fortunately, the design was flexible enough to allow for change. I hope this book will help your home office venture work as well for you, your business, and your home.

References

Chapter 2

1. "Which Remodelings Pay Off?" *Better Homes and Gardens*, Winter 1989-90.

2. "Home Improvement, Home Investment," *Home Mechanix*, September 1993: 51-61.

3. Sherry Harowitz, "Home Improvements Worth the Price," *Changing Times*, October 1990: 67-71.

4. Lani Luciano, "How Remodelers Can Avoid Some Tax Hikes," *Money*, July 1992: 30.

5. Paul and Sarah Edwards, *Working from Home: Everything You Need to Know about Living and Working under the Same Roof* (Los Angeles: Jeremy P. Tarcher, 1990).

6. Ibid.

Chapter 3

1. Judith Schroer, "Author Makes Mark as Small-Business Owner," *USA Today*, 11 May 1992.

Chapter 4

1. Carol Russo, "Building a Home-Office from the Ground Up," *Home Office Computing*, March 1993: 20-21.

2. Ibid.

3. Julie Fanselow, "Zoning Laws vs. Home Business," *Nation's Business*, August 1992: 35-36.

4. Phil Patton, "The Best Gear for Your Home Office," *Money*, July 1991: 106-14.

Chapter 7

1. Raymond Chandler and Robert B. Parker, *Poodle Springs* (New York: Berkeley Publishing Group, 1990).

Chapter 17

1. Paul Schofield, "Computer Networking: The Next Revolution," *The Business Journal*, December 1992.

2. Nancy A. Nichols, "Should You Lease or Buy Your Office Equipment?" in *Step Ahead* (Boston: New England Telephone).

Chapter 19

1. Tom Philben, *How to Hire a Home Improvement Contractor Without Getting Chiseled* (New York: St. Martin's Press, 1991).

Glossary

Artificial light. Light from electrical fixtures.

Batts. Pre-cut lengths of rolled insulation.

Blankets. Rolled fiberglass or mineral wool insulation.

Cathedral ceiling. A ceiling formed on the underside of the roof rafters or joists and conforming to the slope of the roof.

Chair rail. A horizontal trim used to separate the upper from lower (wainscot) portion of a wall. The name derives from its function as a protector against dents from chair backs.

Daylight. Sunlight that comes through windows or skylights.

Drywall. See "Wallboard."

Fire rating. The time required to burn through a floor or wall assembly, as rated by building codes. A typical interior wall framed with 2″ × 4″ studs with ½″ gypsum wallboard on each side is unrated. Replacing the wallboard with "type-X" or "Firecode C™" increases the rating to one hour.

Glazing. The part of a window that lets light through.

Joist. Structural members used repetitively to support floors or roofs.

Kneewall. An outside wall of an attic that extends upward 3′ or 4′, or to about knee height.

Lite. Also spelled "light," a single panel of glazing. A window may contain one lite (picture window) or many lites (French windows).

Mortise. The groove in a piece of wood, into which the tongue, or tenon, fits.

Muntin. A horizontal or vertical dividing strip separating lites of glass or panels in a wall.

Poly. Polyethylene sheeting, usually available in thicknesses of 4 or 6 mil, and in rolls of 3′ or 8′ wide.

Rafter. A long, rectangular member used in series to support a roof.

Roof pitch. The slope of the roof, usually expressed as the number of inches the roof rises for every 12″ of horizontal distance. Common residential roof pitches are usually from 3 in 12 up to 12 in 12.

sf. The measure of building floor or wall area in square feet, width times height.

Sleepers. Flat wood members, usually 2″ × 4″s, laid flat in a repetitive pattern over a floor to level the floor or provide a space for insulation and moisture barrier.

Stud. Vertical wall member, usually a 2″ × 4″ or 2″ × 6″.

Tenon. The tongue of a piece of wood that fits into the mortise (groove) of a joining piece.

Threshold. Weatherstripped wood or aluminum strips installed between the door and floor of exterior and sound-resistant doors.

Truss. A roof framing member constructed from several straight pieces that form a series of triangles.

Wainscot. The lower portion of walls that are finished differently from the upper portion, usually separated by a trim piece called a chair rail.

Wallboard. Wall and ceiling finish material composed of gypsum sandwiched between paper surfacing, and sold under brand names such as Sheetrock™ (also known as "drywall").

Appendix

BOOKS, PERIODICALS, AND PAMPHLETS

Combustion Air

Introducing Supplemental Combustion Air to Gas-Fired Home Appliances (DOE/CE/15095-7, Dec. 1983). U.S. Department of Energy, Small Scale Technology Branch, Appropriate Technology Program.

Computers and Office Equipment

Computerworld, 375 Cochituate Road, Framingham, MA 01704.

Cost Estimating

Means Repair & Remodeling Cost Data, Commercial/Residential, R. S. Means Co., Inc., annually updated, 100 Construction Plaza, P.O. Box 800, Kingston, MA 02364-0800. (617)585-7880.

Design for Disabilities

Branson, Gary. *The Complete Guide to Barrier-Free Housing: Convenient Living for the Elderly and Physically Handicapped*. White Hall, VA: Betterway Publications, 1991.

Hale, Glorya. *The Source Book for the Disabled*. New York: Bantam Books, 1981.

Home-Based and Small Businesses

U.S. Dept. of Commerce, International Trade Administration, Superintendent of Documents. *1990 U.S. Industrial Outlook: Prospects for Over 350 Manufacturing and Service Industries*. Washington, DC: Government Printing Office, 1990.

Applegath, John. *Working Free: Practical Alternatives to the 9 to 5 Job*. New York: American Management Associations, 1982.

Arden, Lynie. *The Work at Home Sourcebook*, Boulder, CO: Live Oak Publications, 1990.

Brabec, Barbara. *Homemade Money: The Definitive Guide to Success in a Homebased Business*. 3rd ed. Cincinnati, OH: Betterway Books, 1989.

Edwards, Paul and Sarah. *Working from Home*. Los Angeles: Jeremy P. Tarcher, 1990.

Entrepreneur Magazine. Good source for new businesses, but lacks the depth of *In Business*.

Galbraith, Oliver, III. *Starting and Managing a Small Business of Your Own*. U.S. Small Business Administration, Off. of Business Development, Starting and Managing Series, No. 1. Washington, DC: Government Printing Office, 1986.

Ganley, John, and others, ed. *Small Business Sourcebook*, Detroit: Gale Research Co., 1983, supplement 1985 (locate this large reference book in the reference section of your library).

Harper, Stephen C. *The McGraw-Hill Guide to Starting Your Own Business: A Step-by-Step Blueprint for the First-Time Entrepreneur*. New York: McGraw-Hill, 1991.

Hawken, Paul. *Growing a Business*. New York: Simon and Schuster, 1987.

Home Business Advisor (newsletter about working at home issues), NextStep Publications, 6340 34th Ave., SW, Seattle, WA 98126.

In Business. Bimonthly magazine. Good source of information for startup businesses.

Inc. Primarily oriented toward businesses somewhere between small and big business.

Kishel, Gregory and Patricia. *Start, Run & Profit from Your Own Home-Based Business.* New York: John Wiley & Sons, 1991.

Laurance, Robert. *Going Freelance.* New York: John Wiley & Sons, 1988.

Money. About money management and acquisition, but much in the way of small businesses.

Morin, William J., and James C. Cabrera. *Parting Company: How to Survive the Loss of a Job and Find Another Successfully.* New York: Harcourt Brace Jovanovich, 1982.

Paradis, Adrian A. *The Small Business Information Source Book.* White Hall, VA: Betterway Publications, 1987.

Resnik, Paul. *The Small Business Bible.* New York: John Wiley & Sons, 1988.

Rosefsky, Robert S. *Getting Free: How to Profit Most Out of Working for Yourself.* New York: Quadrangle/The New York Times Book Co., 1977.

Silberstein, Judith A., and F. Warren Benton. *Bringing High Tech Home: How to Create a Computer-Based Home Office.* New York: John Wiley & Sons, 1985.

Stevens, Mark. *36 Small Business Mistakes— And How to Avoid Them.* West Niyack, NY: Parker Publishing Co., 1978.

Stevens, Mark. *The Macmillan Small Business Handbook.* New York: Macmillan, 1988.

Stolze, William J., *Startup: An Entrepreneur's Guide to Launching and Managing a New Venture.* Rochester, NY: Rock Beach Press, 1989.

Your Own Business: The Izuzu Guide to Small Business Success. Tarzana, CA: Bice & Co., 1991.

Home Remodeling

Branson, Gary D. *The Complete Guide to Floors, Walls, and Ceilings: A Comprehensive Do-It-Yourself Handbook.* Crozet, VA: Betterway Publications, 1992.

McGuerty, Dave, and Kent Lester. *The Complete Guide to Contracting Your Home: A Step-by-Step Method for Managing Home Construction.* 2nd ed. Cincinnati, OH: Betterway Books, 1992.

The National Association of the Remodeling Industry (NARI), 11 E. 44th Street, New York, NY 10017. Good source of free printed information on contractor selection and other remodeling issues.

Superintendent of Documents. *Renovate an Old House?* (Bulletin 212). Washington, DC: Government Printing Office. $3.00.

Woodson, R. Dodge. *Get the Most for Your Remodeling Dollar: How to Save Time, and Avoid Frustration.* Crozet, VA: Betterway Publications, 1992.

Radon

Consumer's Guide to Radon Reduction (402-K92-003, Aug. 1992). U.S. Environmental Protection Agency, Public Information Center, 401 M Street, SW PM-211B, Washington, DC 20460. (202)260-7751.

Spouse and Family

Sommer, Elyse and Mike. *The Two-Boss Business: The Joys and Pitfalls of Working and Living*

Together—and Still Remaining Friends. New York: Butterick, 1980.

Telecommuting

Cross, Thomas B., and Marjorie Raizman. *Telecommuting: The Future of Technology of Work.* Homewood, IL: Dow Jones-Irwin, 1986.

Gordon, Gil E., and Marcia M. Kelley. *Telecommuting: How to Make It Work for You and Your Company.* Englewood Cliffs, NJ: Prentice-Hall, 1986.

Schepp, Brad. *The Telecommuter's Handbook: How to Work for a Salary Without Ever Leaving The House.* New York: Pharos Books, 1990.

BUILDING MATERIALS AND COMPONENTS

Electrical Wiring, Surface Mounted

Wiremold Co., Woodlawn Street, West Hartford, CT 06110. (800)621-0049.

Floor Coverings

Bruce Hardwood Floors (prefinished wood flooring), 16803 Dallas Parkway, Dallas, TX 75248.

Floor Leveling Compounds

Gyp-Crete (installed by licensed applicators). Gyp-Crete Corp., P.O. Box 253, Hamel, MN 55340. (612)478-6072.

Ardex, Inc., 630 Stoops Ferry Road, Coraopolis, PA 15108. (412)264-4240.

Heating, Cooling, and Ventilating Equipment

Room air conditioners: Whirlpool Corp., Benton Harbor, MI 49022.

Split-system air conditioners: Mitsubishi Electronics America, Inc., 5665 Plaza Drive, P.O. Box 6007, Cypress, CA 90630. (714)220-4640.

Through-the-wall heaters: Empire Direct Vent Wall Furnaces, Empire Comfort Systems, 918 Freeburg Ave., Belleville, IL 62222-0529. (800)851-3153.

Through-the-wall heating/cooling devices: Suburban Dynaline DL II Series, Suburban Mfg. Co., 1200 N. Broadway, P.O. Box 399, Dayton, TN 37321. (615)775-2131.

Twinaire window-mounted heating/cooling unit, Suburban Mfg. Co., P.O. Box 399, Dayton, TN 37321. (615)775-2335.

ZoneAire PTAC heat pump or cooling with electric heat, Heil-Quaker Corp., 1136 Heil-Quaker Blvd., LaVergne, TN 37086.

Paints

Wood finishes, penetrating: Minwax Wood Finish, Minwax Co., Inc., Clifton, NJ 07014.

Vapor-barrier paints: BIN, William Zinsser & Co., Inc., 39 Belmont Dr., Somerset, NJ 08875.

The Glidden Company, Cleveland, OH 44115. (216)344-8207.

Stairs, Spiral

American General Products, Inc., 1735 Holmes Rd., P.O. Box 395, Ypsilanti, MI 48197. (800)782-4771.

Stairways, Inc., 4166 Pinemont, Houston, TX 77018. (800)231-0793.

York Spiral Stair Co., Rte. 32, North Vassalboro, ME 04962. (207)872-5558.

Window Treatments

Blinds: Hunter Douglas, Inc., Window Fashions Div., 601 Alter St., Broomfield, CO 80020. (800)438-3883.

Drapes and window quilts: Appropriate Technology Corp. (Window Quilt™), P.O. Box 975, Brattleboro, VT 05301.

Exterior shutters and shades: Environmental Seal and Security Co., Inc., 2621 East Katella Ave., Anaheim, CA 92806. (714)635-5775.

Solaroll Shade & Shutter Corporation, 915 S. Dixie Hwy. E., Pompano Beach, FL 33060. (305)782-7211.

Folding Shutter Corp., 7089 Hemstreet Place, West Palm Beach, FL 33416. (407)683-4811.

Willard Shutter Co., Inc., 4420 N.W. 35th Ct., Miami, FL 33142. (800)826-4530.

Plastic window films: Courtaulds Performance Films, P.O. Box 5068, Martinsville, VA 24115. (703)629-1711.

Metallized Products Div., ITD Industries, Inc., 2544 Terminal Dr. S., St. Petersburg, FL 33712. (813)327-2544.

Shading screens: SunScreen™ and Shade-Screen™, by Phifer Wire Products, Inc., P.O. Box 1700, Tuscaloosa, AL 35403-1700. (800)633-5955.

Vimco, 9301 Old Staples Mill Road, Richmond, VA 23228. (800)777-1503.

Windows, Energy-Efficient and Sound Reducing

Hurd Millwork (Insol-8™), 575 S. Whelen Ave., Medford, WI 54451. (715)748-2011.

Pella Windows (Monumental™ series), 102 Main Street, Pella, IA 50219. (515)628-1000.

COMPUTER SOFTWARE AND SERVICES
Online Networks

CompuServe, 5000 Arlington Center Blvd., P.O. Box 20212, Columbus, OH 43220.

Delphi, 3 Blackstone St., Cambridge, MA 02139. (800)544-4005. (617)491-3393.

Dialog, 3460 Hillview Ave., Palo Alto, CA 94304. (415)858-2700.

MCI Mail, 1150 17th St., N.W., Washington, DC 20036.

Mead Data Central (Nexis), 9393 Springboro Pike, P.O. Box 933, Dayton, OH 45401.

Quantum Link, 8620 Westwood Center Drive, Vienna, VA 22180. (800)392-8200.

DIRECTORIES

Directory of Directories, Book Tower Building, Detroit, MI 48226.

Encyclopedia of Associations, Gale Research Co., Book Tower, Detroit, MI 48266.

Guide to American Directories, B. Klein Publications, P.O. Box 8503, Coral Springs, FL 33065.

Sources of State Information and State Industrial Directories, State Chamber of Commerce Dept., Chamber of Commerce of the U.S., 1615 H Street, NW, Washington, DC 20006.

Standard & Poor's Register of Corporations, Directors and Executives, 345 Hudson Street, New York, NY 10014.

Thomas Register of American Manufacturers, Thomas Publishing Co., One Penn Plaza, New York, NY 10001.

MAIL-ORDER SUPPLIERS OF OFFICE FURNITURE AND/OR EQUIPMENT

Art/Graphics/Design Supplies

Charrette (specialize in graphic design materials), P.O. Box 4010, Woburn, MA 01888-4010. (617)935-6010.

Computer Hardware, Software, Peripherals

Action Computer Supplies, 6100 Stewart Ave., P.O. Box 5004, Fremont, CA 94537-5004. (800)822-3132.

CompuAdd, 12303 Technology Blvd., Austin, TX 78727. (800)477-4717.

Global Computer Supplies, 11 Harbor Park Drive, Dept. 22, Port Washington, NY 11050. (800)845-6225.

Inmac, 2465 Augustine Drive, P.O. Box 58031, Santa Clara, CA 95052-9941. (800)547-5444.

Micro Warehouse, P.O. Box 3014, 1720 Oak Street, Lakewood, NJ 08701-3014. (800)367-7080.

Misco, P.O. Box 399, Holmdel, NJ 07733, (800)631-2227.

General Office Supplies

Frank Eastern, 599 Broadway, New York, NY 10012. (800)221-4914

Moore, P.O. Box 5000, Vernon Hills, IL 60061. (800)323-6230.

Quill, 100 S. Schelter Road, P.O. Box 4700, Lincolnshire, IL 60197-4700. (312)634-4800. West of the Rockies: 5440 E. Francis Street, P.O. Box 50-050, Ontario, CA 91761-1050. (714)988-3200.

Uarco, 121 North Ninth Street, DeCalb, IL 60115. (800)435-0713.

Visible, 3626 Stern Ave., St. Charles, IL 60174. (800)323-0628.

OFFICE FURNITURE AND EQUIPMENT

Backless Task Chairs

Hag Balans Vital Chair, available from Frank Eastern Co. and other mail-order suppliers listed previously.

Computer Accessories

MicroComputer Accessories, Inc., 9920 La Cienega Blvd., P.O. Box 17032, Inglewood, CA 90308-7032. (800)521-8270.

Computer Workstations

Nova Office Furniture, Inc., 421 W. Industrial Avenue, Effingham, IL 62401. (217)342-7070.

PROFESSIONAL ORGANIZATIONS AND TRADE ASSOCIATIONS

Accounting

National Society of Public Accountants, 1010 N. Fairfax Street, Alexandria, VA 22314.

Advertising/Public Relations

American Association of Advertising Agencies, 666 Third Avenue, New York, NY 10017.

Public Relations Society of America, 845 Third Avenue, New York, NY 10022.

Architects

American Institute of Architects, 1735 New York Avenue, NW, Washington, DC 20006.

Bookstores

American Booksellers Association, 122 E. 42nd Street, New York, NY 10168.

Association of American Publishers, One Park Avenue, New York, NY 10016.

Commercial Art

Society of American Graphic Artists, 32 Union Square, New York, NY 10003.

Communications (Business)

International Association of Business Communicators, 870 Market Street, San Francisco, CA 94102.

Computers

Association of Computer Programmers and Analysts, 2108 Gallows Road, Vienna, VA 22180.

Direct Mail Enterprises

American Mail Order Merchants Association, 222 So. Riverside Plaza, Chicago, IL 60606.

Direct Mail Marketing Association, 6 E. 43rd Street, New York, NY 10017.

Franchises

International Franchise Association, P.O. Box 1060, Evans City, PA 16033. For information on franchise exhibitions, phone the Blenheim Group: (407)647-8521.

Home Businesses

American Home Business Association, 397 Post Road, Darien, CT 06820. (800)433-6361; (203)655-4380.

Association of Part-Time Professionals, Flow General Bldg., 7655 Old Springhouse Rd., McLean, VA 22102.

Electronic Bar Association, Paul Bernstein, c/o LAW MUG, 505 N. Lasalle Street-575, Chicago, IL 60610.

National Association for the Cottage Industry, P.O. Box 14850, Chicago, IL 60614.

The Telecommuting Advisory Council, c/o Pat Mokhtarian, Schimpeler-Corradino Associates, 433 S. Spring Street, Suite 10004 North, Los Angeles, CA 90013.

Interior Designers

American Society of Interior Designers, 608 Massachussets Ave., Washington, DC 20002.

Marketing/Market Research

American Marketing Association, 250 South Wacker Drive, Chicago, IL 60606.

Marketing Research Association, 111 E. Wacker Drive, Chicago, IL 60601.

Planning and Organizing

National Association of Professional Organizers, 655 N. Alvernon, Suite 108, Tucson, AZ 85711. (602)322-9753.

Sales and Sales Management

Sales & Marketing Executives International, 6151 Wilson Mills Road, Cleveland, OH 44143.

Travel Agencies

American Society of Travel Agents, 4400 MacArthur Blvd., NW, Washington, DC 20007.

Association of Retail Travel Agents, 8 Maple Street, Croton-On-Hudson, NY 10520.

Writing and Editing

American Society of Business Press Editors, 4196 Porter Road, North Olmstead, OH 44050.

Society for Technical Communication, Inc. (STC), 901 N. Stuart Street, Suite 904, Arlington, VA 22203. (703)522-4114.

Women in Communications, Inc. (WICI), 3717 Columbia Pike, Suite 310, Arlington, VA 22204. (703)920-5555.

Index

More Great Books for Small Business Owners and Do-It-Yourselfers!

Homemade Money 5th Edition — With this all-new edition, you'll be up to speed on the legal matters, accounting practices, tax laws, and marketing techniques sure to make your home-based business a success! *#70231/$19.95/400 pages/paperback*

How To Run a Family Business — From forming the board of directors to setting salaries, you'll find advice to ensure your family business thrives. *#70214/$14.95/176 pages/paperback*

Surviving the Start-up Years — This guide, full of sound advice and concrete examples, will help you get your business off to a successful start. *#70109/$7.95/172 pages/paperback*

Becoming Financially Sound in an Unsound World — You *can* reach financial security! This hands-on guide shows you how to apply proven principles to attain your goals! *#70140/$14.95/240 pages/paperback*

How To Make $100,000 a Year in Desktop Publishing — Cash in on this growing market! You'll discover how to tailor your work for all types of publications. *#70054/ $18.95/280 pages/paperback*

Stay Home and Mind Your Own Business — Make money at home with tips on how to pick a winning product or service, do market research, and set profitable prices. *#70105/$12.95/280 pages/paperback*

Rehab Your Way to Riches — Let a real estate mogul show you how to generate real estate income in ways that limit risk and maximize profits. *#70156/$14.95/208 pages/ paperback*

Success, Common Sense, and the Small Business — As a small business owner, you'll wear a lot of hats! This guide covers the skills you need for a variety of tasks. *#70212/$11.95/176 pages/paperback*

People, Common Sense and the Small Business — Success depends on employee performance. Learn how to get outstanding results by cultivating a highly motivated staff. *#70083/$9.95/224pages/paperback*

Export-Import — Get the vocabulary, insider tips, and rules of the game you need to compete in rapidly-expanding world markets. *#70146/$12.95/160 pages/paperback*

Doing Business in Asia: How to Succeed in the World's Most Dynamic Market — For small and medium-sized American companies, this book offers the information needed to start doing business in Asia. *#70198/$18.95/192 pages/paperback*

Making the Most of the Temporary Employment Market — In an age of corporate downsizing, you must be up to speed on the growing benefits and applications of temporary employment. *#70197/$9.95/176 pages/paperback*

Cover Letters That Will Get You the Job You Want — Open doors with compelling, well-written cover letters. This invaluable guide includes 100 tested cover letters that work! *#70185/$12.95/192 pages/paperback*

The Student Loan Handbook — Discover up-to-date information on all work-study, grant, and scholarship programs available — plus financial planning guidelines and state-by-state appendices. *#70108/ $7.95/168 pages/paperback*

Cleaning Up for A Living — Learn from the best! Don Aslett shares with you the tricks he used to build a $12 million commercial cleaning business. *#70016/$12.95/208 pages/paperback*

Little People Big Business — Day care services are in high demand! This guide covers the requirements for setting up a business, licensing and equipment. *#70067/$7.95/ 176 pages/paperback*

Mortgage Loans: What's Right for You? 3rd Edition — Don't make a big-money mistake on the wrong mortgage! Find the facts on what's suited to your financial situation. Plus information on caps, points, margins and more! *#70242/$14.95/144 pages/paperback*

The Home Buyer's Inspection Guide — Don't get caught in a money-pit! Let an expert inspector teach you the critical structural aspects of property — before you buy. *#70049/$12.95/176 pages/paperback*

Legal Aspects of Buying, Owning, and Selling a Home — This easy-to-read guide gives you the answers to all your legal questions concerning buying, selling, and occupying a home. *#70151/$12.95/176 pages/paperback*

The Complete Guide to Buying Your First Home — Discover loads of hints to help you plan and organize your buy, and avoid common pitfalls for first-time buyers. *#70023/ $16.95/224pages/paperback*

Single Person's Guide to Buying a Home — This buying guide offers you worksheets and checklists that show you what to look for in buying a home on your own. *#70200/ $14.95/144 pages/paperback*

Home Improvements — Discover which improvements will add value to your home and which won't (before you sink a lot of money into it.) *#70207/$16.95/160 pages/ paperback*

The Complete Guide to Residential Deck Construction — You'll love your new deck! Find the information you need to plan, design and construct one by yourself or with professional help. *#70035/176 pages/ $16.95/paperback*

The Complete Guide to Understanding and Caring for Your Home — Even cozy homes have problem areas. With this guide you'll pinpoint what you like (and want to improve) about your house. *#70024/$18.95/ 272 pages/paperback*

The Complete Guide to Remodeling Your Basement — Whether you want a workshop or more family space, you'll do the job right from start to finish! *#70034/$14.95/176 pages/paperback*

The Complete Guide to Being Your Own Remodeling Contractor — This helpful guide will ensure that remodeling jobs get done right! Checklists will help you spot work that's not up to snuff, plus you'll control your costs with handy materials lists. *#70246/$18.99/288 pages/paperback*

Gary Branson's Home Repairs and Improvements on a Budget — Save money with step-by-step instructions that show you how to quiet floor noises, prevent drain clogs, locate wall studs, and hundreds of other easy do-it-yourself projects! *#70247/$16.99/160 pages/paperback*

The Complete Guide to Floors, Walls, and Ceilings — Step-by-step instructions show you how to increase the value of your home by patching walls, soundproofing, installing floors, and more! *#70028/$14.95/176 pages/paperback*

The Complete Guide to Home Plumbing Repair and Replacement — Forget huge plumber's fees! This fully illustrated guide shows you how to troubleshoot, repair, and replace your plumbing. *#70141/$16.95/224 pages/50 illus./paperback*

The Complete Guide to Landscape Design, Renovation and Maintenance — Discover how to prune, renovate an overgrown yard, design landscape, and maintain your yard like a pro. *#70030/$14.95/192 pages/paperback*

The Complete Guide to Decorative Landscaping with Brick Masonry — Beautify your home with patios, walks, brick garden borders, barbecues, and dozens of other step-by-step projects. *#70027/$11.95/160 pages/paperback*

The Complete Guide to Home Security — From doors and windows to lighting and landscaping, you'll learn tips and techniques to theft-proofing your home. *#70029/190 pages/$14.95/paperback*

The Complete Guide to Log and Cedar Homes — Scores of illustrations lead you through all aspects of purchasing or building your log or cedar home — including all phases of construction. *#70190/$16.95/168 pages/74 photos/paperback*

The Complete Guide to Four-Season Home Maintenance — With some simple tips and techniques, you'll minimize costly repairs and replacements — all year round! *#70192/$18.95/160 pages/paperback*

The Complete Guide to Restoring and Maintaining Wood Furniture and Cabinets — Don't let nicks and scratches ruin your treasured heirlooms. Detailed instructions show you how to repair damage and restore gorgeous finishes. *#70209/$19.95/160 pages/paperback*

Measure Twice, Cut Once — Get the right fit every time! You'll learn what each measuring tool does, how to use it properly — even how to make your own. *#70210/$18.95/128 pages/143 b&w illus./paperback*

Basic Woodturning Techniques — Detailed explanations of fundamental techniques will have you turning beautiful pieces in no time. *#70211/$14.95/112 pages/119 b&w illus./paperback*

Good Wood Handbook — Your guide to identifying the right wood for the job (before you buy). You'll see a wide selection of softwoods and hardwoods in full color. *#70162/$16.95/128 pages/250 + color illus.*

Pocket Guide to Wood Finishes — This handy guide shows you how to mix and match stains and other finishes. Spiral bound and durable — perfect for your woodshop. *#70164/$16.95/64 pages/ 250 + color illus.*

The Used Car Reliability and Safety Guide — Take the fear out of used-car shopping! Data from the National Highway Traffic Safety Administration details problems reported on over 800 used car models, plus their safety and theft records. *#70262/ $12.99/320pages/paperback*

Roughing it Easy — Have fun in the great outdoors with these ingenious tips! You'll learn what equipment to take, how to plan, set up a campsite, build a fire, backpack — even how to camp during winter. *#70260/ $14.99/256 pages/paperback*

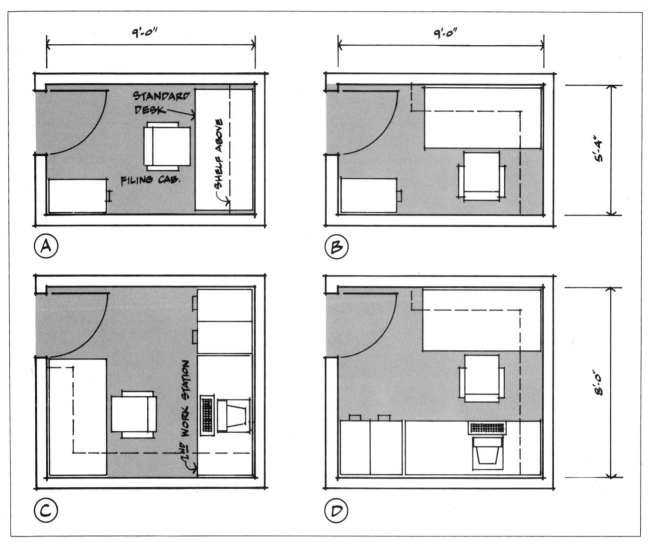

Figure 13-2: Minimum Porch Sizes. *A standard desk requires a minimum width of 5'4", regardless of how you position it or the length of the room, as shown in examples* **(A)** *and* **(B)**. *Three extra feet of width offers not only more space for additional furniture, but much more flexibility for arranging the furniture, as shown in* **(C)** *and* **(D)**. *Note that the space left to walk in, between the filing cabinet and desk in example* **(B)**, *is pretty skimpy at around 18". Placing work surfaces next to an outside wall* **(C, D)** *may not work if the window sill is lower than the average 29" desk height.*

she would like to be able to leave the mess from time to time, without worrying about the impression it makes on visitors.

PORCH PLANNING BASICS

The 5'4" minimum width suggested is based on the width of a standard desk (5') or the space required to fit the same desk turned sideways, with 5' for the depth of the desk and 2'10" for chair and access. If you estimated your space re-

quirements from the guidelines in chapter 3, you'll probably find that the 43 sq. ft. that a 5'4" × 8'0" room yields is far less than what you need. An extra 3' expands space and the choices of furniture arrangement, as shown in Figure 13-2 (above).

Even with a narrow porch, your options grow if the porch is long enough, though a too-long and narrow space might be more evocative of a diner than an office. I'd guess you reach that condition when the length is more than three times the width.

So, if you think you have a space on the porch big enough for an office, you can start planning how the space will be used. Begin with the plan of the porch as it relates to the house. How will people get into the house? How will they get into the office? What clues—other than a sign—can you provide to direct traffic where you want it?

Bumping Out for More Space

If zoning permits, you may be able to gain an extra few feet of width by bumping the wall out over the porch foundation as I did for my friend the accountant, shown in Figure 13-3 (page 113). The extra few feet of width meant more space and flexibility inside and enclosing the porch with materials and forms harmonious with the house improved the home's exterior.

Without changing the floor structure, you can probably increase the width by one quarter. For anything more ambitious, ask a design professional to help you modify the floor structure.

PORCH SUPPORTS

It's also a good idea to get a professional opinion of the porch's underpinnings, whether or not you enlarge it by bumping the walls out. Many wood-framed porches perch above precarious foundations that have settled unevenly, rotted, or been eaten by termites.

Your porch probably sits on piers of one kind or another or a continuous foundation wall. Either method can safely support your new office space, if sized for the additional weight of your office trappings and solid outer walls. Another must: The foundation should extend below the frost line to prevent being shoved around by the soil as it freezes and thaws. You can find out the depth of the frost line in your region by calling the building inspection department of your municipality.

CONVERTING PORCH FLOORS TO OFFICE FLOORS

After making sure the foundation is sound, you will need to address three other concerns: making sure the floor is structurally adequate, level, and warm.

Structural Soundness

If your porch floor is made of wood, chances are it perches above a crawl space that may or may not be semi-enclosed by an open wood lattice, built to keep critters out. If so, it probably prevented dogs and cats from entering, but gave carpenter ants or termites a standing invitation. Before doing any work above, take a flashlight down below to assess any pest damage, as well as any deterioration from water or dampness.

Check the structural adequacy of the floor joists against the table of floor joist sizes in chapter 11 or by getting the advice of an expert. Joists deteriorated or undersized to start with can either be added to or replaced. The right solution depends on what other problems need to be solved, such as raising or leveling the porch floor.

Raising and Leveling a Porch Floor

In addition to sloping, porch floors are commonly set one step below the level of the main house floor. You may want to raise the floor to meet the main floor if your office is to connect directly to the house.

You will surely want a level floor. The easiest way to level a wood floor is probably by adding level sister joists, one nailed to the side of each existing joist. I used this method to both level the floor and frame the bump-out at the accountant's office. The existing floor framing consisted of joists supported by a beam at the house wall and another beam running above concrete piers at the outer porch wall. The new sister joists started at the same height as the old joists, at the house wall, but instead of sloping down to the outside, they were kept level. They cantilevered over the